Donated
To The Library by

THE

DIMONDALE HOME CULTURE CLUB

IN MEMORY OF

FRED MILES

Ernie Harwell

My 60 Years in Baseball

Tom Keegan

TRIUMPH
B O O K S
CHICAGO

The sidebars used throughout this book originally appeared as articles published by Ernie Harwell in the *Detroit Free Press*. The sidebars in Chapters 1, 2, 4, 6, 7, 8, 9, 11, 12, 13, 15, 16, 17, 18, 19, 20, 21 also appeared in the book *Ernie Harwell: Stories From My Life in Baseball*, a *Detroit Free Press* publication. To order call 1-800-245-5082 or go to www.freep.com/bookstore. All articles used with the permission of the *Detroit Free Press*.

Library of Congress Cataloging-in-Publication Data

Keegan, Tom, 1957–
    Ernie Harwell : my 60 years in baseball / Tom Keegan.
        p. cm.
    ISBN 1-57243-451-1 (hardcover)
    1. Harwell, Ernie. 2. Sportscasters—United States—Biography. 3. Baseball—United States—History—20th century. I. Harwell, Ernie. II. Title.

GV742.42.H39 K44 2002
070.4'49796'092—dc21
[B]

2001059207

This book is available in quantity at special discounts for your group or organization. For further information, contact:
Triumph Books
601 South LaSalle Street
Suite 500
Chicago, Illinois 60605
(312) 939-3330
Fax (312) 663-3557

Printed in the United States of America
ISBN 1-57243-451-1
Interior design by Patricia Frey
Microphone image created by Brian Schwartz

To Joe Cullinane,
voice of the Rochester Red Wings
during my youth.

Contents

Foreword

My wife and I were once dinner partners with Ernie and Lulu Harwell on a Caribbean cruise. I really looked forward to those dinners because of the stories Ernie would rattle off every night—they were like trips back in time. He never told the same story twice and he never told them in such a way as to make anyone think that he yearned for "the good old days." All the things he has experienced in his life, in and out of baseball, are absolutely amazing. I got the impression that we could circle the world 10 times, eating dinner with the Harwells every night, and Ernie would never repeat himself or lose our attention.

When you think about it, how many people can you sit across the table from on an ocean liner, a full moon illuminating the evening, as he shares firsthand stories about Babe Ruth (he signed Ernie's tennis shoe), Ty Cobb (Ernie knocked on his door and was granted an interview), Connie Mack, golfing great Bobby Jones, and former heavyweight champion Jack Dempsey?

Ernie's sense of humor never strays too far out of the picture, whether he's talking about his four years in the marines, the winter he and his family spent in Spain, or about the many baseball people he and Lulu have entertained at their house through his seven decades as a major league (in every way) announcer. As a dinner companion, Ernie paints pictures with words the way he paints a baseball game from the booth: not a wasted syllable.

Those dinners whisked by too fast, almost as fast as the dessert disappeared from Ernie's plate every night. You wouldn't know it by looking at him, but Ernie's a big dessert guy.

Ernie has been the voice of the Tigers for so long (since 1960, every year but 1992) that it's not an exaggeration to say that in some ways, he is the Detroit Tigers. It's probably easy for many to forget that by the time he moved to Detroit, he already had stored more memories as the voice of the Dodgers, the Giants, and the Orioles than most announcers do in a lifetime.

Take a cruise with him and you'll hear all about what it was like covering Jackie Robinson in his second year in the majors or being in the booth for the major league debuts of Willie Mays and Brooks Robinson. Ask him about announcing Bobby Thomson's "shot heard 'round the world" as the lead man on the first coast-to-coast telecast of a live sporting event. Everybody forgets about that because Russ Hodges' famous call was taped and Ernie's typically low-key one was not.

Ernie Harwell is the epitome of what a professional announcer should be. Many announcers get down and depressed when the team's not playing well and that would be pretty easy to do lately with the Detroit Tigers. You can never tell with Ernie. He's always right on top of the game he's announcing, right on top of the moment. Ernie prefers to view life the way he prefers his eggs: sunny-side up. I don't know if we'll ever see another announcer quite like him. He's witnessed so many changes in society and in baseball during his life, yet he remains constant. He never changes. And he treats the superstar and the last guy on the roster the same.

I've been very lucky in my time with the Tigers to be around somebody like Ernie Harwell. If anybody should have a statue at Comerica

Park, it should be Ernie. That's my next project, to see to it that the Tigers put up a statue of Ernie Harwell.

After that, I'm going to embark on another project. I'm going to try to find somebody who doesn't like Ernie Harwell. I hope I live long enough to do that because that means I'll never die.

—Al Kaline
November 2001

Acknowledgments

Thanks to my favorite lady (Angie Keegan), my favorite ballplayer (John Keegan), my favorite bass player (Andy Keegan), my favorite drummer (Jim Keegan), my favorite actress (Ellen Keegan), and my favorite Tibetan Terrier (Sammy Sosa Keegan). Thanks also to Celia Bobrowsky and Molly Light of the Tigers, attorney Gary Spicer, "Go Go" Gilbert, Ellen Carlson, Brian Burley, Joe Goddard, Bob Klark of McKean County Federal Prison Camp, and Blythe Hurley of Triumph Books. Special thanks to Daniel Yelovich for furnishing an office with the peace and quiet needed to write the final chapters. This book was written in loving memory of John F. Keegan, M.D., father of 10, lover of baseball.

Ernie Harwell Chronology

- Born in Washington, Georgia, January 25, 1918

- Atlanta correspondent for *The Sporting News*, 1934–1948

- Sports department for the *Atlanta Constitution*, 1936–1940

- Sports director for WSB Atlanta, 1940–1942

- Married Lulu Tankersley, August 30, 1941

- USMC, 1942–1946

- Atlanta Crackers baseball announcer, 1943, 1946–1948

- Brooklyn Dodgers baseball announcer, 1948–1949

- New York Giants baseball announcer, 1950–1953

- Baltimore Orioles baseball announcer, 1954–1959

- Detroit Tigers baseball announcer, 1960–1991, 1993–present

- CBS Radio Game of the Week, 1992, 1994

- Inducted into the Baseball Hall of Fame, August 2, 1981

Chapter 1

A Gentleman Wronged

The proud woman is showing her visitor pictures of her blond granddaughters, each blessed with a clock-stopping face, each one prettier than the last. The neatly bagged clothes and hangers, soaps, and shampoos are lined up near the front door, ready for the Salvation Army pickup.

Outdoors, on a muggy, summer of 2001 afternoon in suburban Detroit, those hard-shelled Japanese beetles are attacking Lulu Harwell's roses. It's always something preventing perfection in the garden, which is as it should be, for a perfect garden would need no gardener. This rose garden needs Lulu every bit as much as she needs it.

In a few hours, Lulu Harwell will begin her nightly ritual of listening to her husband, legendary baseball broadcaster Ernie Harwell, paint baseball games with gentle words delivered with a powerful projection softened by a trace of the South.

1

Mrs. Harwell, sweet Mrs. Harwell, is the definition of serenity as she makes her way over to the couch, near the lifelike stuffed tiger. She sits and smiles a smile so full it borders on laughter.

And then her visitor utters two words, four syllables: Bo Schembechler.

In the blink of an eye, her youthful face ages. The softness in it drains quicker than a popped water balloon. Just an instant ago, her expression was a lake so placid as to be mistaken for a pane of glass. Now it's a tempest, unsafe for passage, even for an aircraft carrier.

"If I saw Bo Schembechler today, I would hope I had a rock in my pocket," she says, her words measured and devoid of humor. "I'd take it out and throw it at him." Lulu Harwell was born and reared in Hazard, Kentucky. She knows a thing or two about throwing rocks.

The sentence hasn't spilled far enough out of the lovely woman's mouth even to reach the carpet and it's as if she can hear the calming voice of her husband, the voice people all over Michigan recognize on elevators, letting her know there will be none of that talk now. Never mind that he is at Comerica Park. Sixty years of marriage means a spouse's presence isn't required for communication to take place.

"Ernie's forgiven everyone, you know," she says. "That's his strong faith. He always tells me I have to forgive everyone too. I guess I have to, but it's hard."

For one thing, it's difficult to know whom to forgive for what. Schembechler, according to most of those on the Tigers' scene at the time, was guiltier of excessive pride and stubbornness in refusing to reverse the decision than of being behind it in the first place, a decision that started with WJR radio and was carried out behind the scenes largely by Jeff Odenwald, the Tigers' marketing director.

"The hurtful thing about it," Lulu says, "is whoever did it, they wouldn't admit it."

Still won't. Schembechler wouldn't return messages left for him at the University of Michigan, where he still keeps an office. Odenwald would not return phone calls left at his home and place of work in Tucson, Arizona, and therefore couldn't be reached for his denial that he played a major role in the short-lived, ill-fated attempt to turn the voice of the Tigers into a shuffleboard player.

Schembechler took the heat for his perceived role as the Grinch Who Stole Summer days before Christmas of 1990, when he let Harwell know that the Tigers were "going in a new direction" in the broadcast booth after the 1991 season.

Miss Lulu—that's what her husband calls her—had plenty of company in decrying the most unpopular decision in the history of the Detroit Tigers.

Irate fans who knew no other voice of summer than the soothing sound of Harwell phoned bomb threats into Domino's Pizza outlets throughout Detroit, a means of letting Tom Monaghan, owner of Domino's and the Tigers, know what they thought of Schembechler's latest misdirection play. Boycotts of Domino's were organized.

Schembechler, a revered football coach at the University of Michigan, became reviled by many overnight. Protesters dumped garbage on the lawn of his suburban home. Newspaper columnists carved him up. Bumper stickers that played on the hottest sports marketing slogan at the time, "Bo Knows" (as in dual-sport star Bo Jackson), cropped up all over Michigan. They said: "Bo Don't Know Ernie."

More than a decade later, looking back on a low point in Tigers history and trying to put the pieces together has the makings of a whodunit.

The central characters:

Jim Long (deceased): The general manager of Tigers flagship station WJR at the time, Long was a quiet, pleasant sort who didn't share his thoughts on important business decisions with many. Whether of his own doing or under orders from corporate headquarters in New York, Long presided over an out-with-the-old, in-with-the-young

Comerica: Love at First Sight on Opening Day?

My first look at Comerica Park will come when I sit at the microphone there on Opening Day 2000.

Most other Detroit baseball people have taken an early peek. Not me. I did participate in the groundbreaking ceremonies, but that was just digging a hole in a parking lot.

The only other time I came near the park was during the summer of 1999, when Alan Trammell, Lance Parrish, and I enjoyed an early dinner in Windsor.

When we returned through the tunnel, I said, "Let's drive up Woodward and measure the distance from the Detroit River to Comerica Park."

We did. It was a little less than a mile. We drove toward the entrance, took a look, but didn't get out of the car.

However I've seen 19 other new parks in my broadcasting lifetime. In 5 of them I've broadcast the first game there.

My first broadcast from a new park was April 15, 1954.

The Baltimore Orioles had begun their modern big-league history with two games in Detroit. They took a train to Baltimore. The players dressed on the train, then paraded through downtown Baltimore to their new home, Memorial Stadium.

When we arrived, workmen were still installing seats and doing other final touch-ups. The Birds beat the White Sox that afternoon, 3–1.

The next time I helped inaugurate a park was in 1965. The Tigers were coming north from spring training and played an exhibition game against the Milwaukee Braves at the new Atlanta park, Atlanta/Fulton County Stadium.

Again, the park wasn't quite ready. The grounds crew was still putting down sod when we reached the stadium.

My next first game featured a rout by the Tigers. On April 18, 1991, the Tigers whipped the White Sox, 16–0, at new Comiskey Park. Frank Tanana was the winner. The Tigers knocked out Jack McDowell early and sent most of the crowd of 42,191 home before the fifth inning.

When Jacobs Field in Cleveland opened on April 4, 1994, I was there to broadcast the game on CBS radio. President Bill Clinton threw out the first pitch. The Indians beat the Seattle Mariners in the eleventh inning on a single by Wayne Kirby.

St. Petersburg, Florida, was the scene of my fifth first-game broadcast. The newest of the American League teams, the Tampa Bay Devil Rays, opened Tropicana Field on March 31, 1998, against the Tigers.

After Hall of Famers Ted Williams, Stan Musial, and Monte Irvin threw out the ceremonial first pitches, the Tigers jumped to an early 11–0 lead and went on to win, 11–6.

—*E.H., April 2000*

movement at the station. He was a staunch University of Michigan football fan.

Jeff Odenwald: Odenwald, who was the Tigers' marketing director at that time, had worked for the Reds, Mariners, and Cubs before joining the Tigers. A human suit. There has been a Jeff Odenwald at every business in every industry in America. Slick. Master of the universe. His magic trick: able to use one eye to look at the person to whom he was talking while the other eye scanned the room in search of a more important person to lock in a conversation. When throwing them back at the bar, his imagination flew all the way into the general manager's chair, where he was certain he would end up.

Saw new team president Bo Schembechler's inexperience in baseball as an opportunity to accelerate his own scaling of the all-important corporate ladder by "helping" Schembechler to execute difficult decisions.

Bo Schembechler: Hard-nosed, authoritative, and a born winner, despite a 2–8 record in the Rose Bowl, Schembechler won the hearts of rabid Michigan football fans by turning the Wolverines into a perennial Big Ten power. He scored more points for loyalty to Big Blue when before the 1989 NCAA Tournament he replaced basketball coach Bill Frieder with assistant Steve Fisher because Frieder had negotiated a departure to Arizona State that was to go into effect at the end of the season. "I want a Michigan man coaching Michigan," Schembechler said, words that gained immortality when Fisher coached the Wolverines to the national championship. Detractors consider Bo an egomaniacal bully. Supporters laud his integrity. He had the unenviable task of informing Harwell late in the 1990 season that he would be offered a one-year contract and then would be shown the door.

Jim Campbell (deceased): Despite being stubborn and demanding on employees, he was the universally well-liked chairman and chief executive officer of the Tigers. Prior to gaining that promotion, he had served the organization as general manager. He was popular with the media and Tigers employees and a longtime friend of Harwell until the Christmas season of 1990, when he became extremely protective of Schembechler.

Tom Monaghan: Then owner of Domino's Pizza and an acclaimed philanthropist, Monaghan once made his private plane available to the Harwell family so they could all attend the ceremony for Ernie's induction into the National Sportscasters and Sportswriters Hall of Fame in 1989, one of only two times Harwell missed a game during his career (the other was for his brother's funeral). Monaghan was often quoted as saying Harwell was an important part of Tigers history.

Ernie Harwell: Anyone who had a grandfather admired for kindness and gentleness and for how capably he handled his job knows Ernie Harwell. He is that grandfather. He is your grandfather. To so many listeners, he is much more. At the time of the controversy, Harwell had broadcast Tigers games for 31 seasons and was told his 32nd would be his last.

The wild reaction to Harwell's firing speaks to more than his longevity, though that certainly played a part in his popularity. That Harwell would be the center of so much attention had a touch of irony to it; his no-frills style of announcing baseball games ensured the listener's attention forever was trained on the diamond—on the actors in the play—not on the narrator. The voice is part of the appeal.

"The Southern accent is perfect for the pace of a baseball game," says Bob Miller, once a member of the Tigers public relations staff, now working for a publicity firm in Detroit. "There aren't a lot of announcers who grew up in the South, but there are many who would like you to think they did."

Harwell hooked the baseball fans of Detroit by relating interesting tidbits from baseball history and teaching the finer points of the game by drawing on anecdotes from the sport's rich past. He hooked them with words that painted the picture of what he was watching, not what he could read on a sheet of statistics. He hooked them as much with what he didn't say as what he said.

Listen closely to a Harwell broadcast and it's possible to hear the vendor's cry between pitches: "Hot dogs! Hot dogs! Hot dogs! Free mustard!"

The pitcher, the batter, the count, the score, the way the fielders are shading the hitter, those are never mysteries during a Harwell broadcast. Even his pet calls, which have endeared him to listeners, are triggered always by the action on the field.

A double play is "two for the price of one." A home run is "long gone." A foul ball becomes a souvenir caught by the lucky man from

Novi (or Windsor, or Bad Axe, or Kalamazoo). A batter taking strike 3 either "stood there like the house by the side of the road," a nod to a poem he recited as a boy while ridding himself of a speech impediment, or "was called out for excessive window shopping." An umpire "gets the family look," from a player or manager, "like when you're a kid and someone takes the last biscuit, you give him the family look."

Harwell's broadcasts are so rich with straight description of the game that these welcome curves stand out. His goal is to make his voice the listener's eyes, and most would agree that few have done it as well.

Frank Rashid, quoted in a column by Jack Lessenberry, perfectly captured both Harwell's style in the booth and others' lack of wisdom in firing him. He spoke in the past tense, believing at the time that

Harwell's career as a Tigers announcer had ended for good, not knowing it would actually be a beginning to a new, more lucrative career than an end of a Hall of Fame career. Harwell would be rehired after a year away, and would spend one year in the radio booth and five in the TV booth before returning to a 162-game radio schedule in 1999. He is signed on for the 2002 season, where he again will team with partners Jim Price and Dan Dickerson on WXYT.

"He was like one of that older generation of symphony conductors who tried not to get in the way of the piece," Rashid said. "His words brought you the game, not the hype. That the Tigers didn't know what a treasure he was showed just how much they were out of touch with their fans."

Based on their reaction to the firing and the absence of complaints about Harwell's performance before it, we know one group that did *not* support the decision: the WJR listeners who followed their Tigers through the voice from the South.

Harwell's contract was scheduled to expire November 1, 1990. Normally, he reached agreement for a new settlement six months before his contract expired. He hadn't heard anything by late September, so he stuck his head in Schembechler's booth and suggested they meet to talk about his future. Harwell said he would like to bring his friend, attorney Gary Spicer, with him. Schembechler scheduled a September 24 meeting that was general in nature. Harwell took notes on that and subsequent meetings and here is what those notes reveal:

"What are your retirement plans, Ernie?" Schembechler asked.

"Well, I would like to keep working, but nothing's certain, of course," Harwell answered.

The men agreed to meet again.

Schembechler phoned Harwell on Friday, October 12 and scheduled a meeting for Monday, October 15.

"I want to warn you, Ernie," Schembechler said over the phone, "it'll be a contract for one year at $200,000."

9

"That's a little low," Harwell said. "And I might want to work past that one year."

"We're thinking we would like you to announce your retirement on the winter Tiger tour," Bo suggested.

"No, I really don't want to retire," Harwell said. "So I couldn't say I was retiring."

"OK, then, Ernie, you make the call on how you would like to announce it," Bo said.

When Harwell and Spicer showed up for the Monday meeting at Schembechler's office, Long was there, which made sense because Harwell worked for both the radio station and the Tigers. Just as the meeting was about to begin, Odenwald entered and took a seat on a couch in the back of the room. It seemed an odd gathering for a marketing director to join.

Schembechler ran the meeting and opened it by informing everyone that WJR and the Tigers wanted to keep Harwell for one more year at $200,000, after which time a new broadcast team would be hired. Harwell's partner of 19 years, Paul Carey, earlier in the year already had informed Long of his intention to retire after the 1991 season, though he kept it a secret.

Odenwald chimed in that they wanted to go in a "new direction," a phrase straight out of the manual for modern marketing under the heading "What to Say When You Don't Want to Say Anything." Sportswriters abhor the term almost as much as do the readers of the stories they write.

Harwell to Schembechler: "Bo, how could you know that I'm good enough to do the job in 1991 and not in 1992? That's like using a quarterback for the first half and telling him ahead of time that he would not be good enough for the second half. I don't want to retire."

Harwell and Spicer pointed out that they had heard no complaints about his work. No negative mail, no critical letters to the editors, no buzz on the radio sports talk shows, no alarming newspaper columns.

"Jim, have there been any complaints to the station?" Harwell asked Long, who shrugged off the question.

Harwell said his health was good, his voice was the same, and his energy level was better than ever. Spicer cited examples of Harwell's loyalty to the franchise and dedication to his trade.

After asking if they had a successor in mind, Harwell was told they did not and was encouraged to help them select one. As Harwell and Spicer were about to leave, Long said that he would have a contract drawn up and would get back to them. Two weeks later, Harwell received a letter from Long stating, "I may be wrong, but I thought you and your agent were supposed to get back to me." Harwell wrote him a letter telling him just the opposite was the case.

Harwell waited for his contract to arrive in the mail and finally received it December 15. He contacted Tigers public relations director Dan Ewald and told him he would like to hold a press conference to announce the decision. If the Tigers preferred, Harwell offered, he could have it away from Tiger Stadium. Ewald said he felt it should be at Tiger Stadium. Harwell told Ewald to invite Schembechler and said he would invite Long. The press conference was set for December 19 in the Tiger Room.

December 18 was WJR sports director Frank Beckmann's first day back at work after back surgery. Long called him into his office and this is how the conversation went, according to Beckmann:

Long: "Ernie's having a press conference to announce this will be his last year. I don't know what Ernie's going to say, but we're going to carry it live and I need you to be there to cover it."

Beckmann: "What, did he make this decision?"

Long: "No."

Beckmann: "Hold on. You mean you're firing Ernie Harwell?"

Long: "He's just a baseball announcer."

Beckmann: "You're not firing a baseball announcer. You're firing everybody's grandfather. You said you don't know what he's going to say? I know what he's going to say. He's going to say he got hosed."

"I left the newsroom with a buddy and tied one on," remembers Beckmann, who later was approached about becoming the No. 2 man in the radio booth but was not interested in taking you're-not-Ernie heat unless he could take it as the No. 1 man.

Schembechler and Long did not show for the press conference that would go down as a dark day in Tigers history. Not far into his opening statement, Harwell put his hand over his brows, scanned the room and said, "Bo Schembechler has been invited here and I don't know whether he is here or not. I can't see him and I can't see Jim Long. Bo? Bo? Jim?"

Harwell came to the press conference armed with the most powerful of all weapons: the truth. He shared what went on during the meeting with Long, Schembechler, and Odenwald and was careful not to put down anyone from WJR or the Tigers.

Samplings of questions and answers from the press conference:

Q: Ernie, do you feel you are getting discriminated against because of your age?

A: That's a hard question. I feel I'm healthy and I can do the job and my mail certainly has not reflected any lapse in my ability and I haven't read anybody writing that Ernie Harwell should be off the air. So, I guess you just have to draw your own conclusions.

Q: Ernie, had you given any indication that you might think about retiring? Had the grind gotten to you on the road?

A: No, I always felt when people asked me I had sort of a standard reply about retirement. I said, "Well, as long as I'm healthy and the good Lord gives me good health and as long as the Tigers want me, I want to keep working." I've been in the big leagues now for 43 years. I've been with the Tigers 31 years and I've missed two games and neither one of those was because of my health. So I really think that I'm healthy.

Harwell invited Odenwald to take the microphone for questions. He took a seat next to Harwell and read a prepared statement.

The final question Odenwald answered should have taken the wind out of the sails of what would become a rallying cry of those in the Tigers' front office and WJR embarrassed at the reaction to the firing: "Ernie shouldn't have had that press conference."

Q: Jeff, back in October, when these decisions were made, did you envision a press conference like this?

A: Yes. Yes. We did tell Ernie, and Ernie alluded to it [during the press conference] that however he wished to handle it, we would abide by it.

After the press conference, Beckmann was the first to ask Carey of his plans and Carey told him on the air that he already had made arrangements for 1991 to be his last season.

Eleven years later, Carey recalls the press conference.

"There wasn't a member of the media there that at one time hadn't been befriended by Ernie," Carey says. "He was universally respected by everyone who ever met him or worked with him. They took it as a personal affront, not letting him decide when he was ready to retire. I agreed. I felt if anybody deserved to determine his own fate, it was Ernie. . . . Two misconceptions arose after that. One was that my decision to retire was some sort of protest over what happened to Ernie. Not true at all. I made my decision well before that. The other was that Ernie was slipping, that he had problems with his eyesight. Absolutely false. There was no truth to that whatsoever."

Beckmann spent the day fielding the questions and complaints of irate callers on the air. Compared to his colleagues at the station, the air wasn't such a bad place to be.

That night, Channel 2 encouraged viewers to phone in with an opinion on the firing. A stunning 97 percent opposed the decision and 3 percent agreed with it. WJR received the same reaction from its public.

13

"We had to spread the telephone calls around the various people in the company because at that time we didn't have voice mails," remembers now-retired Fran Ehlers, who worked 17 years for WJR. "People in the executive offices answered calls and it was very difficult to get any business calls. We got so many pieces of mail there were bags and bags of mail that went unopened. There was no way we could open it all. All the mail we opened favored Ernie."

What few business calls were able to get through weren't much different from the calls from viewers. Affiliates throughout the state threatened to pull out of the Tigers network in protest of the Harwell firing.

All this happened before the next morning's newspapers hit driveways. The headlines and emotion-packed columns fueled the fury.

The *Detroit News* front-page headline asked: "WHY, BO? WHY?"

George Cantor started a memorable column with:

> Thanks a lot, and out with the garbage.
> That's how they deal with legends these days.
> I have never seen anything quite so totally lacking in class and courage as the sacking of Ernie Harwell.

The *Detroit Free Press* front-page headline captured the sentiments of Michigan and beyond: "A GENTLEMAN WRONGED" ran over Mitch Albom's column. Of WJR and the Tigers, Albom wrote, "Hey guys, why not punch Santa in the face while you're at it?"

Jerry Green of the *Detroit News* called it "the most flagrant public relations disaster in the history of sports."

Columnists from New York to Los Angeles and every major market in between chimed in with similar sentiments.

Later in the week, loyal listeners gathered on Long's lawn, demanding he do something to reverse the decision, according to Ehlers. That was far preferable to what was happening on Schembechler's lawn, which Bo-bashers turned into a Dumpster.

Nobody felt the wrath more than Bo. His love-him-or-hate-him personality and big name made him a lightning rod for controversy.

One newspaper account detailed how the current yearbook of the Sigma Alpha Epsilon fraternity of which both Harwell and Schembechler were brothers showed that Harwell was up-to-date on his dues and Schembechler was not. Another reported that Doug Romain, assistant operations manager of the airport control tower, renamed a section of airspace over Detroit Metro from Boshm to Harwl.

Everywhere Schembechler looked he saw "Bo Doesn't Know" bumper stickers. The old football coach must have been looking for someone to flag the media for piling on. He found that someone in veteran *Detroit News* columnist Joe Falls, Schembechler's biographer.

Falls had been on vacation during the Harwell press conference. He returned to work with a bang. The headline stripped across the top of page A-1 that ran over Falls' January 6, 1991, column read: "WJR'S BOSS: I FIRED HARWELL."

Long told Falls that he wanted to fire Harwell effective immediately, but that Schembechler insisted he be given the send-off a legend deserves and convinced Long to let Harwell work through the 1991 season. The following day, Falls came back with a column critical of Harwell for "turning on" the Tigers.

Not everyone at WJR bought that the mild-mannered Long was the mastermind behind the plan to end Harwell's career. The Tigers had just signed a five-year, $15 million extension with the station, and the agreement included a clause that said either side could terminate the contract if it felt that the other side did something to embarrass it.

While everyone else concentrated on Harwell's coast-to-coast support from media and fans alike, Falls was the first to detail what was going on closer to home for Harwell.

"There is a real coolness at Tiger Stadium toward this man now, and it comes from many of the people who considered him a close friend these past 31 years," Falls wrote.

Campbell, Tigers manager Sparky Anderson, and Doc Fenkell, in charge of broadcasting for the Tigers at the time, all withdrew from Harwell, once a close friend. They all embraced the company line that Harwell should have taken his gold watch and gone home instead of telling the truth and expressing his desire to continue working at his profession.

"That's one thing I'll never understand," Ehlers says. "They just froze him out."

Eleven years later, Beckmann, who praises Harwell for always being there for him when he needs advice, expresses why he disagrees with the way Harwell handled his press conference.

"I think you have to know that by doing that, you're going to hurt the team and its image, the radio station and its image, and you're going to hurt the salespeople at the radio station," Beckmann says. "He made a pretty good living for a long time, and if they feel it's time for you to go, why not just say thank you and go?"

Why not? For the same reason men forced out at Ford and General Motors for no deeper reason than the numbers on their birth certificates didn't want to go when they were shown the door by younger, slicker corporate climbers when they knew they still could get the job done. Harwell became a hero to many such men, a poster boy for age discrimination.

"Atta boy, Ernie!" senior citizens hollered at Harwell in parking lots and in line at Kroger stores. "Same thing happened to me. Don't let 'em get away with it. Go get 'em!"

As spring training of 1991 neared, Dale Petroskey, then president of the Mayo Smith Society, the Tigers' fan club, and now president of the Hall of Fame in Cooperstown, led the charge in trying to get the Tigers to change their decision. In a letter to Schembechler dated February 6, Petroskey wrote, in part:

> Dear Bo:
> Consider this a heart-to-heart. You and the Tigers are in deep trouble with your most loyal fans. It takes a lot to make Tigers fans angry, but many are even beyond angry to the point of antipathy. And this feeling is wide and it's deep.
>
> When the Ernie situation broke in late September, the Mayo Smith Society did not pile on like many other groups and individuals. We knew there must be more to the story, and we waited till the other shoe dropped. When it did, we asked our members what they thought.
>
> Frankly, I was taken aback by the feelings expressed in the hundreds of letters which came quickly to our mailbox. There is genuine anger pointed at you and Mr. Monaghan and the organization. Tigers fans are loyal to a fault most times, and the degree of anger in the letters

gives me great reason to be concerned about the future, and you should be, too.

. . . Ernie works for you and WJR, but he belongs to the fans—and we simply want him back.

I have been in public relations all my professional life—at the White House as Assistant Press Secretary to the President, as Assistant Secretary of Transportation for Public Affairs under Elizabeth Dole, and at *National Geographic*. And I've run the Mayo Smith Society for eight years.

Bo, you have a very serious public relations problem on your hands that is not going to go away. They may not be demonstrating in the streets of Detroit or Lansing or Grand Rapids. But there is deep, deep hurt in the hearts of Tigers fans and that will likely never heal if you don't do something to turn it around. They may come to the park—less often, probably—but they won't cheer with quite as much enthusiasm, or pass on the Tigers' tradition to their sons quite as readily.

. . . I know it's tough to admit a mistake. But we all make them. You alone have the stature, well earned over 20-plus years in the public eye in Michigan, to stand above all that has happened in the past several weeks and show some wisdom. Don't confuse wisdom with weakness. Believe me, no one would accuse you of showing weakness or bending to the wishes of the media or the fans if you brought back the beloved Ernie for a few years. They would say you are a reasonable guy who can run a baseball team.

Then get on with the business of the 1991 season with the fans smiling again, and feeling good about you and Mr. Monaghan and the Tigers. By the way, I think you've done a fine job in the off-season and that this is going to be an exciting year. Don't let Ernie's leaving spoil it.

If you want to talk about this, please give me a call.

Best,

Dale

Campbell responded to the letter for Schembechler and didn't count to 10 before typing it. Among its contents:

There is no need for you to answer this letter because as far as I'm concerned, our ties have been severed. Please don't ask me for any further support because you will damn sure be put in your place. . . . I can assure you once again that you have lost me as a friend and one of your most ardent supporters. I would suggest that you and the Mayo Smith Society go your way and I'll go mine. One thing you can count on is the fact that Bo Schembechler will run this organization and he will do a damn good job without your advice or help.

Petroskey, on the phone from his office in Cooperstown, looks back on the turbulent times:

For a guy who grew up loving the Tigers, for them to reach that depth when somebody thought it was a good move to fire Ernie Harwell was a really strange time. He's as big a name as anybody in Tigers history because of his link to the fans.

They were some kind of angry, I'll tell you that. And surprised and bewildered and puzzled by it all and we still are. Why would you do anything to one of your prized possessions when you didn't need to?

Long said he would consider bringing Harwell back, but he said it would take the Tigers' cooperation, which never came.

"They got very stubborn and thought it would pass over," Petroskey remembers. "From a public relations viewpoint, I think they had a bit of a tin ear."

Petroskey was not the only recipient of Campbell's critical words.

Harwell met with Campbell in his spring training office on February 19, 1991.

Campbell: "Ernie, you and I have been friends for over 30 years and we've never had any problems except for that singer [José Feliciano's controversial 1968 World Series anthem put Harwell in hot water for selecting him], but I want to make it clear where I stand with you over what happened last winter. You've hurt this ballclub more than you can ever realize. You've hurt a lot of people, many of them you have hurt financially. You should never have called a press conference."

Harwell: "Jim, all I did was make the announcement."

Campbell: "You didn't have to do any more than that. The media took it from there. Now we've got Bo getting all kinds of phone calls and people throwing things on his lawn."

The next morning, Harwell met with Campbell again.

Harwell: "Jim, yesterday we didn't get to the bottom line."

Campbell: "Oh yes we did."

Harwell: "No, Jim. The bottom line is: do you still want to be my friend?"

Campbell: "We'll have to see about that. It all depends on how things work out."

Harwell: "But Jim, I thought friends were friends regardless of what happened. I thought friends were willing to forgive and forget. I will forgive and forget. Do you think we can still be friends?"

Campbell: "I don't know. We'll have to see how things go."

Translation: Take your pink slip, go home quietly, and we can resume our friendship. Fight to keep your job and we're history.

The front office also grumbled about Harwell doing so many TV, radio, and print interviews in the wake of the December 19 press conference. "My feeling on that was that I had always cooperated when things were good for me, so I wasn't going to disappear when things were going bad," he says. "That wouldn't have been fair to the people who wanted to interview me."

Taking great care not to be perceived as a couple attempting to drum up sympathy, the Harwells kept quiet a pressing family concern. On the very same week of the press conference, Lulu was diagnosed with breast cancer. Charlie Vincent broke that story the following spring. Vincent had asked Harwell why he had been showing up later

than usual, and Harwell told him it was because he had been taking Lulu to radiation treatments. Vincent said he thought that was newsworthy and wanted to write it. Consistent with his lifelong pattern of cooperating with writers, Harwell said he understood.

Ewald, who would have strongly advised against the decision to fire Harwell had he been consulted, and Dave Diles, a retired telecaster who worked in Detroit and on the *Prudential Halftime Report* for ABC-TV, offer interesting takes on those stormy days of 1990 and 1991.

Ewald covered the Tigers for the *Detroit News* for five years before taking a job with the club in 1978. He now handles Sparky Anderson's appearances and teaches English and journalism at Oakland University and Wayne State.

Ewald on Ernie: "I think it's easier for fans to identify with people from the electronic media. They become kind of icons, so to speak, more so than ink-stained wretches. Ernie did it in a way that endeared himself to all facets of society. Detroit is basically a blue-collar town even though there is a lot of money. Ernie's appeal crossed the spectrum from blue-collar to a higher strata of society and did it in a way I never saw anybody do it. He may not have had the national reputation of Vin Scully in L.A. or Harry Caray in Chicago, but here in Detroit he is regarded as the grandfather figure who is always there. His approach is very, very down to earth. He doesn't try to overwhelm people with vocabulary leaving them wondering: what's he saying? Part of his strength and his charm is he's very reachable. He can fit into all aspects of society. Fans like to identify with sports heroes, and they can through him very, very easily."

Ewald on the firing: "There have been a lot of misconceptions on that, I think, and I can only give you my perspective of it. I think it's a perspective that hasn't really been written properly. I don't have the full story even though I was there. I wasn't privy to everything. . . . You've got to understand what kind of guy Bo is. Bo is a no-nonsense guy who knew more about baseball than what he was given credit for. His strength is he is a leader of men, especially in sports. He felt what went on on the field was more important than what happened in the media. WJR was looking for 'a younger type audience,' ways to sparkle up their broadcast in a lot of ways, not just baseball. I think what happened was, someone at 'JR had been talking to Jeff Odenwald. I think the conversation was, 'We think we would like to replace Ernie, but that will never happen.' I don't know for sure, but I think Jeff said something like, 'Oh no, don't worry, I'll take care of this.' He goes to Bo and says 'JR wants to do this and Bo, in his naïveté, figures the most important thing we've got is on the field. He's thinking like an old coach. To my understanding, 'JR wanted to let Ernie go right then, and Bo said, 'No we can't do it that way, he has to have at least another year to say goodbye properly.' Bo insisted he have another year, to which WJR said OK. I think if someone were able to dig out the true story they would find that it originated with Odenwald and whomever he talked to at WJR. I'll die believing that. I would be remiss if I didn't tell you I have a natural suspicion of a lot of marketing types. Some of their methods aren't filled with conscience. . . . Bo wasn't going to let anybody else take the heat. He's not that kind of man. Bo is of the same ilk as Sparky. He would never pass the buck just to get heat off of him. He would figure that's what I'm paid for and I'm stronger than the other guys. He would take it and wouldn't say anything. One of the things that really bothers me is Bo took a lot of unjustifiable vilification for it. He's a man's man. And I have a lot of respect for him. Bo's word is his word. If he tells you something, you can go to the bank with it."

Similar to Ewald, Diles' roots stretch back to the print media. His first assignment for the Associated Press was covering Heisman Trophy–winner Hopalong Cassidy's college football debut at Ohio State. Fritz Howell, regional sports editor for the AP, gave Diles a piece of advice on his way out the door: "Look at every game you cover as a fight between a shark and an alligator and you don't care which one wins." Diles was 20 and a native of Ohio. He needed that talk, and it took root. He thought so much of Howell, who edited his stories for him before they went to the copy desk without telling anyone, that he was with Howell when he died. Diles wouldn't disgrace his mentor by being anything but objective on a story, even an extremely sensitive one.

So when popular WJR morning host J. P. McCarthy called him on his 23-acre Southern Ohio farm he shares with deer and wild turkey and asked him for his take on the Harwell firing, Diles viewed Harwell as a shark and Schembechler as an alligator, and then he voiced his honest opinion. Like so many others, Diles had strong relationships with both men. He had hosted the *Bo Schembechler Show* on Channel 7.

Of Harwell, Diles says: "There is a quote that says the true test of a gentleman is how he treats people who can be of no possible service to him. That's Ernie. He's friendly to everyone."

A shark and an alligator.

"When J.P. asked me about it, I blurted out if Schembechler is president, the buck stops with him," says Diles, who has written eight books on his manual typewriter. "When you allow a radio station to dictate who will do your play-by-play, you're in trouble. Bo saw me at a celebrity golf outing at Tam O'Shanter Country Club and jumped all over me. We got into a shouting match. He shouted: 'I didn't have anything to do with that.' I shouted: 'You should have protected him. Either way you were wrong.' I wrote Bo a two-page letter telling him he owed me an apology. The next time I saw him he acted like nothing happened and we were fine."

Schembechler was accustomed to Bob Ufer, the animated homer who was the longtime voice of Michigan football. Harwell's style was as different from Ufer's as football is from baseball.

A report out of London, Ontario, made some wonder whether Schembechler was the inspiration behind the firing of Harwell.

A *London Times* reporter had overheard another member of the media talking about how the couple that drove Schembechler and minor league director Joe McDonald back to the airport after they were evaluating Tigers minor league prospects at Labatt Park overheard Schembechler call Harwell's announcing style "boring." The reporter went with the story, which greatly strained the relationship between the Tigers and their Double A affiliate in London. The story did not identify the drivers of the car.

Pete Lapkowski drove the car, and his wife, Joan, then an accountant for the since-defunct London Tigers, rode shotgun. Schembechler and McDonald sat in the backseat.

"They were dressed like two older men who had just gotten off the golf course," Lapkowski remembers. "We were all listening to Harwell on the Tiger broadcast."

He doesn't remember much from the broadcast, only that there was a fly ball and then a pause. During that pause, he remembers Schembechler saying, "something like, well, this isn't very exciting."

A smoking gun?

"I really don't think so," Lapkowski says. "If that story hadn't come out in the paper, I might not have made any connection between that little comment Bo made and Ernie Harwell getting fired."

Says Carey, Harwell's partner: "I don't like to preserve negative memories, and that was such an unpleasant time."

Through it all, the mail Harwell received buoyed his spirits, especially the feelings expressed by young listeners.

Tony Hawley, 13, from Belding, Michigan, mailed a three-page letter to Harwell shortly after the press conference. Harwell never will forget this part of it: "Ernie, if you ever need a place to stay, a job, or some money, or even an organ (you know, like a kidney), I'm here to help."

A young boy by the name of Mark Brown, writing under the pen name Tommy Hawkins, authored a book entitled *The Voice Underneath the Pillow* and had his aunt mail it to Harwell. It was a fictitious version of the Tigers and all that was happening. The team is called the River City Tomahawks, the veteran announcer is named Old Pete. Sammy was the boy with the transistor radio under his pillow.

Two pages from the book:

> Sammy knew that baseball would never be the same or as good without that old familiar voice he had known and loved and counted on for so many years. But not just that, Sammy would miss the man behind the voice—the man whose voice for so many years had come from underneath his pillow. "What a shame it is," thought Sammy, "the way some people will throw away the old things and old ways and old people—just because they are old."

For some, watching Harwell work that final season in 1991 was like watching a friend's funeral procession crawl three hours at a time for 162 days. If it was a funeral, at least Harwell was able to hear and read all those nice eulogies. The *Detroit Free Press* and *Detroit News* both printed special tribute sections to Harwell and Carey on the final day of the season. The problem with hearing all the eulogies was that Harwell knew his abilities weren't sick, much less dead.

Harwell's final 1991 broadcast was of the last game ever played at Baltimore's Memorial Stadium, which he had baptized 37 years earlier as the first voice of the Orioles.

At that point, most believed the only way to listen to Harwell calling a Tigers game again would be to listen the way a missionary boy who had left Detroit for Papua, New Guinea, with his family listened.

Isaac Micheals wrote to Harwell: "I am not able to listen to baseball games over here and so I listen to a tape of an old Tiger game with you broadcasting on it and I still go to bed listening to a Tiger game, just like I did when I was eight or nine years old."

Harwell's career as voice of the Tigers apparently was dead. His loyal listeners were left to reflect on his compelling life, one that began on January 25, 1918.

Chapter 2

A Tongue-Tied
Georgia Boy

I n the 20th century's second decade, Gray and Helen Harwell brought
three sons into the rural sliver of the world known as Washington,
Georgia. Population: 2,500. Recreation: watching the paint dry on the
colossal columns of the antebellum homes that graced the town.

For those in a hurry, rapid transit was available: two mules, a big
conductor holding a whip, and a carriage into which as many as eight
passengers could cram. Big, bold letters boasted WASHINGTON
RAPID TRANSIT on the side of the coach.

The Harwells rented a more modest home than the sprawling man-
sions occupied by wealthier folks, though it was by no means a small
abode. Gray, who answered to his middle name and not his first name,
Davis, ran a furniture store with his brother Tom, and, as was custom-
ary in small towns, it doubled as a funeral home, because they were the
ones making and selling the caskets.

Davis Jr., the extroverted oldest son, had his own circle of friends
and was too old to gain much pleasure from the company of his two

younger brothers, the more cynical, introverted Dick, a voracious reader, and Ernie, the precocious, ever-upbeat baby of the family, born January 25, 1918. Dick and Ernie, born less than two years apart, were inseparable, linked by their mutual passion for their father's game of choice, baseball.

As boys so often do, the Harwells lent their father mythical status. Ernie, eyes as blue as they were wide, hair blond and curly, grew particularly impressed when Daddy returned from trips to Chicago and shared the conversations he had had with his pal, the major league baseball player Sherrod Smith, an old friend from Georgia.

Gray visited the furniture mart in Chicago and while in town made it over to the ballpark and sat in the visiting dugout to catch up with Smith, a left-handed pitcher who started his career with Pittsburgh, gained World Series fame pitching for Brooklyn, and finished with Cleveland.

Any big leaguer would have impressed the boys. That this was Sherrod Smith, no humpty-dumpty, made the sparkle in their eyes all the brighter. Smith was noted for having the best pickoff move in the game, and he was noted for far more than that.

He locked left arms with none other than Babe Ruth in the longest World Series pitching duel ever waged. Pitching for the Red Sox, Ruth defeated Smith and the Dodgers in 14 innings, 2–1 in 1916, a story told many times in the Harwell household.

Times were good at home and at work until Mother Nature found the friendly little Georgia town and turned it inside out.

When Ernie was five, boll weevils, those long-snouted, relentless little bugs, hit Washington, devoured the cotton crops, and destroyed the economy. The farmers who had purchased furniture on credit had no means to pay their bills. The Harwell brothers, Gray and Tom, barely had enough to pay their creditors and were forced to close up shop. Like so many other families, they moved to the big city to find work.

They didn't have the means to own a car, but they could afford to keep three African-American servants working for as little as 50 cents a week, including Mammy, as much a part of the family as anybody. She made sure the boys scrubbed behind their ears, saw that they minded Mother and Daddy, and aided in myriad household chores.

The Harwells piled into another family's car and made the 100-mile journey to Atlanta, and what a journey it was. The rains turned dirt roads difficult enough to negotiate when dry into a muddy mess. They slogged along until the mud made them stop. Out of the car they filed and pushed, pushed, pushed, until they were back on their way. And so it went. Stuck in the mud, out of the car to push, back in the car until the mud made the wheels spin in vain again.

Muddied and weary, they made it to Atlanta and found an economically healthier town than the one they left behind. Gray went to work at a branch of the Mather Brothers furniture store chain, known for its homespun motto: "Good and Bad Furniture." Mammy and her husband, Jim, had their own basement apartment in the home the Harwells rented on Piedmont Avenue.

Ernie's passion for baseball reached a new level one October day in 1926. He and his brother Davis listened to Game 7 of the 1926 World Series, pitting the Cardinals against the Yankees, on a crystal set. Such radios required listeners to hunt through a pool of mercury for stations by holding a small piece of wire called a cat whisker. To move would be to lose the station, so the Harwell brothers sat motionless for two hours and listened to Graham McNamee's dramatic presentation of the World Series. One earphone was in Davis' ear, the other in Ernie's.

With the Cardinals leading by a run, the bases loaded, and two men out in the seventh, Cardinals player/manager Rogers Hornsby summoned Grover Cleveland Alexander from the bullpen to face Yankees second baseman Tony Lazzeri. Alexander had pitched his second complete game of that World Series the previous day and had celebrated

The Days of Great Voices Are History

When radio began in the mid-1920s, voice was everything. That's not true anymore. The voice on radio—and its big brother, TV—is secondary to content. I think the modern way is better, but I miss some of the great voices of the past.

The first announcers came to radio from the ranks of singers. Graham McNamee, pioneer sports announcer, took an audition at NBC as a singer and was soon converted to announcing. He and his early rival, Ted Husing, had fantastic voices. Their vocal coloration enhanced every event they covered.

Later, Bill Stern hit the network sports broadcasting scene. Stern entered radio from the stage. He had been stage manager at RCA Music Hall in New York. His voice had a touch of the dramatic and spawned many imitators in his day.

Despite his great popularity, Stern had a weakness. He knew little about sports, but his lack of knowledge didn't faze him. I broadcast the Masters golf tournament with him for two years, 1942 and 1946, and he insisted on talking about the golfers' points instead of strokes. Certainly a basic faux pas.

Husing was different. He added knowledge and dedication to his great voice.

Ted was the first announcer who really studied his sport. He gathered background on the events he covered and always displayed a thorough preparation.

Red Barber was the first baseball announcer to take the Husing approach and prepare himself before a game. But Red did not have a great voice. When I worked with him in Brooklyn in 1948–1949, his voice was so light and weak that our engineer had to turn up the volume full force.

Today's announcers are much better prepared than the old-timers. The moderns work harder, too, but the emphasis on voice is history. Even the studio announcers—with some exceptions—can't match the great voices of Paul Douglas, Andre Baruch, and Don Wilson.

And what about those distinctive news voices? Voices like those of Lowell Thomas, Douglas Edwards, Edward R. Murrow, Gabriel Heatter, and Walter Cronkite. They were classic.

Ray Scott had a great sports voice. His Green Bay Packers broadcasts are still remembered. Of the network moderns, Jon Miller and Bob Costas have a fine sound for play-by-play. Most of the analysts don't worry about voice. The content of what they say is much more important than how they say it.

The best voice I ever worked with belonged to Paul Carey, my partner for 17 years on Tigers broadcasts. Everybody loved that deep, booming sound. And along with his voice, Paul brought dedication and thorough preparation.

I miss Paul and all those other great voices that used to be such an integral part of radio and TV.

—E.H., April 1998

deep into the night, figuring his work was done. Alexander struck out Lazzeri, and the Cardinals won it in the ninth when Ruth was thrown out trying to steal second. And a little boy from Washington, Georgia, was forever hooked on the magic of baseball and radio.

More often, it was the voices of the men calling the games of his beloved Atlanta Crackers that Harwell listened to and mimicked. He went to the house of a neighbor, Thad Johnson, who built radios and listened to the Crackers. If Thad wasn't home, Ernie had to get creative to hear the broadcasts that made him feel as if he had a front-row seat. If it meant he had to wander the neighborhood to find an open window under which he could stand and listen to Jimmy Davenport and Mike Thomas call Crackers games, then wander the neighborhood he did. The cracking of the bat and smacking of the glove mesmerized the young boy, who likewise was entranced by the distant cries of the vendors that could be heard over the radio.

He did more than listen to baseball. He played it and read about it and spent so much time daydreaming about the sport. When Ernie wasn't tossing a baseball against the steps, inventing games with his brother Dick, the boys were wearing out another baseball board game played on a field with a tin base and wooden sides. The ball, a marble, could be thrown fast or slow, depending on which button was pushed.

Their father was fond of telling them baseball was a "talkin' game, passed along from generation to generation."

Doc Green, the druggist back in Washington, was one of Ernie's first baseball heroes. He had played semiprofessional baseball with the Georgia Peach, Ty Cobb, and that alone granted him small-town celebrity status.

Folks gathered around the radio at Doc's to listen to Crackers games, and it was there, during summer visits back to Washington, that Ernie's broadcasting career was informally launched. He wasn't quite ready for prime time.

Doc or one of his customers would lift the young boy onto a stool, push a frosty mug of Coca-Cola in front of him, and urge him to do an imaginary broadcast of a Crackers game. Howls of laughter followed as the baseball-obsessed boy lit up the room with so much enthusiasm and a speech impediment that, among other things, prevented him from pronouncing the letter *s*.

"And Thmith thlides into thecond bathe!" he bellowed to the delight of his audience.

The laughter was all in good fun and no feelings were wounded. The boy's father had the vision to see beyond the counter at Doc Green's and knew the tongue tied in knots wouldn't always trigger such friendly responses. He knew schoolyard taunts had the potential to scar the boy's unbridled enthusiasm for life. One night at the dinner table, while Ernie lisped his way through a conversation, his father declared, "We need to get that boy some help."

Strapped for cash, as were so many families during the Depression, the Harwells nonetheless decided to send their son to the local elocution teacher for weekly sessions.

Passage by passage, Margaret Lackland helped eager young Ernie unfasten his tongue.

Mrs. Lackland had Ernie read passages from various works of literature, including a poem, "The House by the Side of the Road," by Sam Walter Foss.

At first he read:

> There are hermit thouls that live withdrawn
> In the peathe of their thelf-content

In time, and not a short time, it became:

> There are hermit souls that live withdrawn
> In the peace of their self-content

Mrs. Lackland, who counted Benjamin Franklin among her ancestors, also taught her pupils debating skills. Ernie learned well enough to win first place in a local debate competition.

The Tenth Street School awarded a gold medal to the best boy debater and another to the best girl of each graduating class. A panel of judges selected by the P.T.A. president gave a gold medal to Lucy Beacham and one to Earnest Harwell.

Decades later, when Mrs. Lackland was well into her eighties and still teaching speech, she read a magazine article written by her former pupil and wrote a letter to him that, in part, read: "I shall never forget the day you won the medal. Your dad stood there with tears streaming down his face and said, 'This is the happiest day of my life.'"

Those who knew Davis Gray Harwell marveled at how his life was filled with nothing but happy days, despite circumstances that would leave weaker men with broken spirits and bitter hearts.

Several years after he moved his family to Atlanta, the head of the Harwell household underwent brain surgery to have a tumor removed. He was left temporarily paralyzed from the waist down. Years later, in the early 1930s, the paralysis returned and was permanent. There was talk that multiple sclerosis might be the cause. He had no trouble talking, had a sharp mind, and lived until he was 72. Unfortunately, he was limited to a life at home. He couldn't work and was only as mobile as a primitive wooden wheelchair enabled. His days of taking the boys to the ballpark to see the Crackers were over.

His wife and sons became the breadwinners in the family. If this wounded his pride, he refused to show it and forever remained upbeat, thus imparting the wisdom of positive thinking onto his children.

Mrs. Harwell supported the family and in doing so filled the home with sweet scents of baked goods from lemon cheesecake to chocolate rolls to Lady Baltimore Cake. She made sandwiches, as many as 400 at a time, for debut parties. She made wedding cakes and birthday cakes. Customers, sensitive to the family's circumstances, often came to the house to pick up the baked goods. The boys pitched in by riding the streetcar to the drug store to deliver cakes. The ride cost a nickel each way, and the cakes were sold for 50 cents apiece.

Ernie delivered more than cakes. He earned $2 a week tossing the *Atlanta Georgian* onto porches from his bicycle. The 90 customers had a choice of which of the three editions—the first, the market edition, or the baseball edition—they wanted delivered. They paid 10 cents a week for the newspaper only, 12 cents for the newspaper plus life insurance.

Even before Ernie had a paper route, he exhibited an entrepreneurial flair. Without any urging from his parents, Ernie went door-to-door selling magazines. Later, he sold Christmas cards.

Be it his smile, his sparkling eyes, his curly hair, or the pity he inspired as an undersized youth—whatever the cause—little Ernie had a knack for sales. Even so, he wasn't all work and no play Ernie. He found time to pursue his passion. He found time to play ball.

Most of the games were three-on-three or four-on-four with other boys from the neighborhood. The godfather of these games was a bachelor in his thirties who had no social life to speak of and seemingly no passion that extended beyond the game played on the dusty sandlots on those steamy, hot Georgia afternoons.

Blacky Blackstock, a chubby little left-handed hitter who worked at a filling station, never grew tired of hitting grounders and fly balls to the boys. He was always there to correct them when they failed to play the game the right way. He regaled them with tales of his days playing semipro ball. He even taught some of the older boys how to drive a car.

Ernie's first taste of organized ball came when he was selected to the Piedmont Pirates All-Star team at about the age of 11.

In March of 1930, at the age of 12, Ernie experienced a thrill greater than playing for the Piedmont Pirates.

The Yankees stopped in Atlanta on their trip north from spring training to play an exhibition game at Ponce de Leon Park. Harwell snuck down to the front row of the box seats, and when the great Babe Ruth came off the field, he pleaded with him for an autograph.

Ruth called everyone kid, though he pronounced it "keed."

"Keed," he told Harwell, "you ain't got no paper. What am I gonna sign?"

"You can sign my shoe," Harwell told him, and left him no choice. He wheeled his leg over the railing and offered one of his Keds.

The Babe got a chuckle out of the kid's determination and obliged.

"OK," he said. "I'll sign your shoe."

It didn't occur to Ernie that he could have saved that tennis shoe and one day made a pretty penny off it. It was just a tennis shoe and tennis shoes are made for feet, not trophy cases. He kept right on wearing that shoe until it was worn out and then thrown out.

Four years later, Ernie saw the Babe play in a game that counted in the standings.

Ernie's mother had an uncle named Lauren Foreman. He took it upon himself to make sure that Ernie's exposure to baseball would not be hindered by his father's condition.

In 1934, when Ernie was between his sophomore and junior years in high school, Foreman arranged for him to come to Chicago so that he could see a regular-season major league game in person for the first time.

Ernie took the train to Chicago and his great-uncle, no big baseball fan, made plans to take him to see the White Sox play the Yankees. The game was rained out and so was the next day's.

"I don't care how long you have to stay, you're going to see a game," Foreman reassured the disappointed teenager. "I don't care if we have to change your train ticket, you're going to see a game. We'll do whatever it takes."

When the rain finally ended, Red Ruffing of the Yankees faced Ted Lyons of the White Sox. It was Ruth's final American League game in Chicago, and he entertained the crowd with a running catch in foul territory in left field. Lou Gehrig tried to duck from two pitches that ricocheted off his bat and landed over the third baseman's head for doubles. One was identical to the next, and in all his decades of watching baseball, Harwell would never see another hit that followed the path of those two doubles in one day by one hitter.

In October of 1935, Foreman sent for Ernie again, this time so that he could attend the middle three games of the World Series between the Cubs and Tigers at Wrigley Field.

Nine years after Ernie listened to his first World Series game, he witnessed his first one. Submarine-style pitcher Elden Auker was on the mound for the Tigers, and Bill Lee pitched for the Cubs. Marv Owen scored the winning run on a Jo-Jo White single for the Tigers to break a 5–5 tie in the eleventh inning.

Watching baseball was enjoyable, but even watching the Babe didn't do quite as much for Ernie as playing the game.

He was skilled enough to play for the North Side Terrors, an American Legion team. Ernie filled the vacancy at second base created by the departure of Marty Marion, who would go on to become one of the greatest shortstops in the history of the major leagues. Marty's brother Roy Marion was Ernie's double-play partner.

When Ernie rifled those newspapers onto porches from his bicycle, in his head he was taking Roy Marion's feed and firing to Louie Perkerson at first base to complete the double play. In those fantasies, the formidable double play combination would be wearing the uniforms of the Atlanta Crackers, not the North Side Terrors. They would be playing in the Southern League, not the American Legion.

That boyhood dream took on a measure of reality when the Terrors made it to the championship game, played at Ponce de Leon Park, home of the Crackers.

Harwell wore his sleeves long, mimicking those of his boyhood idol, Crackers second baseman Jack Sheehan.

The Terrors lost in the championship game to the Grant Park Aces, though just to gain the thrill of playing at such a grand ballpark as a young teen was an unforgettable victory in itself.

The Marion boys went on to star at Tech High. Harwell attended adjacent Boys High, Tech's bitter rival. Ernie didn't play baseball for the high school. He was too busy making money. Besides, he wasn't sure he hit well enough to play for the highly competitive team. It wasn't until he was on a rifle range in the Marine Corps that he discovered the source of his hitting troubles. He was in need of glasses.

At Boys High, most of the classes were held in little wooden sheds called portables. The trick was to get into the classroom early enough to grab one of the desks in the middle of the room. The potbelly stove turned the back of the room into a sauna, but it didn't have the range to keep those seated in the front from shivering through classes.

Ernie tried his best to pay attention to the teachers, but the Crackers dominated Ernie's thoughts.

"Let's see, they're in Chatanooga and they're probably all eating lunch now," he would daydream.

As he finished up his homework at night, it was more of the same: "Let's see, they are probably all at the hotel, ready to go to sleep pretty soon."

Imagine little Ernie's horror when he awakened after going to bed happy about his beloved Crackers' first-place standing in the Southern League to find they had fallen all the way to last place because they were forced to forfeit 14 games over a technicality. They were in violation of rules limiting the number of experienced players on a roster.

Ernie's knack for sales and passion for baseball merged when he made trips to the visiting team's hotel and pitched himself as a willing and able batboy. He made a habit of going down to the Ansley Hotel, and he approached the manager of the visiting team to offer his services as the batboy. Sometimes the managers forgot about saying yes to the boy and sometimes they remembered. He was paid with a broken bat or a baseball or two too worn out to be of any use to the team.

He had forced his way into baseball, but he had more to offer than retrieving bats and balls. He did his best early baseball work seated in front of a typewriter.

At 16, Harwell took the bold step of writing to *The Sporting News* to offer his services as Atlanta correspondent. He read the publication religiously and noticed they did not include much news from his region of the country.

He knew he would have no shot of landing the freelance work if he confessed his age in the letter, so he did everything in his power to disguise his youth.

He signed the letter, "W. Earnest Harwell" in an attempt to come off as an older, distinguished gentleman. It worked. He landed the assignment, beginning a 31-year association with the publication.

Eventually, J. G. Taylor Spink, editor and publisher of *The Sporting News*, made Harwell one of the ghostwriters for his column. He also used sportswriters Dan Daniel from New York and Stan Baumgartner from Philadelphia.

"Don't forget to put me at these guys' lockers, chatting with them before a game," instructed Spink.

Little did the readers of *The Sporting News* know that Spink never ventured out of his office.

Harwell didn't need to camouflage his age to land a job writing for the *Tatler*, his high school newspaper.

His work for the *Tatler* earned him first place among more than three thousand contestants in the 1936 Scholastic Quill and Scroll awards, in the column writing division. The first winner of the award from the South, Harwell received as a prize a Royal portable typewriter.

In a letter dated May 13, 1936, and written on official Royal Typewriter Company, Inc., stationery from the New York corporate headquarters, W. H. Beckwith, the company's advertising manager, congratulated Harwell in three short paragraphs.

The first typo didn't appear until the third paragraph: "Again our sincere congratulations upon you fine column." No matter. Harwell learned that the "r" key, missing at the end of the word preceding "fine" in Beckwith's letter, worked properly on his new Royal typewriter. He put it to good use.

His column for the *Tatler*, entitled "Turning on the Heat," was gossipy in nature and in part informed what boys had "an eye on" which girls. Baseball updates found their way into his columns as well.

The editor's note that appeared at the top of his *Tatler* swan song in the May 26, 1936, edition read: "This, the last column by Ernie Harwell, marks the termination of the most successful year in feature writing the *Tatler* has ever known. This decidedly is the best column to appear in the 20-odd years of the paper's existence."

In that column, Harwell wrote profile sketches of several graduating students, including the two speakers on graduation night. One line from his profile on Columbia University–bound James Knight, read: "Appreciates Gilley with the dark brown eyebrows."

Of Gerald Cohen, Harwell wrote: "Class valedictorian . . . wants to reform the world (who doesn't?) . . . made terrific grade on Emory scholarship test . . . has nasal tone . . . Cohen, Cohen, gone."

Harwell managed to grade his classmate's voice quality technique and do a home-run call all at once—proof that baseball broadcasting never was far from his thoughts, even long before he did it as a living.

Harwell also worked during one summer on the sports desk at the *Atlanta Constitution* during high school.

Harwell did not conduct any interviews for the tidbits he wrote about the Crackers for *The Sporting News*. He attended games but never introduced himself to players, manager Spencer Abbott, or owner Earl Mann. At 16, he thought he was too young to bother requesting any interviews, so he rewrote stories written in the local papers.

A puzzled Mann asked everyone involved with the ballclub if they had ever met the W. Earnest Harwell whose byline he routinely read in *The Sporting News*. Everyone had the same answer: no.

Finally, after a year of working in the shadows, Harwell introduced himself to Mann. The boy had no choice. He had been assigned to write a full-length feature on the Crackers' owner. He took a deep breath and made the introduction.

Within seconds, Harwell realized his fears were unfounded. Mann, universally loved by all in baseball who came in contact with him, made the boy feel welcome immediately.

Harwell's confidence in arranging interviews grew with each passing year.

He was far more experienced than most 18-year-old boys. Still, he was naive in some ways of the world, as he would learn when he did his first actual interview of a major league player, conducted at the Georgian Terrace hotel.

The Philadelphia Athletics were on their way north from spring training in 1936, in town to play the Crackers. Harwell figured Wally Moses would make an interesting story for *Baseball Magazine*. He called Moses at his hotel, and the outfielder agreed to meet him the next morning.

He wasn't hearing stories about Sherrod Smith from his father this time, and he wasn't merely getting a legend to sign his shoe. He was interviewing a real, live big leaguer, a bona fide hero, whom he was sure would give him the respect owed a professional journalist.

Moses let him into the room and barely paid any attention to him. He was in the midst of a conversation with Bob Johnson and Pinky Higgins, and he wasn't about to let the presence of a teenage reporter deter him from the hot topic of discussion. The ballplayers recounted in graphic detail their exploits between the sheets from the previous night, one man outdoing the other with tales unfit for Harwell's virgin ears.

Harwell managed to pry a few printable quotes out of Moses, and he was paid $10 for the thousand-word story that made no mention of Moses and mates boasting of their off-the-field prowess.

The lesson Harwell learned that shocking morning—ballplayers are just that, ballplayers, not gods—was worth far more than the check he received from *Baseball Magazine*.

Harwell had begun to learn life's lessons and was ready to continue his education at Emory University in Atlanta.

Chapter 3

Meeting Miss Lulu

Sigma Alpha Epsilon fraternity dances were quite the social events in simpler times. The boys wore suits and were frisked at the door, just in case they had any ideas of smuggling alcohol. Girls spent hours shopping for just the right dress, and at just the right price, to wear to the social gatherings. The girls weren't searched. They were trusted because, well, girls just didn't do things like that back then.

Walter Bundy, handsome and among the brightest in his class at Emory University, was more than a little proud at a fraternity dance in 1940. The source of his pride had nothing to do with either his looks or his grades. His date was the prettiest girl at the dance, and that's why he had that little extra swagger that distinguished him from more ordinary fellows.

Miss Lulu Tankersley, brown-haired beauty from Hazard, Kentucky, attended Brenau College in Gainesville, Georgia, on an academic scholarship. Her father, Ford Tankersley, a railroad worker, died in a train accident when she was four years old, and in her only memory of him she is saying good-bye at the funeral. Her mother supported the family from the revenue generated at her beauty shop.

She didn't remarry until a dozen years or so later, to a man who also worked on the railroad.

Brenau was an all-girls school and a formal one at that. A three-piece orchestra played every night at dinner at the college, and the girls all wore nylon stockings and dresses, never pants or tennis shoes. The students dined at the table with professors and, often, the wives of professors. Rowdiness at the dinner table wasn't an issue. In the company of faculty, the girls were all on their best behavior.

Born Lula, she went by her nickname given to her by childhood friends who stole it from the song, "Don't Bring Lulu."

Bundy brought Lulu and made the mistake of introducing her to one of the young gentlemen whose heads she had turned. The rest is romantic history. If baseball is Ernie Harwell's first love, then Miss Lulu, one year his junior, is his true love.

They quickly discovered they both had a passion for reading and a special talent for writing.

Fraternity brothers and sorority sisters filled the dance hall with talk of books and films. Inevitably, the conversation wound its way around to *Gone with the Wind*, the novel that gripped the South like no other and made quite a splash when made into a film.

Harwell's connections to the hottest topic of conversation in the South were far greater than those of most college students.

Without embellishing, he told of how Margaret Mitchell, the novel's author, was on his paper route. Long before he put money in her pocket by buying her compelling novel rife with romance and tragedy, she put money in his pocket when he collected his paper money at her door. He sold her Christmas cards, and he saw her frequently when she came to the house to buy his mother's baked goods.

He didn't have to stop at that. He could also tell the tale of how he assisted *Life* magazine with its coverage of the magnificent film premiere in Atlanta in 1939, however minimal his role. *Life* wanted to use a shot of the premiere for its cover and sent George Karger, the world's eminent theatrical photographer, to Atlanta to carry out the assignment. Knowing that Karger, a native of Germany, would need able assistants to help him get around a city completely foreign to him, an editor at *Life* called Ralph McGill of the *Atlanta Constitution* for suggestions. McGill, who later in life would win a Pulitzer for his efforts to accelerate integration through his work, assigned Harwell and George Tysinger to make Karger's every wish their command.

It didn't take Karger long to infuriate the local photographers, who had no use whatsoever for his pomposity. *Life* had arranged for Karger to shoot an exclusive photograph of Clark Gable and Margaret Palmer, an honoree from the Junior League Ball, posing in front of the *Cyclorama*, a massive, panoramic painting of the Civil War Battle of Atlanta.

Harwell and Tysinger toted Karger's equipment, guarded it, and assisted with the lighting. For their efforts, they gained admission to the exclusive Junior League Ball. They also got to chat with Clark Gable while the photograph was being arranged.

"He was a very nice man, very down-to-earth," Harwell told anyone who was interested, and it would be next to impossible to find anyone back then who was not interested.

Nobody could say the same of Karger, who had come down from New York, where he lived, and acted so superior. The other photographers exacted their revenge on him by showing up for the photo session, climbing onto a platform, and shooting the very picture that was supposed to be *Life*'s exclusive. It ran on the front page of the local paper the very next day, which forced *Life* to change its plans for a cover. The *Gone with the Wind* film premiere was relegated to the inside pages.

The previous night, Ernie saw Gable arrive at the ball with his date, Carole Lombard. Vivien Leigh came with film star Laurence Olivier.

"I was guarding those flashbulbs, otherwise I would have danced with Vivien," Ernie told Lulu, getting a chuckle out of her.

The best Miss Lulu could counter with in trying to match Ernie's brush with fame was to let it be known that she also had been in

It Says Here
That Sayings Hit Home

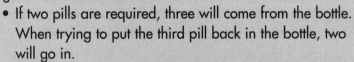

I enjoy sayings, axioms, proverbs, adages—whatever you want to call them. Here are some of my favorites. A few of these I originated, but many were garnered from other sources.

- If two pills are required, three will come from the bottle. When trying to put the third pill back in the bottle, two will go in.
- Definition of a Michigan summer: two weeks of bad ice fishing.
- No matter what your life accomplishments are, the size of your funeral will still be determined by the weather.
- When a person says, "I'll be honest with you," you can't help but wonder, "Wasn't he being honest with me before?"
- Never trust a guy who wears his jacket off his shoulder.
- Beware of anybody carrying a clipboard.
- Avoid any restaurant whose headwaiter is named Heimlich.
- Never eat at a place called "Mom's."
- The fancier the restaurant, the smaller the piece of pie.
- The quality of restaurant food varies inversely with the height of the pepper shaker.
- The higher the altitude of the restaurant, the worse the food.
- "Catch of the day" is whatever the wholesaler offered the chef as a good deal.
- Avoid changing planes in Chicago, Atlanta, and Dallas.
- An airline snack means nine salted peanuts.

- When packing, put all your clothes on one bed. Put your money on another bed. Reduce the clothes by half and double the money.
- Never call home. There is sure to be a crisis.
- It is unsportsmanlike to stop and ask directions. Stay on your own.
- The farther your room is from the hotel lobby, the better the chance is that the key card to your room won't work.
- When you need morning sleep, there will be heavy construction going on outside your room.
- Odds are 3–1 that the next restroom you locate in an airport will be closed for cleaning and slippery-izing of the floor.
- The shorter the time between flights, the longer the distance between airport gates.
- The better the radio reception, the worse the music.
- The bar code in the checkout line will never work on the item you are embarrassed to buy.
- The speaker who says "I'll be brief" will make the longest speech of the night.

—E.H., June 1994

Atlanta the night of the premiere. Traveling by train home from school, she and a few friends had time to kill while waiting for their connection in Atlanta. They piled into a cab and told the driver they wanted to get as close to the premiere as possible. He was able to get within a couple of blocks, close enough for the girls to taste the excitement in the air but too far to see anything of interest.

There was another member of Ernie's family to have even closer connections to *Gone with the Wind*. His brother Dick wrote his first book review for the *Emory Phoenix* on *Gone with the Wind*.

Mitchell received six author copies from The McMillan Co. in New York, and Dick received one of them the day she received them. She inscribed it, "To Richard Harwell from Margaret Mitchell, May 29, 1936." It was the first copy of the book she signed and would be the first article in what would become a vast *GWTW* memorabilia collection.

They became close friends and socialized often, one time too few for the good of all. Dick had made plans to have dinner in Atlanta with Mitchell and her husband, John Marsh, on August 11, 1949. The couple called to cancel the dinner, explaining that Margaret was not feeling well. Instead, they decided to go by themselves to a movie at Peachtree Arts Theatre. On the way out of the theatre, Mitchell was crossing the street when a speeding taxi hit her. Five days later, she died.

Dick's collection and his writings helped to preserve her memory. A renowned Confederacy historian, Richard Harwell wrote four *Gone with the Wind*–related books.

In his review of *GWTW* for the *Emory Phoenix*, he called it "a true expression of the most dramatic era of Southern history." He also wrote: "Her characters actually walk the streets of Atlanta. They seem to grow before the eyes of the reader." The hardback price for the book in 1936: $3.

The whole front page of the Vol. I, No. 3 *Gone with the Wind* collectors' newsletter, dated May 1988, was devoted to him with the headline: "In Memory of Richard Barksdale Harwell."

The first paragraph of his obituary in the newsletter read: "On March 9, the country lost one of its preeminent scholars and historians of the Confederacy; *Gone with the Wind* fans around the world lost one of the last links to Margaret Mitchell."

It was from Dick that Ernie became so interested in writing.

On the evening he met Miss Lulu Tankersley, writing was the last thing Dick's younger brother had on his mind. He was more in the mood for talking. Whatever he said worked well enough that when it came time for Lulu to invite a boy to her sorority dance, she invited

Ernie, instead of reciprocating Walter Bundy's invitation. Ernie thought about the invitation for a good eighth of a second and then accepted it.

Ernie made as many visits to Brenau as his schedule allowed, and it was a busy schedule at that. On top of all the responsibilities of any full-time student, Harwell worked part time in the sports department of the *Atlanta Constitution* for six years during high school and college.

Plus, he was in charge of getting publicity for the SAE fraternity. He came up with the idea of having a bet with Bing Crosby. If the fraternity's team of choice won that year's Rose Bowl, Crosby would have to sing their fraternity's song, called "Violets," on his radio show. If Crosby's team won, everybody in the fraternity had to write a glowing letter to him. Crosby's team won, and all the Greeks sat down and composed their letters.

Ernie also created another source of income and, in the process, introduced college students to big-time entertainment and first-rate live music. He did so by marrying his love for fine music and his creative knack for making a buck. After years of snubbing Atlanta in favor of Boston and New York, the biggest names of the big-band era finally took their acts South. Typically, they arrived on Saturday, left on Friday, and entertained at the Henry Grady Hotel every night they were in town. Harwell concocted a plan and approached the man in charge of booking the bands.

"Why don't you have a college night on Wednesday?" Harwell suggested. "Wednesday is a slow night anyway. Give me 10 cents of every dollar that comes through the door, and I'll spread the word and see to it that a big crowd shows up."

Thanks to Harwell's eye for making a buck, a number of college students were able to boast they saw Tommy Dorsey and Glenn Miller, among many others.

When his schedule did allow visits, Harwell was careful to follow the rules when he visited Lulu. Well, most of the rules.

The girls were allowed to entertain their dates in a designated building on campus. The boys had to sign in and could not stay later than 10:00 P.M. They were allowed to sit alongside their dates on couches. They were not, however, allowed to do anything so risqué as kiss their dates.

Some rules are made to be broken, and no kiss is more exciting than one that's against the rules. Ernie and Lulu looked this way and that, over here and then over yonder, and not a faculty member was in sight. They kissed.

A kiss punctuated by goose bumps. One sweet, innocent kiss. Or so they thought. Little did they know it would become a scandalous act for which Lulu was punished to the fullest extent of the campus law.

Lulu had been elected to the Honor Society. For that, another member of her class who had lost the election never forgave her. She saw an opportunity to retaliate for what she perceived to be a gross miscarriage of justice and she seized it. That Miss Tankersley had won an essay contest judged by a famous alumna fanned the raging flames of the girl's envy.

The girl reported Miss Lulu Tankersley's kiss, her scandalous kiss, to the proper authorities. The wheels of campus justice were set in motion, and this transgression was not to be taken lightly.

As per the rule book, Miss Lulu Tankersley was "campused" for a week, meaning she could not leave campus or entertain special visitors for a week, not to mention the shame of being singled out.

Somehow, Miss Lulu survived the ordeal with her upstanding reputation intact and her feelings for her boyfriend Ernie untainted.

Ernie graduated from Emory in 1940. Lulu graduated from Brenau in 1941. Ernie made a trip to Hazard to meet Lulu's mother and stepfather and to ask for their daughter's hand in marriage.

After a one-and-a-half-year courtship, the former Lula Tankersley became Mrs. William Earnest Harwell on August 30, 1941. The couple was wed in the living room of the home of Ernie's parents because his father's condition confined him to the house. A couple from Hazard stood up for them, and Ernie's brothers, Davis and Dick, were the only others in attendance.

Ernie was years away from having his driver's license, so Lulu drove them to the mountains of northern Georgia for their honeymoon.

They couldn't stay long. They left after Ernie's 11:15 Friday night radio show for WSB and had to return in time for his 6:15 Monday night show. Moreover, they had to leave extra early to accommodate the wishes of a young boy, a lover of baseball, who had written Ernie requesting to meet him. Lulu knew what she was in for right from the start. She knew she was married to a man devoted to his work.

They honeymooned at the Tate Mountain Estates, a modest-budget vacationer's paradise atop a mountain with a heavenly view. The swimming pool was luxurious, the golf course lush, the food delightful.

Years later, when the resort went up in a blaze, Ernie accused Lulu: "You must have burned it down with your passion."

Chapter 4

WSB

One sunny Saturday morning during Harwell's senior year in college, a fellow Emory student approached him on campus. Marcus Bartlett knew Harwell from the speech class they attended together.

Bartlett, program director at radio station WSB, wondered if Harwell would be interested in meeting his boss later that afternoon. Harwell said he could stop by before going to work at the *Constitution*. Bartlett told Harwell to wear a suit and tie.

Unbeknownst to him, Harwell was about to undergo an audition. Bartlett greeted him, handed him that day's *Atlanta Journal* sports page, and asked him to read the account of the Crackers game into a microphone. He was unaware that all of WSB's top dogs were listening to the entire thing.

Bartlett informed Harwell that WSB was in need of a "sports director" and asked him to return Monday with a 15-minute script based on Sunday's baseball results.

He landed the job and was on his way. He was the sports director of a one-man sports staff. The only person he directed was himself. Doug

Edwards, who later would become Walter Cronkite's predecessor as anchor of CBS-TV's nightly news, was the newscaster for WSB.

Harwell decided what would be included in his twice-nightly 15-minute reports. He wrote all of his own material and was determined to be different from the other stations that filled time by reading wire accounts. Typically, 12 typewritten pages of material were needed to fill the 15 minutes. Connie Mack was among the big names he interviewed while working at WSB. Harwell hunted Mack down while attending baseball's annual convention held over the winter in Atlanta.

Guests came to the studio for live interviews, and not just *any* guests. Sports legends ranked among the greatest in their fields hopped cabs and paid their own way to the studio to sit down with Harwell and chat at a WSB mike.

Ted Williams, obsessed with becoming the greatest hitter who ever lived, stopped by in 1942 to appear on Harwell's show. Don Budge, the first tennis Grand Slam winner and owner of a wicked backhand, came in to be interviewed by Harwell. Bobby Jones, golf's biggest name, made appearances.

Heavyweight Jack Dempsey, renowned for packing the meanest punch in history, made the trip into the studio. He was in town to promote a "fight" with a professional wrestler by the name of Cowboy Luttrell. He showed up late for the interview but made up for lost time with a few quality minutes of chatter delivered in a high, squeaky voice.

Having Dempsey as a live guest made promoting a silly event that was beneath the ex-champ's dignity more than worthwhile.

In advance of the Luttrell-Dempsey match, a promoter duped Harwell into covering a local boxing match by appealing to his desire for scoops. The promoter told him he could have exclusive broadcasting rights to the bout. In return for that exclusivity, all the promoter asked was that Harwell would not advertise the fact he would be covering the fight because to do so would be to risk decreasing attendance.

Upon arrival, Harwell discovered the promoter had made the same promise to three other radio stations. They all were given more notice than he was and had typewritten material prepared for their shows.

The Angel, a professional wrestler from a foreign country, brought an interpreter into the studio to conduct his interview, though Harwell strongly suspected the wrestler understood every word and used the aid of the translator only to enhance his mystery and liven up his act.

His shows received a great deal of publicity thanks to a fortunate cross promotion. The *Atlanta Journal* owned WSB and devoted a great deal of space to promote Harwell's upcoming interviews.

Harwell rarely ventured out of the WSB studio to conduct interviews because doing so required transporting the heavy, bulky recording machine used in the pretape era. Loading the machine onto a truck was quite an ordeal, too time-consuming to justify attempting to interview an uncooperative subject.

He knew all about Ty Cobb's reputation as a mean and ornery ballplayer who grew even meaner and more ornery after his playing days. He treated fellow ballplayers with disdain, so he wasn't about to show any courtesy or respect whatsoever to a sportscaster. That's what Harwell was told. Adopting a policy that would serve him well through the years, Harwell decided to judge for himself.

Against Bartlett's advice, Harwell and engineer Mark Tolson drove 120 miles to Cobb's hometown of Royston. Harwell introduced himself to the cantankerous Cobb. It was the beginning of a smooth relationship. Cobb didn't turn him down for the interview. Not that morning. Not ever. Harwell found him to be just as agreeable when they ran into each other at the Masters and at Memorial Stadium in Baltimore one night in 1957.

Harwell, a baseball historian, was particularly fascinated by Cobb's career. He couldn't read or write enough about the Georgia Peach.

It was at Augusta National, home of the Masters, that Cobb mesmerized Harwell with an inspirational story from his cunning past. It

Cobb's 4,000th
Wasn't a Hit in Print

Remember all the hoopla surrounding Pete Rose's chase for his 4,000th hit?

I mention this because it's the 70th anniversary of Ty Cobb becoming the first player to collect 4,000 hits. The historic hit was hardly mentioned in the next morning's *Detroit Free Press*.

The hit came July 18, 1927. Cobb had returned to Navin Field as a member of the Philadelphia Athletics. He doubled off Sam Gibson in the first inning. The headline over the game story read: "FIRST INNING RALLY WINS FOR BENGALS OVER LEFTY GROVE."

The first subhead said: "Fothergill's home run accounts for two scores as Tigers count three times and wipe out rival team's lead." Cobb was still ignored in the second subhead, "Gibson holds Athletics in check after opening frame—Heilmann features Detroit attack with quartet of safeties."

Even the story's lead ignored Cobb's hit. After four long paragraphs he got a mention, but an oblique one. Writer Harry Bullion put it this way: "Gibson stopped Simmons cold and he was effective against Cobb after the first inning when a lucky double slid off Heilmann's gloved hand and helped in the making of two runs."

That's all the coverage the historic No. 4,000 got in the game story.

The *Free Press* ran a column of notes with the headline: "BENGALS IN THIRD PLACE; TY COBB GETS 4,000TH HIT." But the note on the hit came in the fifth paragraph, after Bullion had listed the upcoming schedule and that the Tigers didn't make a double play. Then he mentioned the hit: "When Cobb made his fluke double in the first inning, it was his 4,000th major league safety. He's so far ahead of all records of other batsmen that he will never be beaten or tied."

There was no photo of Cobb, no stats or other mention of his hit.

The Detroit News didn't give Cobb's hit any more attention. It did mention the feat in the headline—the same size head accorded the Detroit team that won the YMCA world basketball title. H. G. Salsinger wrote the game story and passed off the event with one sentence.

He wrote: "Cobb hit a line drive into right field and Heilmann, trying for a one-handed catch, got his glove on the ball but it bounced out and gave Cobb a scratch two-bagger."

Salsinger wrote a column that afternoon but devoted all of it to boxing's lightweight division.

The *News* had no story on the historic double or any photo.

There's no doubt sports coverage has changed in the past 70 years.

—E.H., July 1997

involved legendary sportswriter Grantland Rice, before he had attained fame, and as soon as Cobb mentioned that name, Harwell was all the more interested. Rice was one of Harwell's sportswriting idols.

"Grantland Rice was sports editor of the *Atlanta Journal* in 1904," Cobb started the tale. "He began receiving anonymous telegrams from Anniston, Alabama, trumpeting the achievements of a great young ballplayer by the name of Ty Cobb. Rice crumpled the telegrams and tossed them into the wastebasket. That didn't deter the anonymous champion of Cobb. Finally, curiosity got the better of Rice and he took a train to Anniston to see if there was any truth to the telegrams. With Rice watching, the young Cobb got five hits and stole home."

Rice sent a story to his paper from the local telegraph office. It began: "Ty Cobb was a comet with a fiery tail here this afternoon. He blazed the Annistons to victory with his booming bat and his fleet base running. Here is a young man who someday may make his mark in the baseball world. . . ."

Little did Rice know Cobb was the one sending the telegrams.

The one sent by Rice ended up in the same place as all the previous ones. Rice's assistant sports editor back at the office figured it was just like all the others, sent by the anonymous promoter of Cobb. He tossed it without giving it a second thought.

The Georgia Peach continued to send telegrams and Rice, knowing Cobb was the real deal, ran every word of them. It wasn't until years later that Cobb let the famous sportswriter know that he was behind the anonymous wires.

Harwell used that story as the basis for his first piece in a major magazine that covered more than sports. It ran in the *Saturday Evening Post*.

Perhaps it was Harwell's nonthreatening approach. Maybe it was his baseball-only focus. Perhaps it was his knowledge of baseball in general and of Cobb's career in particular. It could have been that Cobb was impressed with how fearless the young reporter was on the day he drove all the way out to his house, seemingly not even considering he might be turned away. Whatever it was, Cobb never revealed in the presence of Harwell the mean spirit he showed the rest of the world.

Not that Harwell batted 1.000 with prospective interview subjects.

He was asked to serve as master of ceremonies for a banquet that the city of Cartersville, Georgia, threw to honor Tigers slugging first baseman Rudy York after the 1940 World Series. York had just completed a career year, hitting .316 with 33 home runs and 134 runs batted in. York's two-run home run was pivotal in the Tigers' 7–4 victory in Game 3 of a Series they would lose to Cincinnati in the seventh game.

York was a heavy drinker and smoker. He set so many hotel room fires falling asleep while smoking that Charlie Gehringer finally went to management to request another roommate for fear he would go up in smoke.

Harwell figured since he had this sort of access to such a hot story it would be foolish not to bring an engineer and interview York. Well into the 80-mile trip, they realized they had forgotten to pack the necessary equipment to conduct the interview. They returned to the station to get the microphones and arrived early enough to interview York. When Harwell told York he would like to interview him, Harwell couldn't have been more stunned with the athlete's response.

"You have to talk to my agent first," York told Harwell. "You'll have to talk to him and he'll let you know what the fee will be. I don't do any interviews without my agent setting the fee."

Fresh off getting stiffed by York, Harwell was in charge of seeing to it that the slugger was properly lionized that evening, no easy juggling act. He pulled it off and nobody suspected that Harwell thought any less of York than everyone else in the room thought of him.

Harwell's work for WSB enabled him to get a taste of covering a variety of sports.

Bartlett chose Harwell as his sidekick for broadcasting Georgia Tech football games, a duty that resulted in him interviewing Georgia backfield standout Frankie Sinkwich in the preseason "roundup" organized by the SEC. Later, Sinkwich would be remembered for wearing his Marine uniform when presented with the Heisman Trophy.

Sinkwich's response to Harwell's question during the interview taught the young broadcaster to expect the unexpected.

"Frank, you had a little problem with your weight and now you're back and you've lost about 12 pounds," Harwell said. "How do you feel?"

Harwell then let his mind relax for an instant, figuring he had a while before having to ask another question. He figured wrong.

"Lighter," Sinkwich said, and that was all he said.

It was during these years after graduation and before enlisting in the marines that Harwell became friendly with golfing great Bobby Jones, through mutual friend O. B. "Pop" Keeler, one of Jones' closest friends.

There wasn't a bigger name among Atlanta sportswriters at the time than O. B. Keeler, and his expertise on golf was respected well beyond the boundaries of Atlanta. He did have one personal flaw, however. Even fish gossiped about how much Keeler drank. He was not ashamed of his attraction to the bottle and even referred to his home as Distillery Hill in his columns.

Harwell had told Keeler of his growing collection of baseball memorabilia, which started back when Ernie took $32 he had earned from his paper route at $2 a week and purchased baseball guides with the money. He had answered an advertisement placed in *The Sporting News* by statistician Charlie White. From White, he purchased guides by Reach and Spalding covering from 1910 to 1917. He also purchased some old Beadle and DeWitt guides dating back as far as 1860. He collected *Sporting News* magazines from 1920 through 1965.

Ernie's parents were shocked he would blow the money for which he had worked so hard on a pile of baseball guides. It wasn't until he turned around and sold a small portion of those guides to another collector for $75 that they realized their son knew exactly what he was doing. His collection grew to an unmanageable size, and in 1965 he donated it to the Detroit Public Library.

Harwell was 22 when he invited Keeler, who was well into his sixties, to his parents' home for dinner to show off his collection. Ernie's mother fixed a dinner fit for royalty, and the scent of ham and biscuits spiced the air. She timed it perfectly for his scheduled 6:30 P.M. arrival.

Ninety minutes later, just as Ernie's mother decided they would wait no longer, they heard a taxi pull into the driveway. Ernie went outside. From the wobble in Keeler's stance and the gleam in his eye,

Ernie knew the fish were gossiping again about his friend who could drink them all under a rock.

"Psst, Ernie," Keeler beckoned. "I can't make it tonight."

"Thanks for stopping by to let me know, Pop," Ernie said.

Ernie was relieved he didn't have to deal with his mother's reaction to having a drunken man as a guest in her home.

On another occasion, Bobby Jones and his wife were returning from a tournament in Chattanooga and were on their way to a dinner engagement. They dropped off an inebriated Keeler at WSB and asked Harwell if he wouldn't mind escorting him home to make sure he was able to get into and out of a taxi without incident.

Despite his weakness, Keeler had a warm heart and Harwell viewed him as an invaluable resource, a fertile brain to pick.

Harwell's connection to Jones, through Keeler, came in handy when Harwell covered the Masters Tournament for the first time, in 1941.

On the eve of the tournament's first round, Harwell arranged to interview Jones for his 6:15 nightly show from his tower above the 18th green.

Jones agreed to appear on the show. A few minutes after 6:00, rains fell, thunder crashed, and lightning flashed.

Harwell found Jones, cohost of the tourney with Cliff Roberts, and told him, "Bob, you don't have to go out there and do the interview in the rain. I understand. I'll fill the time just fine."

Said Jones, an undergraduate at Georgia Tech and a graduate of Emory Law School: "Oh no, don't worry about it. I'll be happy to do it."

Jones, who once a year for the Masters came out of the retirement that had been forced on him by a bad back at the age of 29, was reluctant to talk about his own game, nothing like the game he had in his prime. But he was effusive in talking about the rest of the field.

In 1941, Harwell reported scores from the tower back to WSB. Much to his chagrin, he didn't get to try to his hand at doing play-by-play of the tournament.

When Harwell received news of what he considered at the time a huge career break, consulting Keeler was one of the first things he did. In March of 1942, Harwell was in the newsroom at WSB, talking with Doug Edwards, when an excited Bartlett stormed into the room, holding a telegram. It was NBC, requesting the services of Ernie Harwell to assist Bill Stern in his coverage of the Masters. It was the first network broadcast of the Masters, and Harwell was on the NBC team, the dominant sports network. There wasn't a bigger name in the business at the time than Bill Stern.

Harwell went to Keeler's home to break the big news to him and to seek advice on how to handle the assignment. Keeler's wife, whom everyone called Mom, sat in the corner of the room, rocking back and forth, knitting while Keeler told Harwell everything he knew about the Masters. Mom, a renowned women's golf writer, had a full set of teeth. She never used them to bite her tongue. Nobody could accuse her of having a phony bone in her body.

"O. B., do you mean to tell me that a national network is using a boy fresh out of school who has never broadcast a golf tournament to broadcast the Masters?" she groused.

Keeler reassured Harwell he would be fine, that there wasn't much more to covering a golf tournament than knowing how to count.

To prepare for his assignment, Ernie joined Lulu on afternoon walks from their Myrtle Street home to the nearby Piedmont Park golf course. They picked a different green to sit behind every day and Ernie pretended to announce the action. On slow days at the course, after the players left the green, he measured the distance of their putts to see how close he had come in his estimates.

When the Masters arrived, Harwell was ready. Stern, his mobility limited by a wooden leg, covered the tourney from a tower. Harwell and Bob Stanton, who worked for NBC out of New York, walked the course with the golfers. Their engineers, toting cumbersome equipment, kept up with them. Harwell and Stanton did their best to find points high enough from which to broadcast so the signals could reach the tower.

That 1942 Masters would be the last one until 1946. The tourney was put on hold, and to aid in the war effort, Augusta National reserved its grounds for the raising of cattle and turkeys. Neither before that nor since has the magnificent golf course ever been mistaken for a cow pasture.

Everything went smoothly in Harwell's first experience with NBC, and he waited for a call from the network offering a full-time job. That call never came. Another one did. When he learned his draft classification was 1-A, he enlisted in the marines in July 1942.

He was stationed in Atlanta the first two years, doing public relations work for the marines, and accepted Earl Mann's invitation to broadcast Atlanta Crackers games in 1943. In an effort to defuse any controversy over a marine working in baseball, Harwell donated his paycheck from the Crackers to the Red Cross. It was a nice gesture, but it didn't stop the civilian complaints from coming into local marine headquarters, and Harwell's superiors told him to put his broadcasting career on hold. He didn't call many games, but it was enough. Mann wanted him back when Ernie finished his tour of duty.

Tongue-tied but sassy, Ernie at the age of six. Ernie Harwell personal collection.

A young marine with his bride. Ernie Harwell personal collection.

Gray Harwell, Ernie's dad, at home in Atlanta during 1942. Ernie Harwell personal collection.

Ernie checks lineups with managers Pancho Snyder and Kiki Cuyler at Ponce de Leon Park, Atlanta. Ernie Harwell personal collection.

Ernie interviews Dodger pitcher Whitlow Wyatt after the 1941 World Series. Ernie Harwell personal collection.

Ernie and Ted Williams in 1942. Ernie Harwell personal collection.

The Baltimore Oriole broadcast team: (left to right) Bailey Goss, Chuck Thompson, and Ernie. Photo courtesy of Greer Inc.

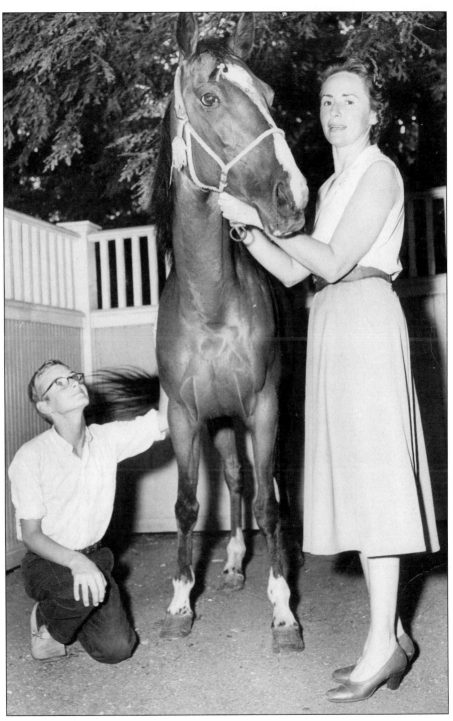

Lulu and Bill (age 12) welcome home Star of Arabia after her runaway jaunt through the streets of Baltimore. Photo courtesy of Ralph Robinson / The Sun Papers.

Ernie introduces Ted Williams at Baltimore's Memorial Stadium during 1951 as the Orioles pay tribute to Ted. Ernie Harwell personal collection.

Two great baseball play-by-play men: Ronald Reagan and Ernie Harwell. Ernie Harwell personal collection.

Orioles manager Jimmie Dykes sinks a putt for Ernie in Yuma, Arizona, during March of 1954. Ernie Harwell personal collection.

He knows 'em all: Harwell with Ty Cobb. Ernie Harwell personal collection.

Chapter 5

"Prisoner, Forward March!"

Guard shack watch can be a lonely duty, and ever so tedious. See the proper credentials, wave the man through, and so it goes all day long. The ability to remain alert and suspicious at all times is forever put to the test.

The guard at United States Marine Headquarters in Washington, D.C., one morning back in the winter of 1944–1945 had no trouble keeping his concentration trained on his duty, and he wasn't about to let one particular grave offender escape his watch.

"Prisoner, forward march!" the guard commanded to the young marine by the name of William Earnest Harwell. "You're going to the commandant's office."

There's a Barney Fife in every crowd, and Harwell had the misfortune of walking past the one in this crowd, an overzealous guard, whom Harwell thought had said, "OK."

"Hey, come back here," the guard ordered Harwell. "What are you doing? You're under arrest."

"Why?"

"You walked through here without gaining clearance," the guard was pleased to inform. "And you're late."

Harwell was, in fact, late. By three minutes. His alarm had failed to sound that morning.

The guard delivered the hardened criminal to the commandant's office, where punishment was meted out.

"Prisoner, step forward!" came the command.

"What happened?" the commandant asked.

When the commandant was brought up-to-date on Harwell's crime, he noted the marine had a clean record up to that point and was lenient with his sentence.

"You are restricted to barracks for one week," the commandant ruled.

Because Harwell lived off base with his wife, this was quite an inconvenience. He made the best of it and spent much of the week in the library reading magazines.

Other than that brush with the law midway through his stretch, Harwell made it through his four years in the military without incident.

As is the case with so many servicemen who don't see combat duty, Harwell doesn't spend much time talking about his time serving his country, out of respect for those who lost their lives, were wounded, or had witnessed battle atrocities that would scar them for life.

"My military career wasn't commendable," says Harwell, who enlisted in the marines in 1942 and was discharged in 1946. "A lot of guys were shot at and others were killed. I guess the most I can say is I did give up time out of my career."

Even to this day, Harwell second-guesses himself for not trying harder to gain admission into officer's school.

Thanks to a writing talent the marines decided to put to use, Harwell had it easier than most, but it's not as if he lived in luxury's lap for four years. The time crawled.

After enlisting in the marines, Harwell was sent to boot camp at Parris Island. It was there that he learned that clichés about drill instructors are based on fact and not at all embellished.

The D.I. was supreme, his authority unchallenged, his boundaries of what was considered good taste in exacting punishment nonexistent. He slapped the boys in hopes that it would make them men. One marine was foolish enough to eat ice cream while in ranks. The D.I. made him put the ice cream on top of his head and stand there until the last drop had melted down onto him, humiliating him, one sloppy drop at a time. Those careless enough to stand in ranks with a dirty rifle were forced to lick from the rifle's surface the oil used for cleaning guns.

To not slap one's rifle hard enough was to risk being ordered down to the ground and commanded to slam the concrete with all one's might for 15 minutes, past the point where raw hands throbbed in excruciating pain.

Middle-of-the-night drills started with the flick of a light switch, then a command to all of the men to hold 60-pound locker boxes over their heads for prolonged periods of time.

Harwell understood it all was toward the goal of getting the men to snap to on command so that when they went to combat, obeying officers would be a reflex, not a decision. That doesn't mean he and his fellow marines had to enjoy the preparation.

Harwell enjoyed the musical aspect of the marches. "Right rear march," was music to his ears. "Oblique march," was a command to which he looked forward.

In contrast, he deplored the spit-and-polish, crease-of-the-pants-must-be-just-so aspect of orderliness. A casual dresser completely comfortable in wrinkled clothes, getting the crease just right forever posed a steep challenge.

It was neither the midnight drills nor the obsession for neatness, neither the sadistic punishments nor the interminable hikes that Harwell found most difficult about his time at Paris Island.

Our Latest National Pastime: Complaints

Complaints! Complaints! Complaints!

Why is everybody always complaining? Why am I complaining about everybody complaining? Doesn't it seem that complaining—not baseball—just might be our national pastime?

Baseball certainly has its complaints. They come from fans and from people in the game. And these complaints, for the most part, are directed toward the owner, the general manager, the manager, the groundskeeper, the writer, and the broadcaster.

Here are the most common complaints aimed at these people and others:

- **To the owner:** You're making too many changes. You're bound too much by tradition. You should spend more for good players. You are paying your players too much. You interfere in the running of the team. You don't take enough interest in the team.
- **To the general manager:** I can never get a good ticket to the game. All the seats have been taken. You are always making bad player deals.
- **To the manager:** You don't have your team bunt enough. You take your pitchers out too quickly. You leave your pitchers in the game too long.
- **To the third-base coach:** You're too aggressive. You send runners home, and they are always thrown out at the plate. You are too timid. You hold up runners, and they never score.
- **To the player:** You don't hustle enough. You make too much money. Why don't you sign autographs? You should speak at our banquet. We'll even give you a free meal.

- *To the umpire:* You always favor the other team. Our team never seems to get any close calls from you. Why can't you hurry up the game? They take too long. You are too quick to toss a player out of the game. You should bear down on the players and control them better.
- *To the concessions manager:* The prices are too high. The hot dogs are cold. Your beer is not strong enough. The lines are too long.
- *To the groundskeeper:* The infield is too hard. Grounders get through too easily. The infield is too soft. We can't turn the double play. Why can't you fix the mound right?
- *To the broadcaster:* You repeat too much. You don't give the score often enough. You're a homer. Why don't you root for the home team more? You're too critical of the players. You're not objective enough, and you never seem to be critical of the players. The commercials are too long.
- *To the writer:* You're too nosy, always prying into the players' private lives. You write too much game detail. Give us more of the human side of the players. You never write positive articles about the home team.

Everybody leads the league in complaints. They are simply a part of baseball—just as they are a part of the outside world. Complaints! Complaints! Complaints!

—E.H., May 1993

"The toughest part about boot camp," he says, "was that you were never alone. You were always with a bunch of guys."

After completion of boot camp, Harwell spent most of his first half of duty in Atlanta, writing press releases and making recruiting speeches.

Looking back, Harwell said: "I was happy to stick around Atlanta as long as I could, but I got the feeling people didn't like the idea I was able-bodied and not in combat."

He was sent to Camp LeJeune, North Carolina, where he spent the summer of 1944.

At the time, the military frowned upon wives joining their husbands. They made conditions as primitive as possible so as to encourage spouses to stay at home.

Nevertheless, Lulu and their infant son Bill joined Ernie when he was sent to Camp LeJeune. They found a home to rent in rural Richmond, North Carolina. The Ritz it was not. They drew their water from a well, bathed in the nearby lake, and made use of an outhouse. Ernie hitchhiked 20 miles to work, sometimes joined by the marine who slept across the street on a cot inside an abandoned filling station.

It wasn't until the next marine who stayed there told him, that Harwell learned there had been a makeshift shower hidden underneath the back porch, a shower of the fill-up-a-bucket-with-water-and-pull-a-string-to-dump-the-water-on-your-head variety.

Somehow, this wasn't what the young marine's wife had envisioned when she walked down the aisle and said, "I do," but this was wartime and everyone had to make sacrifices. Count Lulu Harwell among them. In order to wash baby Bill's diapers, Lulu pumped water from the well into a bucket.

To say she was lonesome and homesick would not be stretching the truth. To say she didn't have a friend in Richmond would not be accurate. It was only one summer, one primitive, bare-bones summer, but the time she spent with the "old woman" next door was time she'll never forget.

Lulu can't remember the old woman's name—Pearl is as good a guess as any, she says—but she does remember everything else about her.

Pearl was a natural-born storyteller, and Lulu would escape in her words, taking journeys back in time to experience the triumphs and tragedies of country folk she came to feel as if she knew.

Pearl told these stories from the greatest of all pulpits for natural-born storytellers: a rocking chair on a porch. Sometimes, birds sang the background music. Other times, the chirp of the crickets added to the soothing effect of the stories. Once in a while, raindrops drummed on the rooftop, which had the effect of making Pearl's yarns all the more soothing.

Another pair of sounds separated by a few seconds forever were part of the background music for Pearl's stories, whether told in the morning, afternoon or evening, whether the yarns were spun on hot and sunny days or cool and rainy nights.

The first sound: spit. The second sound: splat.

She always had a wad of chewing tobacco in her mouth, and when she felt the need, she leaned forward and sent a brown missile of spit arching over the railing of the porch in the shape of a rainbow and crashing down on the front lawn. Spit, splat. Spit, splat. Spit, splat.

"I birthed eight young'uns," Pearl was fond of saying.

Lulu became familiar with the bliss and misery of all eight, none of whom were young'uns by the time Pearl introduced them to Lulu through her yarns, rocking back and forth, passing time: "I birthed [spit] . . . eight young'uns [splat]."

Pearl's propensity for chewing tobacco didn't strike Lulu as odd at all because as a young girl in Hazard, Kentucky, she had seen many an older woman spitting and splatting through stories told on porches.

What happened on the night the Harwells entertained three other couples for dinner was not at all like anything she had experienced back home in the Appalachian Mountains.

Considering it had no indoor plumbing, the shack of a house in Richmond did not make for the ideal place to play host to social gatherings. That didn't stop the Harwells from inviting friends. After all, they were all in the military and all understood the rules of life were different in such times.

Lulu gave it her best effort to put together a tasty meal, and mirth filled the rustic air. The mood changed when mysterious noises grew louder and louder. A hush fell over the room, and it was determined the noises were coming from under the house. Ernie and the men went outside to investigate. They found several servicemen under the house. Either thinking the house was unoccupied or realizing it was occupied by a marine family, they used it to practice a military exercise known as a bivouac (a temporary encampment of military men).

Ernie explained they were entertaining guests and asked them to leave. They left, and the memory of the strange discovery remains.

Lulu's mother, taken aback by the conditions in which her daughter was living, was happy to take her back for a while to Hazard, where she was needed temporarily at the local high school, filling in for an ill teacher.

During their time away from each other, the young couple communicated through letters. Ernie's words never were more creative than the ones he put on paper writing to his wife.

Back in her hometown, Lulu would read the letters, censored by the military, to her students as a means of educating them on the war. She didn't come close to sharing the entire content of the letters, and the students knew it. Ernie's amorous words were for only his wife's eyes and never made it to the ears of the students.

"Read the rest of the letter, Mrs. Harwell," the girls would beg. "Come on, we know there's more. Read it to us."

The blushing face of their pretty young teacher confirmed the students' suspicions. There was indeed more to those missives sealed with a kiss. As to the exact contents, the students' imaginations would have to fill in the blanks.

Ernie wasn't paid a nickel for the written words Lulu found priceless. He was paid to write less passionate copy.

While stationed at Camp LeJeune, Harwell's office duties included editing the battalion newspaper. Soon, he knew, his duty would grow much riskier. The Allied Forces needed the 59th Replacement Battalion in the Pacific, on the islands of Saipan and Peleliu.

At the last hour, Harwell was informed he would not be joining the combat forces in the Pacific because two experienced newspaper men were needed to work on the Camp LeJeune newspaper and Harwell was one of them. Harwell would learn later that most of the men from the 59th Replacement who headed off to battle would die in the Pacific.

Not long after that, Harwell was transferred to Marine Headquarters in Washington and was assigned to work for *Leatherneck*, the official marine publication. Lulu joined him in Washington, where living conditions were not a great deal more modern than in Richmond. They did have a potbelly stove and an icebox, serviced by a man who delivered blocks of ice, and they had to pay only $18 a month in rent.

Harwell repeatedly applied for overseas correspondence. His first assignment for *Leatherneck* away from the mainland brought him to Hawaii, where he wrote about ballplayers playing camp games. Alvin Dark, the New York Giants shortstop, was among those he featured. For another story, he interviewed a dashing young actor stationed at a marine air base in Hawaii. The actor was serving as a pistol instructor. In his interview with Harwell, Robert Stack expressed his frustrations at being branded a one-trick pony as an actor. Initially, Stack enjoyed the attention he received from giving teen actress sensation Deanna Durbin her first on-screen kiss in the 1939 film *First Love*.

"It's time for everybody to move on from that," Stack told Harwell. "That's all anybody talks about when my name comes up."

Stack went on to shake that label and, like Harwell, remained high profile on television well into his eighties and into the 21st century. He became well known for his portrayal of Eliot Ness in *The Untouchables* and later became host of the popular TV show *Unsolved Mysteries*.

As big a name as Stack already had at that point in his career, he wasn't the most well-known person Harwell interviewed during the war.

Harwell thought writing about what happens to the bushels of mail that come to the White House would make for interesting reading. He knew President Franklin Delano Roosevelt was ill and even in the best of times wouldn't likely want to sit down with him to talk about something as off the topic of running the country as the letters mailed to the White House. Instead, he went through the proper channels to arrange an interview with the First Lady, Eleanor Roosevelt. The First Lady granted him the interview, and they chatted in the White House about the mail.

Before Harwell wrote the story, the president died and so, too, did the story. He never did anything with the material he received in the interview with Eleanor Roosevelt, whom he found "most gracious."

The style and tone of *Leatherneck* often was patterned after that of the nation's two most popular magazines, *Life* and *Look*. In one such attempt to give *Leatherneck* the feel of the magazines back home, the editors assigned Harwell and his sidekick, John Jaloki, a photographer from the *Detroit News*, a story that required them to be more creative than they had hoped.

The men were working in China and living in the insurance office of a Mr. Chou, father of five children. Rats abounded in China, and Mr. Chou's boys were in charge of killing the ones that invaded his property. They caught them in cages, from which the rats could be heard pleading for release with loud squeals that echoed through the night. Once removed from the cages, the rats were dunked in buckets of water and drowned. It wasn't how the young American servicemen would have attacked the problem. No matter; they were happy to let the Chinese boys curtail the rat population while they went about carrying out their assignments for *Leatherneck*.

When an assignment called for Harwell and Jaloki to detail a date between a marine and a Chinese girl, it wasn't until after eagerly agreeing to what they thought was a smart idea for a story that they realized Chinese girls didn't date American servicemen. Doing so was enough to ruin a girl's reputation. Also, they found the Chinese reluctant to have their pictures taken out of superstition it would bring bad luck.

Undeterred, they headed for Peking, the forbidden city.

To get their story, the three marines (Harwell, Jaloki, and Red Baskin, the man posing as the date for the story) were forced to find a girl who cared less about her reputation than about her income. They knew where they could find one such girl and headed for the nearest whorehouse.

When they explained what they needed, they were shown into a room where the girls sat on couches so that Harwell, Jaloki, and Baskin could look them over and make a choice. The girls spoke no English, so the marines didn't need to worry about offending them when discussing the field.

"This one's too fat," one said.

"That one's too old," the other countered.

"Her smile isn't quite right," a third voice said.

"She won't do," one added. "Not wholesome-looking enough."

"Not her," his sidekick chimed in. "Too ugly."

"There, right there, second from the right," one man voted.

"Yes, she's the one, all right," the other two agreed.

They paid the agreed-upon amount, and the girl joined them for the day for an assignment that required her to keep her clothes on.

Jaloki shot photographs of the prostitute and the marine walking down the steps on the way to their date, enjoying a bite to eat, and generally doing all the things a young couple would do to make the most of a date. They ran the story decorated with photographs and thought they had no reason to believe their ruse would be exposed.

They soon learned otherwise from marines far more experienced in the nuances of Chinese whores than were these two naive marines. The girl's dress was slit at the bottom in such a way as to identify her as a prostitute.

Despite that experience, Sgt. Harwell, the baseball lover from Georgia, still was far from an expert on houses of ill repute. When an assignment took Harwell and Jaloki to Shanghai, they were in need of a hotel room.

A boy they encountered shortly after arriving in Shanghai assured them he knew of a good hotel and took the two servicemen to it.

"Long term or short term?" asked the hotel clerk.

"We'll be here a few days," Harwell said.

It wasn't long until the men received a knock on the door. When one of them opened the door, they found a woman and a man standing there. The woman with the now-familiar slit at the bottom of her dress did all the talking.

"We need to use your room," she informed him. "Would you mind going downstairs to talk to the girls for a while?"

The men did as they were told and went downstairs to talk to the women who made their livings selling sexual favors.

Harwell also wrote about more serious matters, such as the surrender of Wake Island.

The byline on the *Leatherneck* story that was headlined "THE WAKE STORY" reads:

by Sgt. Ernie Harwell
Leatherneck Staff Correspondent

The opening three paragraphs read as follows:

On Wake Island are two flagpoles. One is being choked at its base by scrubby, green bushes. It is an unsteady, bent shaft, almost hidden in the shadow of a rusted and mangled steel observation tower. It is desolate and lonely—without a flag. A half-mile northward, close to the lagoon, is the other flagpole. From its base of stubborn white coral it rises above the ruin of the island. It is inspiring—the American flag flies from its heights.

One pole was that of the First Marine Defense Battalion when for 15 days in December 1941, it fought off the Japanese attack. The other was erected September 4, 1945, to fly the American colors after the Japanese had surrendered. Three years and nine months—the entire span of World War II—are between Wake's two flagpoles.

Today a naval air station is under construction there. It will be a stopover for peacetime flights into the western Pacific; and, if the time does come again, a stout defense against a recurrence of Japanese aggression.

Harwell also went in with Allied forces to accept the surrender of Mille, the most bombed area during World War II. It was there that the commandant of the Japanese forces posed a pressing question to his captors: "Got any cigarettes?" That same commandant later was convicted of cannibalism.

Nearly every wartime serviceman is haunted by at least one memory, and Harwell is no exception. He was in China as the war was nearing its conclusion. The French had occupied a Japanese barracks and held Japanese servicemen prisoner. Harwell was assigned to the barracks to guard the prisoners. As deaths mounted throughout the war, the age of the "men" the Japanese recruited became younger and younger. All these decades later, Harwell still grows squeamish when asked to talk about guarding that barracks filled with faces too young for war.

"That was not easy to see," he says, reliving a memory he wishes would die. "They were so young. Some of them looked 11, 12 years old."

Looking back with a historian's perspective, Harwell noted the changes wrought by WWII: "Here you had all these boys who had never been away from home and suddenly they are on their own. Unless they came from good, strong, moral upbringings, they were ready to do whatever they wanted. Nobody was going to check up on them. It was a matter of conscience. When they came back they exercised their freedom to do as they pleased far more than before they went over. It was a different sort of life, a noticeable change in the social structure."

Once the war ended, Harwell's discharge was delayed two weeks while military officials searched for his record book. During those two weeks that seemed more like two centuries, Harwell worked as a bag boy for wives shopping for groceries, collected garbage, and spent most of his free time reading in the library.

Finally, he was discharged on his 28th birthday, January 25, 1946. He was free to return to his wife and young son and to resume his broadcasting career in Atlanta.

Chapter 6

The Atlanta Crackers

Businesses were required to rehire returning servicemen after the war ended. Once Harwell heard what WSB had to offer, he wasn't interested. By then, much of the station's airtime was filled with network programming. Harwell was told there was no room for his old, twice-nightly sports show. He wasn't interested in a five-minute report after the 11:00 news, the only opening, and told as much to John Outlar, the WSB station manager.

Outlar became the first of two men in a short period of time to make an off-target prediction about Harwell's career.

"You're making a big mistake," Outlar told him.

Bill Stern, the big shot from NBC with whom Harwell had worked without any problems at the Masters, would become the second. Harwell expressed in a letter his desire to work the golf tournament with Stern again. Stern invited him to help with the coverage again. It didn't go nearly as smoothly for Harwell this time.

Instead of reporting to Stern from the course periodically, as was the case the first time, Harwell was told this time Stern would contact him on the course for updates.

Stern gave Harwell his marching orders: he was to wait at the second green for Bobby Jones and Lawson Little. After Stern's one-minute introduction, he would go to Harwell and listen to his three-minute report.

Stern's introduction lasted so long that Jones and Little were well off the second green and into the third hole by the time Stern went to Harwell.

When Stern went to him, Harwell practiced that nasty habit of his and told the truth, the whole truth, and nothing but the truth.

Standing at the second green, Harwell said, "Jones and Little are on the third hole. We'll try to catch up to them and describe the action."

Huffing, puffing, and talking all at once, Harwell sounded as if he were caught off guard, which was precisely the case. He and his engineer reached the third green in time to broadcast the putts.

At that point, Stern regretted asking Harwell back to work the Masters. He let him know he had goofed and told him what he should have done.

"You should have faked it," Stern said. "Nobody would have known you were faking it. You should have described the drives as if you saw them. This is show biz."

Harwell's response didn't impress Stern.

"I don't work that way," Harwell said.

Stern also chastised Harwell for not stopping the golfers for an interview in the middle of their rounds. Harwell, always one to put the game first, whether it's baseball, golf, or football, told him he didn't think that would be appropriate.

That reaction caused Stern to make what just might be the worst forecast in radio history. "You'll never make it in the radio business," Stern told Harwell. "You're too much of a gentleman."

Earl Mann, by all accounts one of the great gentlemen in the history of minor league baseball, had a decidedly different opinion on Harwell's future.

WATL bought the rights to Crackers games and recruited Wheaties as a sponsor. WATL informed Mann they wanted to use their own man, Stan Raymond, to broadcast the games. Mann balked and insisted he wanted Harwell. The two sides were at a standstill, and Harwell remained busy by handing out free copies of *The Sporting News* and free Chesterfield cigarettes to patients at military hospitals.

"Can you imagine how that would go over today," Harwell says of cigarettes being dispensed to patients trying to get healthy.

It wasn't until the morning of Opening Day 1946 that Harwell learned he had won the assignment and would start work that afternoon. Looking back, he calls that "the most important day of my career."

Ponce de Leon park, the apple of Harwell's eye during his childhood years, became his office. The steep embankment in right field sometimes had a picket fence behind it, and if a ball cleared that picket fence, it was a home run. The sprawling magnolia tree in play in the outfield and the swimming pool behind the stands on the third-base side gave the ballpark a charming feel.

"When the games got boring, the men could go over and watch the ladies swim," Harwell says.

To swim in that pool was to be forever on the lookout for a foul ball crashing off the roof and tumbling into the water with a big splash.

The Harwells ate Wheaties for breakfast every morning during those years and never had to pay for them. Players for the Crackers won a case of Wheaties every time they hit a home run, and Harwell let his listeners know that that every time one of them went deep.

On Saturdays, Harwell broadcast as many as three games. He would do a re-creation of a major league game in the afternoon and sometimes call a Crackers doubleheader the same night.

A telegrapher at the stadium would send abbreviations indicating each pitch—1SC would mean strike 1, called; B1W was ball 1, wide—to a telegrapher at the studio. Harwell would take that sparse information

It's a Calling; Don't Force It

Does a baseball announcer need signature phrases—trademarks by which his listeners identify him?

I don't think so. Granted, Mel Allen's "How about that?" and Russ Hodges' "Bye-bye, baby" were famous and made them distinctive. But there are top-notch announcers today who have no special home-run calls or identifying phrases. Vin Scully and Jon Miller, to name a couple.

So if those phrases come naturally, that's fine. But if they are contrived, they don't work. I've seen young announcers struggle to develop a trademark call—especially for the home run. My advice: forget it, unless it just happens for you. Trying too hard ruins it all.

Most of my special phrases came late in my career. The exception was, "He stood there like the house by the side of the road." I began using this phrase just after I started broadcasting Atlanta Crackers games in 1946. It comes from a poem, "The House By the Side of the Road," by Sam Walter Foss.

Homer once wrote: "He was a friend to man, and he lived in a house by the side of the road." Foss turned around that phrase and ended the fifth and final verse of his poem with, "Let me live in my house by the side of the road and be a friend to man."

I recited Foss' poem when I was in the fifth grade in Atlanta.

My "Long Gone!" call didn't happen until the 1980s, and it came by accident. A batter hit a long drive, and I said: "It's long, it's long, it's long gone." Now I say it for almost every home run.

"Two for the price of one" came about the same way. I don't even remember when I said it for the first time—probably sometime in the 1970s.

The gimmick about the foul balls into the seats started right after I came to Detroit. A batter sliced a foul into the seats behind first base. Just off the cuff, I said something like, "A man from Saginaw will be taking that one home." After that, as I walked through the stands, people would ask: "How 'bout letting a guy from Dearborn [or some other locality] catch one tonight?" And so it grew.

"Instant runs" just crept up on me by accident, too. I first used that phrase sometime in the mid-1960s. I can't even recall when I started my other signature phrases. I never sat down to develop them.

Certainly they are not necessary. Some fans like them; others don't. You just have to be natural and let fans take their choice.

—*E.H., June 1998*

and create the action around it. As a precaution against the telegraph on either end breaking down, he tried to stay a half-inning behind. When the breakdown lasted longer, his creative juices really flowed.

"I'd have the hitters fouling off a lot of pitches," Harwell recalled. "I'd have the infielders having a conference on the mound. I'd even have brawls breaking out, and when the players got home their wives would ask them about the fight. They would say, 'What fight?' Some guys liked to use sound effects. I wasn't too big on those."

One particular re-creation stands out in Harwell's mind because it was an audition of sorts. Brad Robinson worked at Wheaties headquarters in Minneapolis and would make road trips to minor league towns to evaluate broadcasters. Robinson came to the WATL studio to evaluate Harwell, who offered him either a seat in the studio or a sofa in the lobby. Robinson told him it would be more authentic for him to listen from the sofa, because radio listeners didn't have the benefit of sitting in the studio.

Harwell, alone in the studio, was responsible for every station break, and that particular Crackers game, played in Mobile, lasted 21 innings. Harwell emerged from the studio eager to hear what Robinson thought of his announcing abilities. The only thing he heard from Robinson was loud snoring. For all Harwell knew, he had put the man from Wheaties to sleep in the first inning.

Harwell also represented the Crackers in the community and even went with the team on its annual visits to a penitentiary in Atlanta for exhibition games between the Crackers and the prison guards. The inmates cheered wildly for the Crackers.

Harwell approached each broadcast by painting a picture of what was taking place on the diamond. He thought of his father, listening at home in his wheelchair, and included as much game detail as possible so as to make his father feel as if he were at the games. He was, in fact, at one game. Ernie sought and received permission to allow his father to watch a game from foul territory.

Occasionally, Ernie even made a reference over the air to his father, saying things such as, "He hit that one out for the fat man who lives on Clifton Road."

"He listened to all the games and let me know how I did," Ernie recalls. "He wasn't too critical."

Ernie's father wasn't the only one who liked Harwell's announcing style. The New York Giants offered Harwell a job after the 1947 season. By this time, Old Gold cigarettes had replaced Wheaties as sponsor of the Crackers games. Because Giants broadcasts were sponsored by Chesterfield, chief rival to Old Gold, Harwell was not allowed to break his contract and make the big career move. He remained with the Crackers.

The Giants weren't the only New York team with an ear on Harwell. Somewhere, one or more of Branch Rickey's spies was listening closely to Harwell's broadcasts and sending glowing reports back to the Dodgers' general manager.

Rickey is remembered foremost for breaking baseball's color barrier by recruiting Jackie Robinson to play for the Brooklyn Dodgers. Long before that bold move, Rickey proved himself way ahead of the pack on a variety of other sound ideas. He established a farm system that remains the blueprint for all organizations. And he scouted more than ballplayers. He also scouted broadcasters.

During his recruitment of the promising broadcaster of Atlanta Crackers games, Rickey revealed a desire for secrecy that bordered on paranoia, another one of his many traits copied by modern-day baseball executives. Rickey's assistant, Arthur Mann, who was no relation to Crackers owner Earl Mann, acted as the go-between for Harwell and Rickey.

During spring training of 1948, Mann arranged for a secret meeting between Harwell and Rickey to take place at the Battle House Hotel in Mobile, Alabama. Harwell's instructions called for him to take an airplane from Gainesville, Florida, where the Crackers trained, to Mobile. Harwell made the bumpy flight, arrived several hours before the planned meeting, and waited for the man known as "the Mahatma." And waited and waited and waited. Several hours after the scheduled meeting time, Harwell phoned Arthur Mann to let him know Rickey still hadn't shown up.

"Oh," Mann answered, matter-of-factly, "I forgot to tell you, Mr. Rickey had to change his schedule and wasn't able to make it to Mobile."

Soon after that, Mann sent Harwell a letter updating him on the Mahatma's interest in him. It read, in part:

> Dear Ernie,
> Confidentially, Mr. Rickey is definite about bringing you to Brooklyn. He hasn't been able to work out details in his busy mind. I had hopes of getting you down to Vero Beach while he was there and, failing that, getting you together at Mobile. The latter seemed to be OK, and

then he felt that the possibility of a leak at Mobile was too great. Everybody trails him for the purpose of tying up his trips with news. And this, as far as I'm concerned, is simply good reporting.

Mr. Rickey's feeling is that he should see you during the time when Mobile plays in Atlanta for the first time this season. I haven't a schedule, but I'll get one as soon as I reach Brooklyn. Meanwhile, Ernie, I'd plan on a transition this summer but, more important, the long-range plan we talked about, Mr. Rickey wants you definitely to be available for the month of July, at which time our No. 1 announcer will be away for the Olympic Games coverage. This will entail home games and studio ticker broadcasts.

This time, Rickey didn't stand up Harwell, and the men met when Mobile played in Atlanta. Naturally, Rickey didn't tell a soul about the meeting. He didn't even tell Harwell.

Rache Bell, who had coached Harwell in American Legion ball, was a bird dog for the Dodgers, which in effect means he was a freelance scout. He phoned Harwell to let him know someone wanted to meet with him the following morning.

"Well, who wants to meet with me, Rache?" Ernie asked.

"Can't say," Bell said, no doubt after looking in each direction to make sure nobody was listening. "Don't ask any questions. Just be at the Ansley Hotel in the coffee shop at 8:00 in the morning. It's important. You'll see that once you get there."

Harwell recognized the bespectacled man in the coffee shop immediately and knew Bell had not exaggerated the importance of the meeting.

"My plane is waiting," Rickey told Harwell. "I'm in a big hurry and I can only talk with you for 15 minutes, but it is important to me that we talk about what we might be able to do."

Rickey told Harwell of the possibility he would be needed in July to fill in for Red Barber.

Harwell was indeed summoned to Brooklyn in July of 1948, though the source of No. 1 broadcaster Red Barber's absence was not the Olympic Games; rather it was a perforated ulcer that resulted in his hospitalization.

During a meeting with Rickey to discuss his midseason transition to the Dodgers' broadcast team, Harwell requested the terms be expressed in a contract. Rickey obliged and wrote a letter on official Dodgers stationery with the following letterhead:

BROOKLYN NATIONAL LEAGUE BASEBALL CLUB
215 Montague Street, Brooklyn 2, New York

In a two-page letter dated August 4, 1948, and delivered to Harwell at Hotel Bossert in Brooklyn, Rickey wrote:

Dear Ernie:

As a result of our meeting in my office on the morning of July 29, 1948, I am pleased to reduce our understanding to letter form, the conditions of which are:

Beginning this day the Brooklyn National League Baseball Club, Inc., agrees to employ you and you agree to accept employment as play-by-play announcer and broadcaster for Brooklyn Dodger baseball games at Ebbets Field and for Brooklyn games in other National League parks for a minimum of one month and at a salary of $1,000 for that period.

Inasmuch as the illness of Mr. Walter Barber is of a temporary nature, your employment at this time must necessarily be regarded in the same light. You, therefore, agree to remain employed beyond a month and to the termination of the baseball season, if needed, with your salary of $1,000 per month to be prorated through the extra period, if any.

The Brooklyn Baseball Club agrees to pay for your room at the Bossert Hotel and normal living expenses for yourself while employed by us in Brooklyn, and to sustain you in like manner, plus transportation, while on the road for live broadcasts.

You understand that during Mr. Barber's convalescence Connie Desmond has moved from junior status to senior status, and that you will assume Desmond's old share of the play-by-play and other broadcasting duties. This situation, as you understand, is not measured precisely by time or effort. Rather it is a task to be worked out by mutual cooperation, as Messrs. Barber and Desmond have done for so long and with such pronounced success.

As part of the consideration of our arrangement, you agree to offer your services to us for the 1949 season as Brooklyn Dodger play-by-play announcer and broadcaster, having in mind that Mr. Barber's health will be a determining factor in our ultimate acceptance or rejection of the proffered services. You have given us until November 1, 1948, to act upon your offer and, if accepted, you agree to sign a contract calling for a salary of $15,000 for Brooklyn baseball announcing through the 1949 season.

If at all possible, and in consideration of your economic welfare, we will make this decision before November 1st, and you agree to cooperate with us in extending the deadline, should your position in the professional field permit.

Wishing you utmost success at the Dodger microphone, I am

Cordially yours,

Branch Rickey, President

With that letter from one man who already had achieved exalted status in his field to another who one day would do the same, the longest major league broadcasting career in history was launched.

Earl Mann, who was losing not only his broadcaster but a friend as well, wasn't about to let that happen without getting something in return for his Crackers, and so it came to be that an announcer was traded for a catcher.

Chapter 7

Traded for a Catcher

H ow is it that a man can hit .471, slug .706, never commit an error, do all this in the big leagues at the age of 22, and never get another shot to play anywhere but in the minors?

Such was the fate of Cliff Dapper, backup catcher for the Brooklyn Dodgers in 1942. He compiled those statistics in eight games, not enough to draw any conclusions. Still, shouldn't a man who has had nothing but success be given a chance to fail before being deemed a failure?

Again, how could this happen?

Dapper was called upon to serve his country early in the 1942 season, and he wasn't the same player when the war ended. He could trace his decline to the Aiea Barracks in Hawaii, where he was stationed while serving in the navy.

"I was in the upper bunk, and Bob Lemon was in the lower bunk," Dapper recalled from his home in Fallbrook, California. "Something happened that made me hurry out of bed. I jumped out of the top bunk, hit the deck hard, twisted my leg, and broke it right down by the ankle. I was laid up for quite a while, hobbling around on crutches for a long time."

The barracks was loaded with professional athletes and tough to beat on the baseball diamond. Still, tension ran high in the barracks because it required only a look out the window to see all the ships lined up at Pearl Harbor, ready to be manned by the men from Aiea for an invasion of Japan. It never came to that.

Al Matuza of the Chicago Bears broke the best news any of his mates had ever heard. Matuza had been listening to the radio in the wee hours of the morning when he heard about the dropping of the atom bomb on Hiroshima and the Japanese request for surrender terms. Matuza let out a holler that awakened everyone in the barracks, and soon everyone was hooting and hollering.

"We were right across the street from the Bachelors Officer Quarters, and we all charged across there, raided the back of the barracks, took all the beer they had, and drank the night away in celebration," Dapper recalled. "We knew the war was over and knew we didn't have to go into Japan. We really raised hell."

Dapper and Lemon, the Cleveland Indians pitcher, were discharged together at Terminal Island in December 1945, and by February they were back to working for their respective baseball organizations. Dapper reported to the Dodgers, was assigned to St. Paul of the American Association, and then was demoted to Mobile.

In 1947 the Mobile Bears won the league championship, led by George Shuba, Cal Abrams, and Chuck Connors, who later gained acting fame playing the title role on the popular TV show *The Rifleman*.

"Didn't matter how high you threw the ball to first base," Dapper says. "Connors would catch it."

After the 1947 season, Dapper briefly thought he had found a path back to the major leagues. The Tigers had drafted him and were in need of catching depth. The transaction was nullified, however, because another player already had been drafted off the Mobile roster, thus freezing the rest of the players.

"That was my last chance to get back," says Dapper.

Late in the 1948 season, Branch Rickey needed an announcer and Earl Mann needed a manager. Trading a player/manager for an announcer makes no sense. This deal made perfect sense. The Brooklyn Dodgers got the voice of Ernie Harwell and the Crackers got the brains and brawn of Cliff Dapper, who had been catching for Montreal, in a trade for the ages.

"Best thing that ever happened to me," Dapper says. "I had the best years of my baseball life, got to know Earl Mann, a great man to work for, and I was glad to get Ernie Harwell into the Hall of Fame."

He endured teasing from Lemon and many others in good humor. "What kind of a two-bit ballplayer gets traded for an announcer?" Lemon was fond of asking Dapper.

A lucky one, Dapper routinely answered.

There have been one-sided baseball trades: in 1900, the Giants dealt 246-game winner Amos Rusie to Cincinnati for zero-game winner Christy Mathewson. Rusie did not win a game after the deal, and Mathewson won 373. George Foster was traded for Frank Duffy and Vern Geishert. Four players, including Nolan Ryan, were traded for fading Jim Fregosi.

There have been bizarre trades: Lefty Grove once was acquired by a minor league team in exchange for the team paying off a construction debt on an outfield fence.

There even once was a manager-for-player trade when controversial Oakland A's owner Charles O. Finley sent Chuck Tanner to the Pirates for catcher Manny Sanguillen and $100,000.

And once, two managers were even traded for each other in midseason. That happened in 1960, Harwell's first season as the voice of the Tigers. Bill DeWitt, president of the Tigers, and Frank Lane, running the Cleveland Indians at the time, decided to swap managers, leaving both managers feeling as if their dignity had been stripped. Joe Gordon went from Cleveland to Detroit, and Jimmy Dykes went in the other direction.

Reese Was a Classy Boy of Summer

When Hall of Famer Pee Wee Reese died, my baseball generation lost a friend and a hero. I'd known Reese since his second year in the big leagues. We rode the trains together, played golf together, were partners on the radio, and fellow members of the Hall of Fame Veterans Committee.

He was one of the warmest, friendliest players I've known—the personification of class.

I first met Reese in 1941. He and pal Pete Reiser were coming through Atlanta on a Brooklyn Dodgers exhibition trip that spring. Pee Wee and Pete came to the studios at WSB and appeared on my sports show.

Injuries wrecked Reiser's promising career, but Reese went on to become an All-Star and a Hall of Famer. He was team captain, No. 1, and the true leader of the Boys of Summer.

When I broke in with the Dodgers as an announcer in August 1948, Pee Wee was the first to make me feel at home. I taught his wife, Dottie, how to keep score. He was an avid hearts player. Hearts was our game on those long train rides, and I often slipped him the queen of spades and quickly ducked when he angrily fired his cards at me.

Jackie Robinson was usually in those games. Also Gil Hodges and Billy Cox. That was the entire Brooklyn infield. All of them are gone now, along with Roy Campanella, Rex Barney, and Carl Furillo. Those Dodgers were my first big-league team, and they still have a very special place in my heart.

None was classier than Pee Wee. Later, when I broadcast with the Giants, we still would visit each other. Along with his personal warmth, Reese had a tremendous sense of humor and was very adept with the gentle needle. One of his favorite targets was Giants manager Leo Durocher, his onetime Dodgers skipper. Reese had succeeded Leo at shortstop when Durocher retired as a player.

After Pee Wee's playing days ended, he went into television and radio. For years he was Dizzy Dean's partner on *The Game of the Week*. I had the pleasure of working with Pee Wee on the NBC radio broadcast of the 1968 World Series. He was in the booth with me in St. Louis when Jim Northrup's triple off Bob Gibson in Game 7 drove in two runs and sent the Tigers to the championship.

Just a few years ago, Reese joined me on the Hall of Fame Veterans Committee. The last time I saw him, Lulu and I had dinner with Pee Wee and Dottie the night before our voting session. He was the same old Pee Wee. Warm, friendly, and the epitome of class. Like his friends, I will miss the Captain.

—E.H., August 1999

Neither before nor after the Dapper-for-Harwell swap was a player ever traded for a broadcaster.

Hence, being a player who retired with a lifetime batting average as high as .471, albeit in only 17 at bats, is only the second-most exclusive of Dapper's baseball clubs.

Branch Rickey, the man who engineered the deal, once said the best trades are the ones that are never made. In this case, the deal worked for everybody.

Financially, Dapper's most successful years came after his 24 years in baseball as a player, coach, and manager. Dapper made a fortune as co-owner of an avocado farm with former Dodgers great Duke Snider. Snider sold his share long ago, and Dapper leases his land to nursery growers who grow flowers and organic vegetables.

"Baseball's been very, very good to me," says Dapper, who eventually made it back to the majors as a coach for the Brooklyn Dodgers. "And avocados were very, very good to me."

Dapper hopes he one day will meet the man for whom he was traded.

"Next time you talk to Ernie Harwell," Dapper says, "tell him I said hello."

Chapter 8

Dem Bums

Hilda Chester is ringing her cowbells. Hilda is letting Johnny Mize have it—is she ever. Gene Hermanski again takes advantage of the inviting right-field porch, only 297 feet from home plate, to blast another home run.

"That's another Old Goldie for Hermanski," says Ernie Harwell, the new announcer just up from the minor leagues. Harwell grabs a carton of Old Gold cigarettes and rolls it down the screen that stretches from the radio booth to behind home plate. The public address announcer, Tex Rickard, leaves his seat by the dugout, grabs the Old Gold carton, and delivers it to Hermanski as he crosses home plate.

Shorty's Sym-Phony, a collection of tone deaf "musicians," butchers another tune to the delight of the audience. Bobby Thomson strikes out and is serenaded back to the dugout by the world's most off-key tuba player.

Cookie Lavagetto is gone by now, having retired the previous season. His most loyal disciple, Jack Pierce, sees that although he may be gone, he must not be forgotten. He surrounds himself with helium balloons, each one marked with one word: *Cookie*.

It's Ebbets Field late in the 1948 season, and Harwell has walked into the middle of the most passionate love affair between baseball players and baseball fans in the history of the major leagues. "Dem Bums" broke a lot of hearts. All were in agreement that it was better to have loved and lost than never to have loved at all. Players and fans alike traveled to the attractively flawed ballpark packed into trolley cars and they were nearly as close together during games, thanks to the construction of a stadium that put ticket holders right on top of the action.

Before taking their seats, those holding tickets had to pass through stiles that weren't nearly as sophisticated as modern ones. Two people were required to man the gates. The stile boys operated the four-part gates by depressing levers with their feet to allow customers to gain admission. Typically, the stile boys were teenagers and the ticket takers were adults.

Joe McDonald, the man who would become an executive for the Tigers years later when Harwell was in the booth, started his long career in baseball as a stile boy at Ebbets Field, getting paid 50 cents a day. With forged working papers, he went to work at the age of 13. The Dodgers received advance notice when a spy from the Labor Department came to inspect the place to make sure they weren't breaking any labor laws. During such times, the underage boys such as McDonald would spot the spy and hide behind a post until he passed out of sight.

"At the end of every day, I would get paid the 50 cents and have to pay a penny for Social Security," remembers McDonald from his home in Lakeland, Florida, where he scouts for the Colorado Rockies. "When I turned 65 and received my statement from Social Security, there was no mention of that penny. I love my country, but I would like to know what happened to that penny."

From his post as a stile boy, McDonald received a promotion to the press gate, where he came to know the sportswriters and broadcasters.

McDonald remembers legendary New York columnist Dick Young giving him a ride home from his final day at Ebbets Field, the day before he began his service for the air force.

He also remembers seeing Ernie Harwell and Dodgers broadcasters Red Barber and Connie Desmond walking past him every day.

"Ernie and Connie were very friendly," McDonald remembers.

Off the air, Barber wasn't as gregarious, but that did nothing to make McDonald any different from the rest of Brooklyn. He, too, was involved in what he called "a love affair between Red Barber and Brooklyn."

"Red was a Southerner and you could detect it in his voice," McDonald said. "The people of Brooklyn spoke in a distinctly different dialect, yet we just loved the man. I don't think anyone ever even mentioned that he spoke like a Southerner. It was weird. There was just this immediate, successful marriage between Brooklyn and this guy Red Barber.

"These guys were dynamic," McDonald said of Barber, Harwell, and Desmond. "They didn't have television. Radio on the porch, that's where it was at. It was such a different way of life, pretelevision. Going to a game was more precious because you couldn't see it on TV. It was a different world and it was more fun. There was nothing like seeing it in person then. And for the road games, you'd listen to Ernie, Red, and Connie."

Jackie Robinson and Duke Snider, Roy Campanella and Pee Wee Reese, Gil Hodges and Carl Furillo, Preacher Roe and Carl Erskine—it was into this collection of remarkable talent in the freshly integrated major leagues that Harwell walked when he made his debut in what would be the first of an unprecedented seven decades of major league broadcasting. By the time Harwell became Barber's temporary replacement in the booth, Leo Durocher had been relieved of his managing duties in midseason and was replaced by Burt Shotton.

And Now, the One and Onlys

It takes the "onlys" of life to add sparkle to our existence. For instance: the only girl you ever loved; the only friend who defended you; the only teacher who thought you might be a success.

Here are some of my onlys during my journey through baseball.

Only player to ask to sit in the radio booth and hear me broadcast: George Brett.

Only player to ask me to review his speech when he was honored in pregame ceremonies: Ted Williams.

Only umpire to let me rub up baseballs before a regular American League game: Jim Evans.

Only manager to cry when I spoke in Baseball Chapel: John McNamara.

Only former sports announcer to invite me to lunch at the White House: President Ronald Reagan.

Only player I was traded for: Cliff Dapper.

Only player to deliver a message to my radio booth while in uniform: Eddie Murray.

Only player to rent me his home: Jim Essian.

Only coach to rent my home: Jimy Williams.

Only player whose wife furnished me with her spaghetti sauce: Sal Maglie.

Only player to give me stock in his paint company: Denny McLain.

Only manager to fight with me: Leo Durocher.

Only anthem singer to sing a Harwell-written song in duet with me: Robert Merrill.

Only executive to chastise me for erroneously "postponing" a game on my broadcast: Jim Campbell.

Only executive to fly me to spring training in his private plane: Branch Rickey.

Only manager whose movie star wife interviewed me on TV: Durocher.

Only anthem singer who sang "Georgia on My Mind" in duet with me at a Detroit charity luncheon: Pearl Bailey.

Only player to cohost a cruise with me: Jim Northrup.

Only manager who let me take pregame practice with his team: Burt Shotton.

Only anthem singer who let me select his wife: José Feliciano.

Only player whose wife I taught to score a game: Pee Wee Reese.

Only player to induct me into the Baseball Hall of Fame: Ralph Kiner.

Only player to shop for my wedding gift the day before he pitched a World Series game: Whitlow Wyatt.

Only player who became a movie director and cast me in his film: Ron Shelton.

—E.H., June 1997

Back-to-back rainouts delayed Harwell's first broadcast. He rode the subway, walked through the gates of Ebbets Field, and stood in a big-league ballpark for the first time since his Uncle Lauren took him to Comiskey Park in 1934. He was a stranger in a strange land, a Southerner in New York, a minor league broadcaster in a ballpark packed with customers who knew everything there was to know about the ballplayers Harwell had never met. He asked for and received directions on how to get to Ebbets Field via the subway. Once he got there, Desmond introduced him to one stranger after the next.

"Hey, Ernie!" was just the music his ears needed.

It was Russ Meyer, the right-hander who would pitch for the Cubs during that August 4, 1948, game. Meyer had pitched for Nashville in the Southern League and recognized the voice of the Crackers when he saw him on the field.

Meyer didn't last long. He protested so loudly and profanely when Jackie Robinson was called safe stealing home in the first inning that he earned a quick ejection from the ballgame. To the chagrin of the announcers, many of Meyer's profanities spilled out of radios throughout New York.

Branch Rickey, a pioneer in yet another way, became one of the first to authorize announcers joining the team on the road for live broadcasts that replaced the in-studio re-creations.

Harwell's first trip was to Boston. Braves Field had no booth for the visiting announcers and didn't even accommodate them with decent seats. They were assigned seats in the upper deck in right field, too far away to read the break of pitches, the hops of grounders, and the true flight of fly balls.

Barber was well enough to join Harwell and Connie Desmond in the booth for the first time September 9, 1948, at the Polo Grounds. The old redhead's timing was impeccable. Rex Barney, the Dodgers' 23-year-old flame-throwing right-hander, tossed a no-hitter that night and beat the Giants, 2–0. It was not the Dodgers' year, however, and they finished third.

It was from Barber that Harwell had his belief reaffirmed that to report more than the game details unfolding in front of him would be to cheat the listeners. Like Barber, Harwell didn't believe in cluttering broadcasts with too much in the way of opinion. Barber was demanding with those who worked for him in the booth, especially young statistician Bob Pasotti, at whom he was known to fire pencils.

"Some people found Red hard to work with, but he was a great help to me," Harwell says. "He was the first one to really go down and talk to the players, managers, and umpires, and he would always stress the importance of finding out yourself from the source instead of taking somebody else's word. He reported the game down the middle."

Unlike Barber, Harwell did not see anything wrong with socializing with the players. Barber suggested that to do so was to compromise one's integrity. "He didn't say it a lecturing way," Harwell says. "He just stated his opinion and left it at that."

History remembers Barber as one of the great baseball announcers, a talented trailblazer who spawned a legion of legendary broadcasters, including current Dodgers voice Vin Scully, considered by Harwell to be "the best in the business."

In contrast, Desmond became known as a man who drank his way out of a job after Barber left to call Yankees games.

Barber maintained an all-business relationship with the players, and Harwell treated them as he treated anybody else, with a friendly nature. As the train chugged from one city to the next, Harwell played hearts with Robinson, Reese, and Hodges and enjoyed meals with them. He occasionally enjoyed a round of golf with various Dodgers as well.

And Harwell's work for Rickey was not limited to calling baseball games. After Ted Husing bolted to announce Baltimore Colts games, Harwell was recruited by Rickey to announce football games for a Brooklyn football Dodgers franchise that drew little and won never in a short-lived, upstart professional football league known as the All-America Conference. Bob Chappius, who had starred at University of Michigan, was signed to play quarterback. Rickey convinced Pepper Martin, former member of Rickey's St. Louis Cardinals baseball team known as the "Gashouse Gang," to become the team's place-kicker. Rickey's football instincts languished on the opposite end of the spectrum from his unrivaled baseball genius.

"If baseball players can play a game every day, I see no reason why football players can't play two games a week," he groused. "We need two gates a week to make this thing fly." That idea went nowhere, and the team folded after one season. The league also folded, though four of its teams were swallowed into the NFL.

Meanwhile, Harwell's option for 1949 was exercised by Rickey.

The Dodgers had high hopes for a big season in 1949. They left spring training confident that better days were ahead. On their way north, they stopped in Atlanta for an exhibition series against the Crackers at Ponce de Leon Park. The Ku Klux Klan tried and failed to put its racist stamp on the series. The hooded ministers of hatred threatened that if Robinson set foot on the field he would be promptly assassinated. Robinson responded to the threat the way he did to all racist taunts early in his career: by strengthening his resolve and barreling ahead with nonstop hustle that became the signature of the franchise. If the threat worried Robinson, he didn't reveal it. He played the series without incident and was on his way to not only the batting title but also the National League MVP award as well.

"To me the most impressive thing about Jackie was his combative attitude, the way he always wanted to win," Harwell says. "He was very aggressive, and he didn't let anything stand in his way. I think that made him an ideal choice to break the color line. Rickey had to pick a player who was good, near great, and he had to get a guy who was aggressive and who had the qualities of leadership. Jackie answered him in all those phases."

Harwell took particular delight in watching Robinson aggravate pitchers while running the bases. "He'd dance off first base, like you read about Cobb doing," Harwell remembers. "He'd get in a rundown, and they'd throw the ball away. He would hit a ground ball, and because of his speed, infielders were forced into errors they wouldn't normally make. Pitchers were always on alert. He was fast but he wasn't superfast and he had great timing. He would dance off the bag, and they had to throw over a lot. No matter if he was playing cards or baseball, even in his relations about race, he was aggressive. He didn't hold back, although he did hold his temper the first two or three years."

With the benefit of hindsight, Harwell views Robinson's successful baseball career as, "the most significant event that's happened in sports. It has changed the whole face of American sports. I don't think we ever would have had the Latin players, guys like Clemente, the Alomars, Pedro Martinez. They would have been barred."

At the time, Robinson's historic significance wasn't trumpeted as major news.

"It was hardly mentioned in the *New York Times*," Harwell remembers. "They didn't even have a full house in '47 when they played the Braves. In the *Times*, they didn't even emphasize his debut. It was in about the fifth or sixth paragraph, considered sort of incidental. As people looked back, it became more significant. The fact is that when the experiment Rickey and Jackie got together on succeeded, Rickey began to get a lot more credit for it. If it hadn't been a success, the whole idea might have died for a while."

With Robinson leading the way, the Dodgers waged a tug-of-war for first place with the Cardinals all summer long. Stan Musial led the Cardinals' offensive attack, and shortstop Marty Marion, Harwell's predecessor at second base for the North Side Terrors, was the cornerstone of a rock-solid defense. Most veteran baseball observers predicted the Dodgers would collapse under the weight of a so-so pitching staff. In the end, it was the more experienced Cardinals that caved to the pressures of the pennant race. The Cards lost four in a row in the final week of the season. The Dodgers clinched the pennant by defeating the Phillies, 9–7, on the final day of the season, which was also the final game Harwell would broadcast that year.

"In those days, the network picked one announcer from each pennant winner to do the World Series," Harwell recalls. "Obviously, Red Barber was the No. 1 announcer for the Dodgers, and he did the World Series. I watched the games from the press box with the sportswriters. It wasn't like it was a disappointment because you didn't expect to do it."

Casey Stengel's Yankees won the World Series in five games. In Game 2, the only win for the Dodgers, Preacher Roe pitched a shutout at Yankee Stadium.

Away from the field, the Harwells enjoyed the move to the big city. Lulu became friendly with the Dodgers' wives and met with them regularly for dinner in Manhattan while the team was on the road. On one such occasion, Lulu and Mrs. Jackie Robinson, Rachel, were talking about how much they missed their husbands during long road trips.

"Jackie always brings me nice presents when he returns from a trip," Rachel told Lulu. "He came home from the last trip and bought me the most beautiful black satin lace negligee you can imagine. How about Ernie? What presents does Ernie bring home for you from road trips?"

Lulu scratched her head once and couldn't awaken any thoughts that would impress Rachel Robinson, so she scratched her head again and at least came up with something. "Sometimes," Lulu started, "Ernie brings me those little soaps from the hotels."

All was well at home in Roslyn Heights until, one afternoon, Lulu looked out the window at the Harwell's son Bill, and her maternal instincts told her something was terribly wrong.

"He was playing out back and fell down in a way that I knew wasn't him," Lulu says, looking back at the scare of her life. "He was very agile and it just didn't look right."

While in kindergarten, Bill was diagnosed with polio; it was determined he likely caught it from the little girl next to whom he sat on the school bus. Bill was confined to the living room couch for a month as his mother catered to his every need.

Between Dodgers seasons, Ernie was working for CBS radio as part of its football roundup team. Red Barber was the studio host, and he would play traffic cop for several reporters stationed throughout the country. Barber would call upon the reporters to give play-by-play of the games they were at for brief stretches and then switch to another site. Ernie was set to go to Iowa to do the Nebraska-Iowa game when he learned of Bill's diagnosis. He canceled the trip. When Bill was well enough to travel, Ernie took him to Atlanta, to his parents' home, and took him on daily trips to a swimming pool, which at the time was considered good therapy for polio victims. Bill recovered, though the polio left a subtle mark: one of Bill's legs is shorter than the other.

Things continued to progress well on the career front for Ernie Harwell. The Giants approached him and asked him about crossing town for the 1949 season, but Harwell rejected their overtures because he "didn't think it was right to leave [the Dodgers] so soon." He stayed one more year with Barber and Desmond, getting along better with both men than they got along with each other.

After the 1949 season, the Giants again came calling. This time, given the chance to be one of two announcers, instead of one of three, Harwell couldn't say no. He received permission from the Dodgers and was ready to join Russ Hodges in the Giants' broadcast booth.

Lulu soon would find out that though the move was easy on the family, it didn't sit so well with everyone in their lives. She discovered this upon taking Bill and Gray, the Harwells' second son, two years Bill's junior, to the pediatrician's office.

"I'm thinking about sticking one of your boys with a crooked needle," the doctor told Lulu. "Your husband is going across the bridge to work for the other side and that just isn't fair."

Chapter 9

It's Gone!

He takes his poodle, Giant, for strolls every morning and then settles in on the couch to watch his favorite television network, TVLand, alone in his Bay Area home. *I Love Lucy* has stood the test of time in the opinion of the greatest baseball player Ernie Harwell ever saw. The same can be said for *The Honeymooners, The Dick Van Dyke Show*, and *The Jeffersons.* "They make me laugh and I like to laugh in the morning," Willie Mays said days before he turned 70 on May 6, 2001.

His eyes aren't nearly as sharp as they were when he could stare from first base and read so clearly the tendons above the catcher's right wrist that he could determine how many fingers he was putting down, thus knowing what pitch was coming. He would relay the stolen sign to the hitter. Nothing about the septuagenarian hints at his once-blinding speed. Everything about him, from his thick chest to his massive hands, still screams power after all these years.

Mays has made his share of enemies through the years with his sometimes-prickly behavior. Yet mention 1951, his rookie season, and the anxious edge flows from him and is replaced by a sense of calm. He made his major league debut on May 25, 1951.

"When I came to New York, the Giants did a good thing for me," Mays says. "They found me a place to stay because they felt New York was kind of fast and I could get in trouble fairly quickly. They found me an apartment, on 155th Street. They found me a nice couple to live with. Every morning, the kids on the street would knock on my window to wake me up, and I would play stickball with them for an hour. I would leave for the park in time to get there at 11:00. Then when I came back home after the game, at about 4:30 in the afternoon, the kids let me eat. Then I had to play with them for another half hour."

He bought the winners ice cream.

"There were no losers in those games so I had to buy them all ice cream," he says. "The ice cream parlor was at the end of the street, next to the barber shop. The cops would block the street off for me so we could play. We had such a good time."

And during those times of fun and games with the boys who lived in the shadow of the Polo Grounds, Willie Mays learned a very valuable baseball lesson.

"On my block, instead of throwing it in the air we had to bounce it," Mays says. "Guys would hit it on the ground and it would curve. I learned to follow it and stay right on top of it. I was right on it. Sometimes guys would throw it in reverse and it would break inside. I was a good breaking ball hitter and I learned it from those games."

Mays used the word *good* to describe one of his baseball skills. It is not a word often associated with the Say Hey Kid. *Great* is more common.

Ask Ernie Harwell to name the greatest player he ever saw, and he answers before the question has been finished. "Willie Mays," Harwell says. "And I always say that without hesitation. Willie's joy of playing impressed me more than anything else. The verve he played with, the boyishness he showed on the field. He was naïve when he first came up and got over that pretty soon. He had so much ability and could beat you so many different ways. He knew exactly what to do and it was just completely natural with him. With Jackie Robinson, it was a little less natural; it was more determination than natural ability. Willie was a natural born baseball star from the beginning."

Mays learned about the major leagues reading the Birmingham newspaper on Sundays. "Joe DiMaggio was the player I liked reading about the most," Mays says. "They always wrote about how he was an all-around player. That was the kind of player I wanted to become."

Harwell, who had joined the Giants' booth in 1950, noticed a spark that lifted the team when Mays came on board in May of 1951.

Harwell remembers Mays feeling overmatched at the start and going to Giants manager Leo Durocher and telling him he felt he wasn't ready for the major leagues, asking him to send him back to the minors. Harwell disagreed with Mays and agreed with Durocher, who told the young ballplayer from Alabama he indeed was ready to play in the majors. He went hitless in his first 12 at-bats.

"Even then, you could tell he was special," Harwell says. "The first time you saw him taking batting practice, you knew. That doesn't make me any great scout. It wasn't difficult. Everybody could tell."

Harwell and Mays do agree on one thing: the most famous catch ever made by Willie Mays was not his best. Each man has another he thought was better than the catch Mays made sprinting acres back toward the wall to rob Cleveland's Vic Wertz of extra bases in the 1954 World Series.

The best catch Mays ever made?

"Bobby Morgan in Brooklyn, last of the ninth, bases loaded, he hits a ball to left-center," Mays says. "I ran. I dove parallel. I catch the ball, knock myself out. When I came to, I saw two people. I saw Jackie Robinson and I saw Leo Durocher. My first instinct as I was coming to was why is Jackie out there? He's the opposition. Later on, I found out he's trying to find out if I caught the ball. And Leo's worried about me.

It's Not Stretching the Truth

There's no sustained thrill in sports that can match a pennant race. Here are some of the things bound to happen down the stretch:

- The managers of the contending clubs will say, "It all depends on pitching."
- Television camera crews will go on the road with the team.
- Each TV station will feature interviews with loud fans in loud bars.
- A rookie reliever will pick up a surprise victory.
- A noncontender will use an unknown pitcher against a contender. The other contenders will protest; the unknown probably will win.
- Radio stations will be flooded with new songs about the team.
- The newspaper will send three more staffers to each game.
- Each paper will issue a special section with profiles of the players.
- Ads to buy and sell tickets will appear in the classifieds.
- More players will do TV and radio commercials.
- The teams' front offices will say: "We're making every effort to strengthen the team, but we're not going to wreck our farm system."
- A key player will suffer a severe injury and miss the rest of the season.
- Sudden rains will create unwanted doubleheaders.
- A player will say, "This is what baseball is all about."
- Another will say, 'Now it's fun to come to the ballpark."
- Bumper stickers saluting the team will spring up all over the city.

- Some fans will be surprised when the ballpark is not sold out for every game down the stretch.
- Disgruntled millionaire players won't understand why the club can't renegotiate their contracts in the final three weeks.
- The magic number suddenly emerges.
- All the dopesters become Iffy, and everybody tries to figure out which team has the schedule advantage.
- The team wins three straight and one of the coaches refuses to change his underwear.
- Although losing a game, a team will clinch the division and will be accused of backing in.
- Another team will be accused of choking when it loses two in a row.
- One team will be favored because "it's been through this kind of pressure before."
- Underdog players will say, "We're as good as those high-talented guys because we put our pants on one leg at a time."

—*E.H., August, 1991*

He wasn't worried about the ball. He was trying to find out if I hurt myself. That was the best catch that I think I made."

The Mays catch that stands out in Harwell's mind? The year was 1951, the ballpark Forbes Field in Pittsburgh, the hitter Rocky Nelson, the hit a searing line drive to left-center.

"He determined he couldn't catch the ball with a glove-hand stab across his body, so he reached out and caught it with his bare hand," Harwell remembers. "It was the final out of the inning and when he got back to the dugout, all the veterans gave him the cold shoulder, acted like nothing special happened. Willie wasn't aware of the gag veterans often played on rookies. He walked up and down the dugout and was surprised nobody said anything."

Mays knew he would have a receptive audience in Durocher.

"Did you see that great catch I made?" Mays asked Durocher.

"No, I was having a drink of water and didn't see it," Durocher said. "Go out and do it again next inning."

Inning in and inning out, Mays captivated the crowds at the Polo Grounds with speed and power, smarts and style. He wore a cap too small for his head so that it would fly off when he raced after a fly ball as only he could.

"I think entertainment is the key to playing sports," Mays says. "When the cap flew off, people identified with that. The basket catch, people identified with that. You have to entertain them. Just like going on stage. On the base paths, if I knew I was going to be safe I would fall down, let the people ooh and ah, and then I'd get to the base. Sometimes I would knock the cap off just to see how things would go. I learned the basket catch when I was in the service. I thought Leo was going to stop me, but he never said anything. I missed two balls 10 years apart. I missed one in Pittsburgh and I missed one in the Polo Grounds."

He didn't miss much of anything on the field, thanks to extraordinary instincts. In Durocher, Mays found a father figure who made sure he didn't bite off too much of the Big Apple off the field.

"Leo knew the nightlife in New York very well, and he knew I could easily get in trouble being the star of the ballclub," Mays says. "I wasn't much for nightlife then and I'm not much for nightlife now."

With a well-rested Mays sparking them and with the double-play combination of gentlemanly Alvin Dark and fiery Eddie Stanky as the team's "backbone," according to Harwell, the Giants roared all the way back from a 13½-game deficit to the Dodgers on August 12 to move into first place. They won their last seven regular season games. Meanwhile, the Dodgers needed to go 14 innings on the season finale to defeat the Phillies and force a three-game playoff for the National League pennant and the right to play the Yankees.

Bobby Thomson's two-run home run led the Giants to a 3–1 win in the first game, played at Ebbets Field. The series moved to the Polo Grounds and the Dodgers won to force a win-or-go-home game in the first nationally televised series in baseball history.

The Dodgers took a 4–1 lead, and 20-game winner Don Newcombe needed only three outs to send the Dodgers to the World Series. Two singles, one out, and one double later, Newcombe was pulled from the game. From the dugout phone, Dodgers manager Chuck Dressen asked bullpen coach Clyde Sukeforth which right-handed starter looked sharper for emergency relief duty, Carl Erskine or Ralph Branca. Sukeforth told Dressen that Erskine had just bounced a curveball in the dirt, so Branca was the man.

With unlucky No. 13 on the mound, the rookie Mays on the on-deck circle, and first base open with two men on, Dressen decided not to issue an intentional pass to Thomson. Meanwhile, Mays fidgeted in the on-deck circle.

"I was nervous Leo was going to pinch hit for me," Mays says. "He told me a million times after that he never would have pinch hit for me, but I know he would have done anything to win that game, so you never know."

It's not likely Durocher would have had more confidence in anyone then on the bench than he had in his rookie sensation, but as Mays says, "you never know."

Thomson made it a moot point by belting a line drive into the left-field seats.

On his drive to work that morning, Ernie remembers feeling a pang of sympathy for his Giants broadcasting partner, Russ Hodges. It wasn't really fair to Russ that he had to broadcast the big game on radio like everybody else while Ernie got to be the only one calling it on television, Ernie thought.

Harwell remembers five radio broadcasts that day: the announcers from the Dodgers and Giants did the game, as did Liberty Broadcasting and Mutual Broadcasting. Harry Caray called the game for KMOX in St. Louis.

Harwell and Hodges had alternated between television and radio throughout the series, and it was Harwell's turn to become the voice of television for the big day. Though he always has preferred calling games on radio to television, he figured he lucked out because he was the only TV voice, as opposed to one of many on radio. He figured wrong.

The call Hodges made that day of the most famous moment in baseball history has been played more than any broadcaster's call: "The Giants win the pennant! The Giants win the pennant! The Giants win the pennant!"

Bobby Thomson's "Shot Heard 'Round the World" off of Ralph Branca became immortalized because a Dodgers fan listening on his radio at home taped it, thinking he could use it to lord over Giants fans after the Dodgers won the game, and he was certain they would win. Because the Dodgers lost, the man didn't want the tape and Hodges bought it from him for $10. Video cassette recorders weren't yet invented, so there is no record of Harwell's NBC-TV call, a simple one: "It's gone."

Broadcasters use an outfielder's body language as a tool for reading borderline shots. In reading the way Andy Pafko backed up, Harwell wondered if he had made a mistake. He breathed a sigh of relief when it cleared the fence. And then what did he do?

"I let the picture tell the story," Harwell says.

The picture was an outbreak of raw emotion, the spilling over of feelings that had been building for weeks. The picture was pandemonium. The picture was Eddie Stanky leaping on Durocher's back. The picture has been shown over and over, though never with Harwell's voice preceding the celebration.

In a sense, Harwell's chance of going down in history that day was similar to Mays'. Harwell was one booth over, and Mays was one batter over. Still, the greatest player Harwell ever covered played in the greatest game Harwell ever worked.

Back home in Larchmont, Lulu, always one to root for the team that employed her husband, was ecstatic. She wanted to celebrate with the neighbors. Gray was upstairs taking a nap when Lulu and Bill ventured onto the street to find cocelebrants.

The neighbors had always been very friendly, always very inquisitive about Ernie's job. They thought it interesting that an insider who walked among their idols lived on the block. All those feelings were swallowed into a greater emotion when Lulu and Bill encountered the long, sad, ravaged faces on the block. "Just about everyone we ran into was a Dodger fan," Lulu remembers. "They weren't in much of a mood to talk."

Just as well they didn't feel like talking because there is no telling what they might have told Mrs. Harwell at that moment. They might have called her the wife of a traitor. They might have told her she was married to the Benedict Arnold of the broadcast booth. Realizing they would be better off celebrating alone, back in a home full of Giants loyalists, Lulu and her oldest child returned to the house.

Before that magical season, Hodges had let Harwell know the Red Sox were looking for a play-by-play announcer and let him know he was confident he could get Harwell the job. Harwell decided not to pursue it, and the job went to Curt Gowdy.

If Harwell had gone after and landed the Red Sox job, he never would have witnessed the most dramatic moment in baseball history and never would have seen the baptism of one of baseball's all-time greats. His reluctance to uproot his family again and a fear he would be labeled as a carpetbagger for leaving jobs too soon made Harwell stay put.

The Miracle of Coogan's Bluff overshadowed what happened in the 1951 World Series, which featured three of the greatest outfielders of all-time. Like Mays, the Yankees' Mickey Mantle, then 19, was a rookie.

119

Joe DiMaggio was in his final year. Stengel's Yankees beat Durocher's Giants in six games, giving Stengel his third consecutive World Championship. Durocher lost to Stengel.

Durocher and Stengel had another run-in once. To say he lost to Harwell in a fight on a train in one of the two seasons following 1951 would be to stretch the truth. If anyone had been scoring, Harwell guesses it would have been scored a draw.

Up until the point he scrapped with Durocher on the floor of a moving train, Harwell had only been in one fight in his life. He and a few fraternity brothers at Emory piled into a car and headed over to Peachtree Street. Freshmen were required to wear beanies at the time. Harwell spotted a Georgia Tech freshman walking toward him and decided to mess with him. He ran past and tried to swipe the beanie off of his head. He didn't quite get hold of it, so he turned around and came back to grab it again. This time, the Tech freshman was wise to him and greeted him with a sock to the nose. The two had at it on Peachtree Street, and that was the extent of Harwell's fighting experience when Durocher rubbed him the wrong way on a train ride.

"I'm cowardly and peaceful most of the time," Harwell says.

Most of the time.

Harwell had seen Durocher bully the weak, making "stooges" out of them. He wasn't interested in becoming Durocher's latest victim. Harwell was reading the newspaper on the train when Durocher flicked his fingers into the paper, pushing it into Harwell's nose. Instead of taking it (and whatever verbal abuse would have followed), Harwell rose up out of his chair and tackled the former shortstop. They rolled around on the ground until they ran out of steam. They never mentioned the incident to one another and got along well after that.

Durocher rubbed elbows with the Hollywood stars and made sure everyone within earshot knew all about it. He was married at the time to glamorous actress Laraine Day, best known for her performances in the Dr. Kildare movies.

"She had the most beautiful skin you've ever seen," marvels Lulu. "And she was quite nice. She had a little of the Hollywood in her, but not too much of it. I remember she had a massage every day during spring training and she loved to snack on chocolate candies."

Durocher and Day, an odd couple to say the least, given her grace and clean-cut image and his gambler-from-the-streets persona, were fond of giving parties, and the Harwells were on the invitation list. Dancing actress Cyd Charisse and her husband, the singer Tony Martin, were among the famous couples that played charades with the Harwells.

Baseball's popularity in New York was such that an invitation from Durocher wasn't the only means of meeting celebrities. Durocher had no hand in the Harwells meeting Henry Fonda.

Ernie and Lulu went out one night to see the Broadway hit *Point of No Return*. Heywood Broun Jr., a sportswriter who doubled as an actor, had a bit part in the play.

"Henry Fonda would like to meet you," Broun informed Harwell.

Fonda explained he lived and died with the Giants and caught broadcasts of their games whenever possible. He said he couldn't wait until intermission for updates on the status of Giants games and arranged for the stagehands listening to the Giants on the radio to signal him from the back of the theater. A flashing of two fingers, followed by a flashing of one finger, followed by a downward thumb meant the Giants were losing 2–1. Three fingers followed by a circle and an upward-pointing thumb meant the Giants were leading 3–0.

During their meeting, Fonda hadn't the slightest interest in discussing either the play, the differences between acting in Hollywood and Broadway, or for that matter anything that didn't have something to do with his beloved Giants.

Lulu enjoyed her trips to the city to have dinner with Giants wives while the team was on the road, and the social life in the big city was to the liking of the Southern couple. A visit from Ernie's parents was among the richest memories of the New York years. Making a rare flight, Ernie's parents made seeing the ocean for the first time in their lives a priority. Ernie drove them to Jones Beach. As a salty breeze fanned their faces and the rumble of the waves tickled their ears, they looked in awe at the vast and beautiful Atlantic.

"I remember the people from the airlines being so nice, going out of their way to help Ernie's father," Lulu remembers. "His parents were so nice. His father never once complained about his situation. Not once."

On the field, the Giants couldn't match the thrills of 1951 during the remainder of Harwell's New York stay.

Military service took Mays from the Giants after he played just 34 games in 1952. The only games Mays played the rest of that summer and for all of the 1953 season were played for the military.

"We played against the marines and they were the worst," Mays says. "They would knock you down all the time. They were dirty. As soon as I would step in the batter's box, bam, upside my head. I would hit it over the fence, come back up again, bam, back up in there they came. After I got through, they would carry me off the field and cook me a couple of big steaks. They were fine when the game was over. During the game, they were mean, boy. They were mean."

And without Mays, the Giants weren't nearly as fierce. In 1952, the Giants finished in second place, 4½ games behind the Dodgers. In 1953, they faded all the way to fifth place.

The Giants won more than the pennant in 1954, when Mays won the MVP in his first season back after military service. They swept the Cleveland Indians in four games, but Harwell wasn't there to call the action.

In a small-scale precursor to what would happen to Harwell decades later in Detroit, he was unceremoniously dumped without explanation. As would be the case in Detroit, though again on a much smaller scale, the sportswriters rushed to his defense when he was fired. The *Herald-Tribune*'s Roger Kahn, who later would author *The Boys of Summer*, widely regarded as the best baseball book ever written, slammed the Giants for firing Harwell. Max Kase of the *Journal American* and brothers Arthur and Milt Richman of the *Daily Mirror* and the *United Press International* also supported Harwell, as did Arch Murray of the *New York Post* and Dick Young of the *New York Daily News*.

Harwell wasn't out of work for long. The St. Louis Browns uprooted to become the Baltimore Orioles, and the Orioles needed a big-league announcer.

Chapter 10

Star of Arabia

Harwell called Orioles games from the beginning of the franchise in 1954 through the 1959 season. For their final two and a half years in Baltimore, the Harwells lived in a house unlike any they would ever call home.

The vintage mansion at 12 Blythewood Road, built in 1850, was fit for royalty, replete with high ceilings, a vast living room, two staircases, four porches, nine bedrooms, seven and a half baths, and three acres of land. It was affordable only because it was in somewhat of a state of disrepair. Even at that, its splendor was undeniable. It blended smoothly into the street with a dozen homes, each with a unique charm.

The dining room chandeliers, copies of those at the White House, drew gasps from first-time visitors. The spiral staircase in the front of the house inspired similar reactions. The back staircase led from what back in the day was the butler's pantry to the second floor.

No fewer than 88 shutters decorated the outside of the house, and that didn't count all the indoor shutters, which tucked neatly into crevices.

The boys, Gray, on the verge of entering teenage years, and Bill, a full-fledged teenager, could shoot their arrows at targets without fear of sending one into the neighbor's yard. It proved the ideal setting for treasure hunts. The myriad trees and the birds that convened in them captured Ernie's fancy and became backyard conversation pieces.

Nearly every new day the property revealed another neat feature. One such day came when Ernie was digging in the yard with the intention of planting a bush that would be nurtured by Lulu. He stumbled upon a brick walkway. He kept digging and to his delight discovered that the path led all the way into the woods.

It was a path traveled by human feet and one night by a horse's shoes.

It was a quiet Baltimore summer night, with a silence interrupted mainly by the chirp of crickets. Nothing in particular was out of the ordinary, except, that is, for the majestic horse roaming free through city streets and swanky residential neighborhoods, college campuses and open fields.

The nuns from Notre Dame College rushed to the window to catch glimpses of the horse galloping in the night. They gasped in wonderment at its beauty and its mystery. A stray horse? In the heart of Baltimore? Where did it come from? Where was it going? Is it real? Yes, it's real.

The rare car passing by came to a sudden stop as the driver gawked, put his tongue back in his mouth, and cruised slowly away. Crawlers of the night, not an easy crowd to impress, would tell to captive audiences the story of the horse without a rider, the chestnut-colored, muscle-bound, four-legged creature with the star-shaped white blotch on its forehead.

Meanwhile, the Harwells slept soundly, completely unaware that their filly, Star of Arabia, had broken free from the fence out back and had gone on an unguided tour of the outside world.

Ernie was on the road, of course. Aren't baseball wives always alone to deal with it all when the world is turned upside down? Isn't the husband always on the road when the pipes burst and flood the basement, when the boy chases a fly ball, runs smack-dab into a tree, and is knocked out cold?

The two teenage boys slept. The infant twin girls slept, though not through the night, never through the night. The twins would grow up to be so different from each other, one a blonde, the other a brunette, one tall, one short, one left-handed, one right-handed, one brown-eyed, one green-eyed. Naturally, when they were infants, they never awakened in the middle of the night at the same time. Their mother was a baseball wife, after all, and baseball wives never have it that easy.

Lulu was up and down throughout the night, which wasn't always such a good thing but was a blessing on the night Star of Arabia stayed out past her curfew. One of the twins awakened hollering with all her lungs for a feeding; otherwise, the Harwells might have seen the last of Star of Arabia.

While she was up, tending to her baby's needs, Lulu glanced out the window and saw an image that would stay with her forever. There was Star of Arabia, leading a procession down the street. A cop car rolled slowly behind the filly. A small army of men carrying flashlights marched behind the squad car. Lulu, as if she didn't have enough on her plate at the moment, headed downstairs to claim the horse.

She opened the door as a humbled Star of Arabia, weary and in pain from her gallops on concrete, lazily marched up the driveway.

"Don't you worry about a thing, lady," a police officer told her. "For some reason, this horse turned right up your driveway. We'll take care of it. You just go right back to bed. Sorry for the disturbance."

Exhausted, Lulu could feel but one emotion: pity for the poor horse that didn't know her limits and had bloodied hooves to show for it.

In her haste to greet Star of Arabia, Lulu had locked the door behind her, preventing her from getting back inside, where she was desperately needed because by now both babies were crying. A police officer broke into the house by cutting a hole in a window.

Grand? It's Really a Goofy Old Game

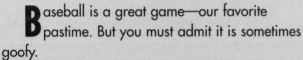

Baseball is a great game—our favorite pastime. But you must admit it is sometimes goofy.

Take a look at the presidents of the two major leagues. The National League president is Bill White. White is black. The American League president is Bobby Brown. Brown is white.

Baseball is one of the few businesses in which competitors are also partners. No wonder the owners make so many illogical decisions.

In baseball's literature, we celebrate the ultimate symbol of failure (the mighty Casey striking out) and focus an inordinate amount of attention on confusion (Who's on first?).

The first rule in the baseball rule book says, "Baseball is a game played between two teams of nine players each." Yet in the American League (and in most minor leagues) each team has ten players.

Rain checks are used for indoor stadiums. Umpires ruin new balls before each game by rubbing them with mud from the Delaware River.

Old men wear knickers and young men grow beards. The highest-paid performer in the minor leagues is a mascot called "The Chicken." In the major leagues the hirelings make more money than their bosses.

A batted ball that hits the foul line is called fair. The word "strike" (which means to hit an object) is used when a batter misses a pitch or doesn't even swing at it.

In what other sport does a dog own a world championship ring?

In baseball, spring training begins in the winter, and the
World Series is confined to North America.
The left-hand batter's box is on the same side of the field as
right field. Over the door of the visitors' clubhouse the sign says
"No Visitors."
Finally, if baseball is such a great family game, why don't we
honor Pop Fly as the Father of Baseball?
I tell you, baseball is a goofy game.
                                                            —*E.H., June, 1991*

The next morning, when Ernie called from the road and asked,
"What's new?" Lulu had an answer for him.

"Pick up a paper," she said. "Associated Press wrote all about it."

Mother of four, and caretaker for a curious horse, Lulu had two
more appointments to fit into her calendar: one trip to the veterinarian
and another to the blacksmith.

Star of Arabia learned a valuable lesson that adventurous evening:
the grass on the Harwells' side of the fence is greener, and a whole lot
softer, than the ground outside the fence. The horse learned the hard
way that a peaceful life isn't such a bad life, and a peaceful life it was
at the Harwell household.

Well, most of the time, anyway.

It was not necessarily so if your name happened to be Mel Ott and
you were a Hall of Fame baseball player working as an announcer for
the visiting Detroit Tigers and you accepted a gracious invitation to
join several other members of the Tigers' traveling party, including
broadcaster Van Patrick, for a picnic at the Harwells'.

Baltimore lent itself to picnics. All that was required of the host was
to make a trip to the waterfront to buy crabs, steam the crabs, put them
in a big basket, make a big bowl of coleslaw, throw some newspapers

down on the picnic table, toss a hammer and tong on the table, and let everybody go at it.

Ott was among the greatest power hitters to ever hammer baseballs over fences, or crabs on a picnic table for that matter. A left-handed hitter, Ott drilled 511 home runs during his magnificent 22-year career with the New York Giants. A lifetime .304 hitter, Ott averaged 32 home runs and 121 RBIs during a 10-year stretch from 1929 through 1938.

He spent six of those seasons as player/manager and gained fame as the only manager ever to lead the league in home runs when he did so in 1942. Ott's laid-back approach to managing didn't produce too many winners.

Ott's exaggerated leg kick during his swing became his signature, and it was that very leg and what happened to it in the backyard of 12 Blythewood Road that became the source of embarrassment for the hosts of the picnic.

No man can hit 511 home runs in the major leagues without extraordinary strength, and Ott still had plenty of it left after his retirement. Yet he was no match for the Harwells' teething nephew. Rhee needed relief for his aching gums, and there was no teething ring in sight, so he settled for the next best thing. He reached out and grabbed Ott's leg and gave it a good hard bite. Ott let out a loud yelp. Maybe nice guys aren't the best guys to manage baseball teams, but if your nephew is going to bite a man in the leg, it's best that he bite a nice guy. Ott reassured the horrified hosts that they need not worry, he understood fully. And order was restored at the peaceful home on Blythewood Rd.

Peaceful, that is, unless your name happened to be Juanita and you were the pet monkey of one of Milton Eisenhower's servants. Dr. Eisenhower, the Harwells' neighbor, was president of Johns Hopkins University at the time. His brother, Dwight, was also president at the time: president of the United States of America.

Juanita occasionally escaped, and when she did, she inevitably found her way to the Harwells' backyard, at which time Muddy, the family dog, would chase the poor monkey up a tree and stand sentry under it. If Muddy couldn't be coaxed back inside, Lulu would go next door to let the owner know Juanita was stuck in the tree house . . . again.

Dr. Eisenhower lived at the house without a wife. He was a regular spectator at Orioles games and was not a snob by any means, but he was not as regular a guy as, say, Ernie Harwell, either. Lulu picked up on that quicker than Ernie did. Not long after moving into the exclusive neighborhood, Ernie discovered one morning that there was not an egg to be found in the refrigerator.

"No problem," he told his wife. "I'll just knock on Milton's door and ask him if he has any eggs."

"Oh, Ernie, you can't just knock on somebody's door to borrow eggs in a neighborhood like this," she said. "Besides, Dr. Eisenhower probably doesn't even know where they keep the eggs."

Ernie settled for toast for breakfast that morning.

Milton did come to the house for dinner one night and sat down at the organ to belt out a few tunes. (Juanita, the servant's monkey, was not invited.)

Milton's more famous brother visited the street at least once, on the day his niece was married, and Milton informed all the neighbors of the proper etiquette should they meet the general. "Please call him Mr. President," instructed the president of Johns Hopkins University.

The Harwells never met Mr. President. Ernie was on the road, of course, when he paid his visit. Lulu was at home, but the closest she came to meeting Dwight D. Eisenhower was to meet his protection. Members of the Secret Service knocked on the door and asked if they could use the tree house out back to keep vigil over the president, and that was where they spent the evening.

131

Lulu caught a glimpse of President Eisenhower after his motorcade pulled onto the street and was taken aback to discover he was wearing a thick cake of facial makeup, having just finished a television interview.

Milton Eisenhower had no complaints whatsoever about the fare he was served at the Harwells. The same could not be said for Jungle Jim Rivera, the left-handed-hitting outfielder. When the White Sox came to town, Harwell golfed with Rivera and Sammy Esposito, the Sox third baseman. He invited them to the house for lunch afterward.

Harwell and Rivera became friends when Jungle Jim played for the Crackers, after Earl Mann used his connections to gain Rivera an early release from a penitentiary in Atlanta.

"God blessed Lulu with hospitality and she has taken full advantage of it," Ernie boasts of his wife. Because an old friend of Ernie's was at the house, Lulu took particular care in preparing a tasty lunch. While eating that lunch under the chandeliers fit for the White House, Jungle Jim Rivera looked up from his plate and asked the hostess, "Lulu, do you serve this slop to everybody?"

Oh, well, can't please all the people all the time.

Ernie worked some Baltimore Colts games, missing the great Johnny Unitas by one year, and became friendly with legendary football coach Weeb Ewbank and his wife, Lucy, who enjoyed playing the organ. The Ewbanks lived in a woodsy section of town, a comforting environment under most circumstances, but one that added to the Harwells' jitters on the evening the Ewbanks came to dinner at the Harwells. The hosts were rapt listening to their guests tell the tale of the neighbor who recently had been murdered. The perpetrator had broken into the house, peeled an antique sword off the wall, and used it to murder the resident.

The chills Ernie and Lulu felt listening to that story couldn't compare to the ones they experienced upon returning from lunch one afternoon. Their eyes simultaneously locked on their son Gray and a pal of his on the steeply pitched roof of their house, a parents' nightmare.

They stopped in their tracks, as if moving would shake the Earth and bring the boys tumbling off the roof to a terrible fate.

"Be careful up there," they hollered.

They already were caught where they shouldn't have been, and carrying candles, no less, so the boys decided to finish their mission. Gray had always suspected there was a secret room tucked beneath the roof, and on this ill-advised mission he confirmed his suspicions. The boys opened the secret door and discovered a room full of ancient newspapers. This, they determined, was the place where masters hid their slaves when Yankees stormed through the neighborhood intent on freeing all the slaves.

Harwell became a popular broadcaster in town, but nobody can please everyone. Lulu discovered this when she asked one too many questions of a painter giving an estimate of the house with 88 shutters.

It was quite an ordeal, finding the right painter at the right price for such an immense project.

One particular painter came highly recommended. His estimate came in lower than all the others, and his personality was pleasant enough, an important consideration considering how much time he would have to spend at the house. He needed to pass just one more test to land the job at the house owned by the potential customer whose last name had slipped his mind.

"So, are you a baseball fan?" Lulu asked him.

"Sure, isn't everybody?" he asked.

"Are the Orioles your favorite team?" she asked and should have quit there.

"Oh, yeah," he answered.

"How do you like Ernie Harwell, the broadcaster?" she asked.

"Oh, he's OK," the painter answered. "But I like the other guy a lot better."

He flunked the test and lost the job. Her undying loyalty forced Lulu to take the higher bid.

Two of the "other guys" with whom Harwell shared the radio booth in Baltimore made it to Cooperstown as well, as winners of the Ford Frick Award: Chuck Thompson and Herb Carneal.

Bailey Goss and Howie Williams worked with Harwell in 1954, the Orioles' first season. In 1955, Thompson replaced Williams. Harwell marveled at Thompson's talent, and his style reminded Harwell of the great Ted Husing.

Thompson and Harwell also teamed on Colts broadcasts, a duty that required them to attend a booster club banquet. At the end of the evening, an irate fan let Thompson have it for mispronouncing one of the Colts' names.

"You're not pronouncing Szymanski's name right," the fan let Thompson know. "You're saying, "Sismanski." The correct pronunciation is, "Szymanski."

He wasn't finished.

"And tell that Ernie Hardwell, too," he added.

So much for his credibility on the topic of pronouncing names correctly.

During their broadcasts of Colts games, Harwell and Thompson were not allowed to say, "The extra point is good" because that too closely resembled the slogan of Gunther Beer, which was: "It's good like Gunther." They were the chief competitor of National, the brewery that sponsored the broadcasts. Instead, they were required to say, "And it's through the uprights," or, "He converts the extra point," or anything else they could think of that didn't include the word *good*. Members of the same family owned the two breweries, and that's how fierce and petty the battle grew between family rivals.

After the 1955 season, National became the sponsor of Colts games, and Gunther won the rights to the Orioles' games. Gunther announced that Harwell and Thompson would not be retained to call Orioles games because they had become too closely associated with National.

Thompson continued to broadcast Colts games and gave up the Orioles for the 1955 season. Harwell stayed with the Orioles and went to work for Gunther, but not until after an intervention by a waiter at a Chinese restaurant, a fortunate piece of timing that led to a friendship between the waiter, Wally Lee, and Harwell.

Gunther sent a representative from its New York office to meet for lunch in Baltimore with Harwell and David Woods, his representative in contract negotiations. The New Yorker said he was in the mood for Chinese food, so they headed to the nearest such restaurant, the China Inn.

It was Harwell and Woods' first trip to the China Inn. As soon as the three men were seated, Lee asked them to sign a petition urging Gunther to keep Ernie Harwell as the voice of the Orioles. Because it was the man from Gunther who suggested they eat Chinese, he knew Harwell and Woods had nothing to do with the petition being presented at the lunch table. That fortunate coincidence factored in Harwell's remaining as voice of the Orioles.

The switch in beer sponsors meant a switch in partners for Harwell. He found Carneal, his new partner, every bit as talented and enjoyable as he had found Thompson. The two men had similar low-key broadcasting styles and came to enjoy each other's sense of humor.

The sponsors changed, and so did Harwell's partners in the booth, but other things remained pretty much the same. Like their ancestors, the St. Louis Browns, the Orioles lost more often than they won. The first season in Baltimore was the worst. While Harwell's former team, the Giants, swept the Indians in the World Series in 1954, Harwell toiled at the other end of the spectrum. The Orioles, managed by Jimmy Dykes, went 54–100 and were saved the embarrassment of finishing last by the Philadelphia A's, who stumbled to a 51–103 finish.

As so often is the case with teams bad enough to lose 100 games, the 1954 Orioles were packed with memorable characters.

Harwell looks back fondly on trips to the racetrack with Clint Courtney. "He was the goofiest bettor I've ever seen," Harwell remembers. "And he would always win on the last race and make enough to pay for his gas for the ride home."

Don Larsen went 3–21, and the wins could have represented how many hours a day he slept. "He always wanted to have company, somebody to talk to," Harwell says. "He liked to have a few drinks, but that wasn't what kept him up all night. He just liked to talk all night."

Vern Stephens led the team with eight home runs and 46 RBIs, numbers Harwell recites without looking them up.

"We called them the Kleenex team," Harwell remembers. "They would pop up one at a time. There were bad lights and a gigantic ballpark that didn't have any fences within the stadium at that time. Very few home runs were hit, and there was a lot of foul territory."

Dykes, Harwell says, "was the only man I ever knew who chain-smoked cigars." The Orioles were in Boston at the end of the season when one of the writers passed Dykes in the hall of the hotel and gave him the friendly greeting, "What goes, Jimmy?"

"I do," Dykes responded.

He was about to be fired and he knew it. Mr. and Mrs. Clarence Miles, Eastern Shore socialites and owners of the Orioles, came to Boston to announce the managerial change. Harwell and pals had to choke back laughter when exposed to Mrs. Miles' affected manner of speech when she asked, "Did you boys motor up from Baltimore?"

In 1955, Harwell was reunited with Paul Richards, his friend from the Atlanta Crackers. Richards replaced Dykes in the dugout. His smarts were wasted on a talent-short team that won 57 and lost 97. The Orioles improved under Richards, going 69–85, then 76–76, 74–79, and in 1959, Harwell's last season in Baltimore, 74–80. Armed with baseball knowledge that borders on encyclopedic and forever able to bank on an elephant's memory, Harwell can rattle off those records accurately without looking them up.

Harwell never hesitates when asked to name the smartest baseball man he ever has known: "Paul Richards." The manager was fond of saying, "I never want to hurt anybody's feelings . . . unintentionally." When he wanted to hurt someone's feelings, such as an umpire's, he drew on language more foul than a pop-up back to the press box.

"Umpires told me he knew words they had never heard before, yet he read the Bible every day," Harwell remembers. "He could recite the Gettysburg Address and the second verse of 'The Star-Spangled Banner.'"

Sometimes it pays to be a genius. Other times, a man can be too smart for his own good.

With Harwell calling the action from the radio booth, Richards' smarts fouled things up, but good, once. Richards was of the mind that it was foolish for a catcher to use his big, bulky catcher's mitt to tag a base runner coming from third base on a fly ball. Instead of doing it the conventional way, Richards figured it would be better for the catcher and pitcher to exchange gloves, because the pitcher had to pass by the catcher on his way to backing up the play anyway.

The plan hit a snag worthy of a slapstick comedy routine. Bill Wight, the pitcher, was left-handed. As required by the position, catcher Joe Ginsberg was right-handed. This caused great last-second confusion, and as they were fumbling with their gloves, the out-fielder's throw sailed to the backstop.

"Back to the drawing board," Richards sighed.

Richards always brought his golf clubs on the road and sometimes, in a failed attempt to fool his players, put the name Ernie Harwell on the carrying case.

Years later, Richards died on the 18th green of a course in his home-town, Waxahachie, Texas. Harwell attended his funeral and was in accord with everyone that if Paul Richards had to go, there wasn't a better time or place than on the 18th green, tallying the score of his final round of golf.

The Orioles' records weren't impressive. Other aspects of the organization, however, did gain favorable reviews from Harwell. He was impressed with how smoothly Jack Dunn, president and general manager of the minor league Baltimore Orioles, guided the transition to the major leagues. It was Jack's namesake grandfather, owner of the Orioles in the early 1900s, who was credited with finding a wayward youth named Babe Ruth at St. Mary's Industrial School. Dunn's other discoveries he sold to the major leagues included Max Bishop, George Earnshaw, Lefty Grove, and Ernie Shore. Harwell and Jack Dunn III became friends and spent time together on the golf course.

Veteran Baltimore sportscaster Vince Bagli describes Harwell as "kind of an ugly golfer. He didn't have a good swing. All he did was win. He would always take your $3." Bagli enjoys telling the tale of Harwell and Dunn at a course where the clubhouse that overlooks the 18th green had a large picture window. Harwell sculled one out of the trap, shattered the window, and without changing his expression, wryly asked Dunn: "Is that a one-stroke penalty or a two-stroke penalty?"

The closest Harwell comes to cursing on the golf course, according to Bagli, is when he screams, "Come back, all is forgiven," at a ball heading out-of-bounds.

Most of the good times with the Orioles came off the field during the early years of the transition to the big leagues. The Orioles had so little in the way of quality experience that they decided to rush prospects to the major leagues before they were ready to face the world's best pitching.

Harwell befriended one such overmatched hitter, and the down-home young man from Little Rock, Arkansas, who had made his major league debut at the age of 19 in 1956, enjoyed visiting the Harwells and had many a catch with Bill and Gray. During Harwell's tenure as Orioles play-by-play man, the infielder with the snazzy glove batted just .249 with 10 home runs and 72 RBIs in 959 at-bats.

Nobody had any way of knowing at the time that Brooks Robinson would achieve so much success he would gain induction into the Hall of Fame in 1983. Nobody could have guessed he would become so popular that more babies in Maryland would be named Brooks than in all the rest of the world.

Brooks had a big debut and told Harwell he called home and told his father, "This isn't going to be so tough up here." He immediately went into a prolonged slump and learned otherwise.

Robinson never grew conceited over his fame, never lost his down-to-earth personality, and never forgot his humble beginnings as a ballplayer. He demonstrated this one spring morning at Orioles training camp, long after he retired.

Baseball writers spend so much of their springs bored stiff, waiting out the hours in the sun while the millionaires stretch the aches and pains out of their bodies. Coworkers shoveling snow back home would never want to hear it, and wouldn't believe it anyway, but most baseball writers list spring training as among the most overrated assignments in the business. A small group of writers was happy to avoid boredom one morning by swapping stories with Brooks Robinson, who can laugh and make others do the same with the best of them.

Their fun in the sun was interrupted when a woman frantically shouting "Brooks! Brooks!" caught the Hall of Fame third baseman's attention. Holding a baby, the woman beckoned the legend.

"Excuse me, boys, looks like I've got to go meet the latest baby named Brooks," Robinson said with a laugh.

Sure enough, when Robinson stopped by to see the woman, she was armed with what she was certain would supply Robinson with the biggest thrill of his life.

"Brooks, say hello to our baby boy," she said, her smile stretching from first base to third base. "You'll never guess what we named him."

"John?" Robinson played along.

"Nope," the woman said. "Guess again."

"Robert?" he offered.

"Nope," she said. "Guess again."

"I give up," Robinson said, feigning bewilderment.

"Brooks!" she bubbled with so much enthusiasm.

Robinson's initial expression defined shock, before it melted into unbridled glee. The woman was convinced she had given Robinson a memorable first in his life. She went home and told all her friends how she had made Brooks Robinson's day.

As for humbling debuts, Robinson's couldn't stack up against Harwell's introduction to Baltimore.

The Orioles were in the first week of their first season when Harwell received a call from Norm Almony, vice president in charge of marketing for National Beer, the brewery that sponsored the broadcasts. Almony explained he would be entertaining a group of National's top salesmen and he wanted Harwell to schmooze them. Ernie obliged and showed up at the Oasis, a strip joint on the infamous Baltimore Block.

The Oasis was smoky and dark, better to hide the dancers' flaws that way. Sid Gray, the club's emcee, blended in well with the decor. He was long on miles, short on nutrition, with a smile shallower than a wading pool.

"Ladies and gentlemen," Sid Gray shouted into his microphone, "let me introduce our great Orioles announcer. He's doing an outstanding job and we love him. Let's hear it for Ernie Harwell."

At that moment, if a man sentenced to a lifetime in Siberia without a winter coat had offered to trade places, Ernie Harwell couldn't have said yes quickly enough.

Harwell had no choice but to become, however briefly, the only fully clothed person to stand. He stood up and waved to the crowd, which didn't wave back. Their attention was trained elsewhere. He sat back down as quickly as he could.

Gray decided to introduce Harwell again.

"He's great, folks," Gray said. "The best. Ernie, stand up again and take another bow."

Reluctantly, the new broadcaster in town did as he was told and stood up for a second time.

Gray, proud of having made a stooge out of Harwell, put the announcer in his place, which was his seat.

"Sit down," Gray barked. "Nobody wants to look at you."

Gray was right. Nobody wanted to look at Harwell. They preferred to look at the women, warts and all.

Harwell's official welcome to Baltimore was a great deal classier. Baseball giants flocked to Baltimore to celebrate the moving of the St. Louis Browns to Baltimore, where they became the Orioles. Hank Greenberg, Lefty Grove, and Connie Mack were among those in attendance at various ceremonies. The Orioles opened in Detroit at what then was known as Briggs Stadium.

When the Orioles returned from their season-opening trip, a big contingent of fans was at the train station to greet them. Harwell was given equal treatment to the ballplayers in a parade through the streets of Baltimore. Richard M. Nixon, then Dwight D. Eisenhower's vice president, threw out the ceremonial first pitch at the Orioles' home opener at Memorial Stadium, against the White Sox.

A sit-down-and-shut-up command from a go-go joint emcee notwithstanding, the city of Baltimore did come to enjoy listening to Ernie Harwell. He enjoyed working there and, when the time came, found it difficult to part with Carneal, his likable and talented partner. Harwell's family dreaded the idea of leaving 12 Blythewood Road, a splendid home. But they all swallowed hard and did what they had to do.

Detroit beckoned.

Chapter 11

The Tigahs

The gentleman from Swifton, Arkansas, had such an efficient batting stroke that it took him on a tour of the country, all expenses paid, with a handsome salary. The more cities George Kell visited and the more times he hit them where they weren't, the more Swifton kept calling him home.

Kell played for teams based in Philadelphia, Detroit, Boston, Chicago, and Baltimore during a 15-year playing career he ended with a lifetime batting average of .306. And he played so well that he was a guest of honor in a pastoral town in upstate New York one summer afternoon in 1983, a town called Cooperstown.

It's possible to take a boy out of Swifton, especially a boy whose talents were bigger than Swifton, but not nearly so easy to take Swifton out of a boy.

To spend any length of time at all talking with Kell is to hear many, many times how much he enjoys the retirement that has him spending most of his time on a farm in Swifton and most of the rest of his time in a "high-rise apartment" in Little Rock. He stays busy serving on the boards of a couple of banks, his church, and the rural electric board. He apologizes for memory lapses and explains, "I had a stroke three weeks ago. It didn't affect my speech, just my memory a little."

To hear Kell talk about his two places of residence is to think about someone from television's Mayberry talking about a trip to Mount Pilot.

Kell and Harwell first became friendly when the former was winding down his playing career in 1957 for the Orioles. At the age of 35, Kell still had enough left in his body and bat to hit .297. Still, something told him it was time to move on, time to make room for another third baseman from Arkansas, a teenager by the name of Brooks Robinson.

Kell tore ankle ligaments with 10 days remaining in his final season as a player and informed manager Paul Richards of his intention to return home to Swifton. Richards asked him to stay with the club. Kell didn't have anything better to do, so he spent time in the radio broadcast booth, and Harwell put him to work as a color commentator.

"I picked up a lot from Ernie Harwell in those 10 days," Kell remembers.

He took some of what he learned to work with him when he landed a job with CBS television, doing pregame and postgame shows for telecasts of the Game of the Week. Dizzy Dean and Buddy Blattner were in the booth.

Kell was excited to learn the identity of his first pregame guest, the incomparable Casey Stengel, one of baseball's great characters and a mile-a-minute talker. As part of his homework for the assignment, Kell phoned his friend Harwell for advice.

"What do you think would be an interesting topic?" Kell asked Harwell.

After thinking about it for a few seconds, Harwell suggested to Kell that he ask Stengel to explain what factors go into who bats where in the lineup.

"Ask him to explain what qualities he wants in a hitter for each spot in the order," Harwell suggested.

"Good idea, I think I'll do that," Kell said.

Harwell didn't see the interview and was curious how it went the next time he ran into Kell.

"It was fine, but Casey talked for 15 minutes and never got past the leadoff hitter," Kell told him.

Kell moved from that job into the Tigers' radio booth in 1959. After the 1959 season, the sponsorship for Tigers broadcasts changed from Goebel Beer to Stroh's Beer. That change in sponsorship spelled the end of Van Patrick's career as voice of the Tigers.

"Mr. John Stroh, top man at the brewery, called me into his office and told me he was making me the No. 1 broadcaster and would be hiring a No. 2 broadcaster," Kell remembers. "I asked him, 'What about Van?' He told me, 'Van's been selling Goebel for 15 years. People associate him with the other beer. I can't have him selling my beer now. It's like I told Van, it's different with you, George. You've only been doing it one year. Nobody really associates you with the other beer the way they do Van.' It was not an easy time for Van or me. Van sort of blamed me for it."

Asked for a recommendation during that meeting with John Stroh, Kell did not have to think about it for long.

"Ernie Harwell of the Orioles," Kell told him.

"OK, I'll bring him in and interview him," Stroh said.

Kell phoned Harwell to let him know he would be getting a call.

"What about Van?" Harwell asked.

"He's out, no matter what," Kell told Harwell.

Stroh interviewed Harwell and let Kell know what he thought of the man he recommended.

"He told me, 'I like him. He's a lot like you. You're the same type people.' He got the job," Kell remembers.

Kell says he did not recommend Harwell as any repayment for informally introducing him to the trade in Baltimore.

"I take a lot of pride in myself, and Ernie Harwell always impressed me as a guy I would like to spend time with, a guy I would be proud

My All-Time Tigers, Picked Using My Rules

During my 34 years of Tigers broadcasting, I've often been asked to name an all-time Tigers team. So I'm going to do it.

My selections will be restricted to those players I've seen in action from 1960 through the 1993 season. You'll likely disagree with my picks, and that's what makes it fun.

My first baseman is Norman Cash. He was a batting champion with home-run power. I'll pick another first baseman, Cecil Fielder, who hits the ball harder and farther than anybody I've ever seen.

Second base belongs to Lou Whitaker. Steadiness and longevity put him on my team. Lou is underrated as a hitter. In the clutch or with two strikes on him, he is one of the best.

I have no doubts about shortstop. It has to be Alan Trammell. Tram does everything well. He will lead the team in batting this year for the seventh time in the past 14 years. His shortstop play is as consistent as I've ever seen.

At third, I debated but decided to take Aurelio Rodriguez over Don Wert. Both were good. But Rodriguez had a better arm—a true rifle—and was a better hitter than Don. I always felt that Aurelio, with his great arm, should have switched to pitching.

My outfield would consist of Al Kaline, Willie Horton, and Rocky Colavito. Kaline, the Hall of Famer, was the consummate professional. He was a consistent hitter who often could supply the home run. Nobody in my American League time ever played right field better than Al. Horton was less talented in the field but was a powerful clutch hitter. He contributed many clutch RBIs. And don't knock the Rock. Colavito was one of the Tigers' most colorful stars. His home-run power was awesome, and he had an outstanding arm.

I'll take two catchers, Bill Freehan and Lance Parrish. Bill lasted longer and was probably better on defense. He was also a great leader. Parrish could throw well and gave the Tigers consistent longball power.

Because it's my team and I can do what I want, I am going to pick three starting pitchers and three relievers. My right-handers are Denny McLain and Jack Morris. Denny was sensational in 1968 with 31 victories, including one in the World Series. He followed the next year with 24. And he won 20 games in 1966.

Jack Morris lasted longer with the Tigers and through the years was a more dominant pitcher. He was the team's ultimate stopper.

My left-hander is Mickey Lolich, 1968 World Series hero with three victories over the St. Louis Cardinals. Mickey was a true workhorse. He pitched more than 300 innings in four straight seasons, and in 1971 and 1972 won 25 and 22 games, respectively.

For my bullpen, I pick Mike Henneman, who set the all-time Tigers save record; John Hiller, the left-handed ace in the 1960s and 1970s; and Guillermo Hernandez, who helped the Tigers to a Series title with his 32 saves in 1984.

For my pinch-hitter, my choice is Gates Brown. He handled the toughest job in baseball in great style and is certainly the best Tiger I ever saw in that role.

That's my team.

—E.H., October 1993

to call a friend," Kell says. "Whenever I met him, I was impressed with him. He's an amazing man. I'm 78 and Ernie's 83 and he can run circles around me. He's one of those one-in-a-million people, like Ted Williams and Barry Bonds, guys who can just keep going on and on without ever losing any of their talent."

Like so many employed by the Tigers at the time of Ernie's firing, even those who think as highly of Harwell and go back as far with him as Kell, Harwell's former partner quickly dismisses the subject and moves on to another subject when it's broached.

"I don't blame him for not wanting to be done," says Kell, who was a close friend of Jim Campbell's. "He was in perfect health. I don't have any idea who was behind it. They didn't ask the television people what they thought before doing it."

Harwell and Kell shared the radio and TV booths from 1960 through 1963, when Kell decided he missed Swifton and his family too much. He was talked out of retirement for the 1965 season to work in the television booth. In that job, he was able to spend most weekdays at home in Swifton because in those days most televised games were on weekends.

After Kell left, first Gene Osborn and then Ray Lane joined Harwell in the radio booth.

Harwell called Michigan State football games in 1963 and welcomed the experience, but didn't fret when that opportunity dried up after a year.

"The thing about football is it's so forgettable," Harwell says. "You do a game and do another game the next week and sort of forget about the game once it's over. And guys don't stay around as long as in baseball."

For Harwell, Detroit became a professional home like no other. The man who had worked in Atlanta, New York, and Baltimore took root in Detroit. The move to Detroit marked a crossroads in his personal life as well. At his previous addresses, Harwell was both a father and a son. In Detroit, he would be a father, a grandfather, and a great-grandfather.

Both of his parents died early in Harwell's first spring training with the Tigers. He left Lakeland after his father's death on February 15 to attend the funeral and help his mother. Harwell was back in Lakeland for a day when he received word that his mother had died on February 21. He returned to Atlanta for a second funeral, taking a melancholy journey back in time, going through his parents' home with Aunt Ruth. Every room, including the cluttered basement, held memories, each enriching his deep appreciation for how fortunate he had been to be raised by Gray and Helen Harwell.

"She had taken care of him so long and done such a great job with him, her job was over," the third son remembers. "It wasn't a case of her not being able to live without him. She was looking forward to living. She wanted to travel around, see the kids and the grandkids. The Lord just took her at that time."

His parents lived long enough to take great pride in their son's accomplishments but never had the chance to see him win the hearts of Tigers fans with five decades of broadcasts.

Harwell never will forget the details of the first Tigers regular season game he called. Rick Ferrell, a former catcher who in 1984 would gain induction into the Hall of Fame, was a front office executive for the Tigers when Harwell came to town. On the final day of spring training in 1960, Ferrell came into the press box and announced a blockbuster trade. The Tigers, Ferrell announced, had traded batting champion Harvey Kuenn to the Indians for home-run champion Rocky Colavito, a deal that was roughly as popular with the baseball fans of Cleveland as was the Tigers' decision to waive Hank Greenberg after the 1946 season.

Indians fans were afforded the opportunity to let Colavito know how beloved he was on Opening Day because the Tigers opened their season in Cleveland.

The Indians had no spot for Kell and Harwell in the press box, and they were seated in the upper deck behind home plate at a makeshift table.

"Bitter cold day," Harwell remembers. "A biting wind was coming off Lake Erie, and it was about 35 degrees. All I wanted to do and all George wanted to do from the first pitch was get back to the hotel. The game went 14 innings."

Harwell had witnessed Colavito hit four home runs in Baltimore the previous year but would not see him get a hit on this day. The slugger/matinee idol went 0 for 6. It didn't take long for Cleveland fans to be proved right about the trade. Colavito enjoyed much more success in Detroit than Kuenn did in Cleveland.

That same year, the teams traded managers in midseason, when the Tigers dealt Jimmy Dykes to the Indians for Joe Gordon.

Harwell, the man who was traded for a catcher, the man who traded Atlanta for New York and New York for Baltimore, had found a permanent home in Detroit. His reputation in the business steadily grew, and by 1963 he was assigned to announce the World Series for NBC radio. Burdened by a bad cold and a burning sore throat, Harwell nearly couldn't answer the bell for Game 1.

"The night before the game I was in my hotel room in New York and couldn't get to sleep," Harwell remembers. "Part of it was nervousness, and part of it was my bad throat. Announcing a World Series had been my ambition my whole life, and here I was on the edge and I was starting to think I wasn't going to be able to work."

At 3:00 in the morning, Harwell willed himself to his feet, slowly dressed himself, made his way to the lobby, and asked the bell captain at the Commodore Hotel where he could find an all-night drugstore. He walked down Madison Avenue and bought over-the-counter medicine at the drugstore across the street from the Waldorf.

On his walk back to the Commodore, Harwell ran into legendary crawler of the night Harry Caray, then a broadcaster for the Cardinals. Caray was not in search of cold medicine, but whatever fluids he poured down his throat had an uplifting effect. Caray flashed his signature smile and slapped a hello on Harwell's back.

"Harry was out tomcatting," Harwell remembers with a laugh. "He wasn't doing the Series. He was just there to have a good time."

Harwell worked the World Series with Joe Garagiola and was paid on a per-game basis. Naturally, both men were pulling for a seven-game series. They fell three games short. The Dodgers swept the Yankees.

Harwell fell $1,500 short of what he had hoped for, but it was from that World Series that the man who was at the premiere of *Gone with the Wind* gained a measure of immortality in another film classic, *One Flew Over the Cuckoo's Nest*.

A slice of Harwell's call of Game 2 can be heard coming out of a radio in the film as a mental hospital staffer wheels a medicine cart out of a room. Harwell's delivery is decidedly calmer than that of Randle P. McMurphy, the patient portrayed by Jack Nicholson. With a number of agitated patients crowding around him, Nicholson's character stares at the blank television and does imaginary play-by-play.

"My 15 seconds of fame," Harwell says of *Cuckoo's Nest*. Harwell also can be seen and/or heard in *Tigertown*, *Cooperstown*, *Aunt Mary*, *Cobb*, and *Paper Lion*.

After that Game 2 broadcast, Harwell was able to sneak in calling the Michigan State–USC football game played at the Coliseum on the eve of Game 3 at Dodger Stadium.

Calling the World Series and seeing the world were highlights of Harwell's early years in Detroit. The Harwells spent the winter before the 1965 season living in Mallorca, Spain, where Gray spent much of his senior year in high school and the twins, Julie and Carolyn, attended school at the age of six.

The winter was a cold one and Gray, not wanting to see his father shiver, bought him a present to keep his head warm. Berets were all the rage in Spain at the time and Gray, figuring it was best to, when in Spain, do as the Spanish do, bought a beret for his father. As much to let his son know he appreciated his warmth as for any other reason, Ernie wore a beret in the booth for decades, and it became something of a trademark.

"People thought either I was a cab driver or a director of dirty movies, so I had to give up the beret," Harwell explains.

He replaced that hat with another one given him by a Farmington Hills neighbor, Pasquale Ferrari, who had purchased it while visiting his mother in Rome. That fisherman's cap now keeps Harwell's head warm on cold nights at Comerica Park.

Memories of that winter in Mallorca warm the hearts of all the Harwells. They rented a two-bedroom hotel suite on a Mediterranean beach for $83 a month, plus a meal that cost $1 a night. The proprietor of their favorite restaurant, Los Candiles, was a woman known as The Black Panther, a moniker that spoke to her past as the leader of a Dutch underground group during World War II. Amelio, the bartender, was all of 12 years old. He doubled as a waiter, and when things got slow he buried his nose in comic books. The Harwells never will forget the trip they took to Formentor, at the top of the island of Mallorca. World-famous travel writer Temple Fielding owned a home there and called it the most appealing place in the world to reside. Easy for Fielder to say. He never had to drive down the mountain with a car that lost its brakes, as did the Harwells. Construction workers had been blasting at the bottom of the hill, which made stopping a good idea for those driving cars. It wasn't an option for Gray Harwell. He steered the car right through the blasting area without stopping. Fortunately, it happened to be between blasts. Somehow, their wild ride down the hill ended without incident as the car came to a peaceful stop.

They survived that ordeal, just as Julie survived her brush with what qualified as modern medicine in Mallorca.

While reading the local English newspaper, Harwell had recognized a man's byline from *Variety* magazine and figured it wouldn't hurt to call him and pick his brain for advice on how to make the most of their winter in Mallorca.

"Bruno showed us around, and we became pretty good buddies," Harwell remembers of the helpful writer whose last name he can't recall. "Every time I saw him, he introduced me to a new girlfriend."

Bruno let the Harwells know the procedure for seeking medical attention should one of them come down with an illness while on the island: go to the druggist and purchase the proper fluid and then go to the local bar, Pepi's, where the town nurse could be found. She supplied the syringe and gave the shot to the ailing Julie. And then, after giving the shot, she washed her hands. Not before, after.

The Harwells had arrived in Spain around Halloween and returned home shortly after Valentine's Day. What Ernie and Lulu didn't realize until shortly before the flight home landed was that Gray had packed a souvenir knife in his bag. They feared a scene at customs, but the tension was broken when one of the agents recognized the announcer of the Tigers and was eager to the break the news to him about the recently announced changes in the booth.

"Hey Ernie," blurted the customs agent. "You've got a new partner. George Kell is going to the TV booth and Gene Osborn is going to be your partner."

That's how Harwell learned he no longer would be sharing the booth with his pal Kell.

"That was my greeting when I got back to America," Harwell remembers.

Harwell had a new partner in Osborn. Soon Harwell would be paired with Ray Lane, a combination that would cover a team that forever would hold a special place in Detroit history for reasons that extended beyond nine innings and 27 outs.

Chapter 12

Healing Tigers

S moke curled into view beyond the left-field fence as word of danger on the streets of Detroit began to spread throughout Tiger Stadium. Harwell and Ray Lane were in the booth and made mention of the smoke before getting word from WJR not to mention it again.

By the time the game ended that day in the summer of 1967, everyone was under strict orders to go home and stay home. They were told to avoid the freeways, lest they run the risk of having their cars toppled. Harwell heeded the warning, and when he got home to Grosse Pointe, the first thing he saw when he walked in the door was a brand-new television. Lulu had purchased one ticket in a raffle that day and won the TV. His humor untainted by the troubles in his city, Ernie cracked, "Have you been out looting again, Miss Lulu?"

Lulu hadn't heard about the riots. Soon she would hear plenty about them. She would hear rumors that the rioters planned to cut a path to the suburbs. Gray's girlfriend, Sandy, had to spend the next couple of days with the Harwells for fear that heading home wouldn't be safe.

One young man with the Tigers didn't heed the orders from club executives to head home to safety. Willie Horton's steering wheel wouldn't let him do so. Horton was a big name in Detroit baseball circles since he hit a home run that crashed off the bottom of the light tower in right-center at Tiger Stadium in a high school city championship. He and Alex Johnson, who would go on to win a batting championship in the major leagues, led Northwestern High past Cass Tech. Horton was a catcher and an underclassman. His legend was born with that long home run.

Years later, when the city he so loved erupted in violence, Horton couldn't bring himself to stay away from the fray. He ventured into the streets with his Tigers jersey on.

"Really, to tell you the truth I don't know why I did it," Horton says. "I saw things that were unreal. You see so many things burning you think it's a war. You see all that and you don't really understand what's going on."

He saw rocks flying through windows. He saw cars and buildings ablaze. He saw confused young men driven to violence.

"I just started driving," Horton remembers. "I started out at Livernois and ended up on 12th. You just try to talk to people. Some of them stopped and listened to me. Some of them kept on doing what they were doing. Some of them scratched their heads and tried to figure out what I was doing there. I didn't even think about how dangerous it was. I was just trying to do what was best. When I got home, my uniform looked like it had been in a fire. To this day, I'm glad I did that. From that point on, I tried to get more and more involved in bringing peace to the city."

It was some journey that brought Willie Horton to 12th Street. The journey started in the Virginia coal-mining town of Arno, near the Tennessee border. Willie was the youngest of 21 children reared by Clinton and Lillian Horton. When Willie was 10, the family moved to Detroit and took up residence in the Jefferson Homes, a high-rise housing project in the shadow of Tiger Stadium.

Horton, best pal James Slate, and whatever other kids they could recruit from the projects were fond of playing a game called Strikeout against the Tiger Stadium wall.

"We took a spike and made a square box on the wall, or we'd paint it and hope we didn't get caught," Horton remembers. The box was the strike zone.

Horton and Slate earned money at their paper routes and their jobs bagging and carrying groceries for shoppers from the A&P on Trumbull. They spent the money on Saturdays at the arcade and at movie theaters on Grand Avenue Boulevard.

"Sometimes we'd spend whole days going in and out of movie theaters," Horton remembers. "There were a lot of small theaters and a couple big ones. We saw movies at the Grand River Theatre. I remember one day we saw Elvis Presley at the Fox Theatre. We saw the movie in which he sang "Ain't Nothin' but a Hound Dog" there. I cried all the way home because I thought Elvis was dead. We had so many things going on then."

Horton and Slate "slipped in" to Tiger games without paying.

"We got caught slipping in the back gate one day," Horton remembers.

Rocky Colavito, then playing for the Indians, and Don Mossi felt sympathy for the boys and introduced them to clubhouse managers John Hand and Rip Collins. It led to a job for Horton. The job didn't last long because it was evident that his baseball talent was something special and he was too busy playing ball to launder ballplayers' socks and jocks.

As he did on the day he thought Elvis died, Horton had difficulty sorting fact from fiction when he walked smack-dab into the middle of riots that resulted in 43 deaths. The fracturing of his city made Horton all the more determined to help the Tigers make it to the World Series in 1967. The Tigers fell one game short, losing to the Angels on the final day of the season when Dick McAuliffe bounced into a double play for the first time all season.

Horton's Theatrics Were As Good As His Play

Today is Willie Horton's day. I'm pleased he is being honored at Comerica Park with a much-deserved statue and the retirement of his Tigers No. 23. Willie is Detroit's own—a wonderful man and a true friend.

If life is a landscape, Willie is a garden of emotions. The centerpiece of his garden is a blooming hypochondria. You won't find that flower listed in seed catalogs and it might not be in everybody's garden. But during his baseball career, it was a thriving example of Willie's way.

Horton never met an ailment he didn't anguish about. Always treating each ache or pain with an overdose of exaggeration, he was the Tigers' Moaner Lisa. To Willie, a simple headache loomed as a brain tumor. The sniffles indicated at least pneumonia, and a boil on his leg meant immediate amputation.

One afternoon at Tiger Stadium, Willie made a diving catch in left field, suffering an injured leg. Rolling over on his back, he looked to the heavens and shouted for help.

Judging by his theatrics, one quickly discerned that left field had qualified as Willie's deathbed. Here is the unforgettable scene we saw that afternoon.

Trainer Bill Behm struggled up the dugout steps to begin his slow gallop toward Horton.

Next came manager Mayo Smith to check on his suffering slugger. Mayo's sprint onto the field couldn't equal his usual speed to the buffet or bar—the only places he had been training for the past 20 years. On the way toward Willie, Smith suddenly went down. A leg cramp sent him sprawling off the turf.

Trainer Behm faced a dilemma. Horton was almost near death—at least in his own mind. On the other hand, Behm's manager and boss was suffering with his charley horse and demanding attention.

The answer's obvious: attend the boss.

So, Wondrous Willie was treated second. He recovered and lived to play left field for the Tigers.

Because he has always been one of my favorites, I'm certainly happy that Willie survived.

—*E.H., July 2000*

The Tigers' role in healing a wounded city would be delayed a year.

"After losing like that on the last day, everybody went to spring training early," Horton remembers. "We had the best team in baseball and we knew it. It wasn't no individual play. Most of us all came up together in the minor leagues and we didn't feel any pressure because we had so much confidence in each other. We always had the feeling somebody was going to pick somebody else up. That's what winning is all about. That's what a team is all about, that closeness."

The 1968 Tigers brought the divided city of Detroit together on a nightly basis to root for a team that had one of those magical seasons that become embedded in memories and never fade. They were noted for winning games in the late innings, which made their method of winning the World Series entirely appropriate. The Tigers fell behind, three games to one, and won the last three games.

Denny McLain, a character the likes of which seldom has been seen in any sport, won 31 games.

"His confidence was what made him such a great pitcher," Harwell says of McLain. "And that confidence led to his undoing. It made him think the rules don't apply to him."

Horton remembers a story that speaks to McLain's sharp mind and innate disdain for rules and the authority figures who try to implement them.

"We were playing winter ball in Puerto Rico," Horton recounts. "We're on the bus playing cards and our manager, Wayne Blackburn, said, 'That's it. No more playing cards on the bus.' He took the cards away from us. Mac looked right at him and said to us, 'We're still playing cards.' Blackburn said, 'What? How are you going to play cards with no cards?' Denny showed us how to play cards by looking at license plates."

McLain went from playing cards by looking at license plates to *making* license plates (see Chapter 13). Throughout it all, he has remained a teammate of Horton's. Once a 1968 Tiger, always a 1968 Tiger.

"We all felt his pain in one way or another," Horton says. "He's part of it. We all came up together."

McLain had numerous businesses he was certain would make him a millionaire. He even convinced some teammates of that and recruited them as investors.

"He had a paint company that some of the players went in on," announcer Ray Lane remembers. "We were flying out of the Bay Area after a series with Oakland, and McLain gets up out of his seat and comes up to where Ernie and I were sitting. He pointed out the window at the Golden Gate Bridge and said, 'See that bridge? Just yesterday, my paint company landed the contract to paint that entire bridge.' He was dead serious."

No harm in trying, but Lane and Harwell didn't bite. McLain would need to look elsewhere for investors.

McLain was the central figure of the team, the guy who generated the most stories, the most controversy, even on a team that had no shortage of characters, all of whom had their roles to play.

Gates Brown forever delivered the clutch pinch hit. In a bold stroke of genius that shocked a nation of baseball followers, conservative manager Mayo Smith made the radical move of switching Mickey Stanley from center field to shortstop for the Series so that he could play Horton, Jim Northrup, and the great Al Kaline together in the outfield.

"Nobody I polled about that the night before the World Series thought it was a good idea," Harwell remembers.

It worked brilliantly.

"It was the right thing to do because Mickey was the best athlete on the team and we needed to get Al in there," Horton says. "Al had one of those off years and then he got to the World Series and had a great World Series, which was something we all wanted for him. Al was more like a daddy for all of us. I call him an Abraham Lincoln leader, a quiet leader. Norm Cash was a loud leader. And Gates Brown was an in-between leader."

Mickey Lolich, who had been called to duty temporarily by the National Guard during the riots the previous year, won three games in the World Series. He beat Cardinals ace Bob Gibson in Game 7.

Throughout the 1968 season, Ernie Harwell and Ray Lane called the action from the booth that hovered over home plate.

"Best announcing team Detroit ever had," McLain says. "Ernie brought the franchise to the public, and Ray Lane added his sparkle."

It was Horton who made the pivotal play in the Series when in Game 5 he threw out Lou Brock, who was trying to score from second with two outs on a single to left. Brock did not slide.

"We studied information on the other team more than most teams did then," Horton says. "We knew Lou picked up bad habits on the bases. It said on the report that because Lou Brock stole so many bases when he was running on a ball hit to the outfield, the outfielders would lob the ball back in, figuring they had no chance, and Lou would drift on the bases. Bill Freehan saw Lou break stride and he let the ball come through. If Lou hadn't broken stride, Freehan would have told Don Wert to cut off the throw. Lolich was pitching and when he reached the middle innings he would start getting into second gear. I knew Mike Shannon wasn't going to pull him, so I gave him the line and the ball was hit right in front of me. I charged it and all I was thinking about was hitting Coyote in the nose."

"Coyote" was Wert, the third baseman. Gates Brown was "Gator." McLain was "Dolphin" because he was such a big fish in card games. John Hiller, the team's best reliever, was "Ratso," after Ratso Rizzo of *Midnight Cowboy*. Hiller and Pat Dobson didn't care for getting to bed early. McAuliffe was "Mad Dog." Kaline was "the Lion," Jim Northrup "the Fox." Earl Wilson was "Duke," after John Wayne. Norm Cash was "Stormin' Norman." Horton was "Boomer," or "TNT," or "Willie the Wonder."

"Freehan was "Big Ten" because he had that Big Ten walk," Horton says with a laugh. "Not too many people remember, but Elroy Face and Eddie Mathews were on that team. They didn't play, but just having them there meant so much to us. Elroy Face always drank moonshine. Eddie Mathews, I guess he probably drank a little bit of everything."

The Tigers franchise was a model for success then, and when White Sox broadcaster Ken "Hawk" Harrelson, former power hitter for the Red Sox, reminded Horton of that during the summer of 2001, the old Tiger swelled with pride.

"If I can get some of that pride back in that uniform, get the young players to feel the way we felt about the D," Horton says. "My shirt never hit the floor. I had so much love and respect for that D. That's how we were raised through the Tiger organization. I want that to be important to today's Tigers. I want them to feel it's just as important what you do off the field, how you carry yourself. We had dignity, pride, and respect in people. Ken Harrelson said he was so glad to see me and Al [Kaline] back involved. He said it hurts me to see this team after all those years coming in here learning from you guys, how y'all went about playing the game."

Ernie and Ray Lane (right) with Denny McLain (center). Ernie Harwell personal collection.

The Harwell twins, Julie (left) and Caroline, surround Amelio, a then-12-year-old bartender, writer, and night clerk at Los Candiles Hotel in Majorca, Spain. Ernie Harwell personal collection.

Ernie chats with Hank Aaron, who displays a recording of the song "Move Over Babe, Here Comes Henry," written by Bill Slayback and Ernie. Ernie Harwell personal collection.

Three Hall of Fame broadcasters: (left to right) Curt Gowdy, Ernie, and Bob Elson.
Ernie Harwell personal collection.

David Eisenhower examines Ernie's base-ball collection at the Detroit Library. Ernie Harwell personal collection.

With Giant and ESPN star broadcaster Jon Miller. Photo courtesy of John F. Cummings, © 1989.

With longtime partner Paul Carey, Ernie leaves a Tiger Stadium press conference after his firing on December 19, 1990. Photo courtesy of Nick Brancaccio / The Windsor Star.

Ernie and Lulu visit Florida neighbor Erskine Caldwell, author of Tobacco Road *and* God's Little Acre. Ernie Harwell personal collection.

Author Elmore Leonard visits Ernie at Comerica Park. Photo courtesy Bill Eisner, © 2000.

Then and now: Lulu and Ernie in Atlanta during 1941 . . .

. . . and in Lulu's rose garden, 1998. First photo courtesy of H. T. Allen. Second photo courtesy of Focal Point, © 1998.

The Harwell clan at Ernie's Hall of Fame induction, August 1981. Ernie Harwell personal collection.

Ernie broadcasting playoff games for CBS radio. Ernie Harwell personal collection.

It hurts Horton to see the Tigers flirt with 100 losses summer after summer. The hurt vanishes when he sees a familiar old figure, youthful as ever, bouncing around Comerica Park. Nostalgia drips from every syllable when Horton reminisces about the old Tigers. His tone changes to reverence when he discusses the voice of the Tigers.

"Every time I see Ernie Harwell I get chills," Horton says. "That's how much I look up to him. All you have to do is see him walk across that field and you forget about the kind of season we're having. He don't have to speak, just seeing him is enough. There is some gloss around that man, something special about him. I've gotten a lot of mileage out of the things he's told me."

Horton remembers meeting Harwell for the first time.

"From day one, he wasn't no stranger," Horton remembers. "The first day I met him he seemed like he knew me all my life. You don't know why, but he's somebody special God put here. You ain't gonna find a better person."

When he lost his parents in a car wreck in 1965, Horton took comfort in Harwell's words.

"The things he said gave me that inner strength I needed," Horton remembers. "I know he's done it for many other athletes. He gives you so much and never asks for anything in return."

Horton's contributions to the Tigers and the city of Detroit are immortalized in one of the six statues at Comerica Park.

"I closed my statue speech by saying I couldn't have done it without people like Ernie Harwell," Horton says. "He taught me how to understand the game. He taught me how it's about the fans, you have to recognize the ballgame don't start with you. He made you realize how to carry yourself off the field."

Horton searched for the right way to express why the mere sight of his friend, the youthful octogenarian, gives him chills. He found it.

"It's like there is always a light that shines around him," Horton says. "Wherever he goes, there's that light shining around him."

Horton marvels at how much has changed with the Tigers and in the city and how his friend surrounded by shining light hasn't changed a bit.

Horton spent three months of the 2001 season evaluating the Tigers' minor league system and preparing a report for owner Michael Ilitch. Player development is the only answer for the Tigers because the building-via-free-agency option is a path blocked by a catch-22: the only way to fill the seats of Comerica is to win games, and the only way to do that in the near future is to buy free agents. The only way to be able to afford free agents is to fill the seats.

The Tigers organization is in need of reconstruction, the way Detroit was a city in desperate need after the riots of the summer of 1967.

"I think what our team did in 1968 healed the city for many years to come," Horton says with pride. "Not only the city, the whole state. People ain't never forgot that. I was part of it. My teammates were part of it."

There was only so much a ballclub could do to repair a downtown that remains impoverished.

Harwell's biographer was in Detroit to cover an early season Yankees series in 1995, and he remains haunted by a conversation he had with an emotionally spent taxi driver.

As massive Tiger Stadium slowly shrunk in the rearview mirror, a lady of the evening caught the backseat passenger's eye, hiked her red double-knit skirt, and managed to shoot a come-hither look with those big bloodshot eyes of hers. The cabbie blew into his steamy coffee cup, took a swill, and placed the cup back in its holder. He tried to rub some innocence into his eyes and used the passenger as his confessor. The lady of the evening and so many more like her ate at the cabbie, making him feel as if his life lacked meaning.

"That's all I do all night," he lamented. "I take the hookers from a john to the crackhouse, from the crackhouse to a john. All night. John, crackhouse, john, crackhouse, john, crackhouse. That's my life.

How do you like my life? Think you want to trade places with me anytime soon?"

It's not the Detroit of Willie Horton's youth, when it was movie theater to movie theater, a game of Strikeout outside the park, nine innings of Tigers baseball inside the park.

"It's not the same world," Horton laments. "It's sad."

Chapter 13

Commissioner McLain

I t's Friday, September 21, 2001, 10 days after the terrorists' attacks on the World Trade Center towers and the Pentagon.

Here at the McKean County Correctional Institute, tucked in rolling hills on the edges of the Allegheny National Forest, security hasn't changed a bit. At the fork in the road, to drive straight is to drive toward the prison secured by shimmering barbed wire and armed guards. Tension runs high inside those walls. Gang activity percolates.

To take a left at the fork is to drive toward the minimum-security federal prison camp. No walls. No fences. No armed guards. No chance anyone is going to escape because to do so would be to run the risk of being transferred to a place nobody could mistake for a country club. That looming possibility is enough to disprove the axiom that states there is no honor among thieves. In this small slice of northern Pennsylvania there is indeed an honor system for convicted thieves, and it works. A mix of white-collar criminals and minor drug offenders undergoing drug treatment make up the inmate population. Violent offenders are housed down the street.

To arrange an interview with an inmate requires undergoing a security check, swapping multiple faxes, signing numerous documents, reading pages and pages of regulations. Once on site, only one document must be filled out and signed. Nobody oversees the interview.

"It's basically a dorm," says Denny McLain from his plastic chair in the otherwise empty visitors room. "I always describe it as a Days Inn, minus the bathroom."

Minus a bathroom and plus a roommate.

McLain, baseball's last 30-game winner and most famous two-time loser, is in the midst of an eight-year, one-month sentence. He was convicted of conspiracy, mail fraud, theft from a pension fund, and money laundering. His release date is listed as July 7, 2004, though McLain expresses confidence he will be released as soon as October 2002.

The way he repeatedly mentions "52 months," the duration of his stay up to the point of September 21, 2001, leaves the impression he counts the days every day.

"I have good days and bad days," he says. "With only 13, 14 months left, I have more good days than before. It changes from minute to minute."

"It changes from minute to minute." With those words, McLain proves he is capable of seeing himself accurately after all. His mood does change from minute to minute. He seems happy when lost in stories from his glory years with the Tigers and on stage in Las Vegas. The smiles vanish as he is overcome again by the cruel that-was-then, this-is-now reality of his life.

Nearly every time he mentioned the name Ernie Harwell, a smile came to his pudgy face, the biggest smile coming at the first mention.

"How can you write a book about Ernie Harwell?" McLain hollers from the door of the visitors' room before taking his seat. "He's never done anything bad in his life. What can you say about Saint Ernie? I don't think you'll find anyone on earth to say anything bad about Ernie Harwell. It's nice to know somebody who nobody says anything bad about."

McLain can't put himself into that category. Highly intelligent, witty, opinionated, and knowledgeable on a breadth of topics that stretch far beyond baseball, McLain always has had a knack for getting himself into trouble. As the years passed, his list of enemies grew as swiftly as his circle of friends shrank.

His once devoted and forgiving wife, Sharyn, daughter of Hall of Fame shortstop Lou Boudreau, divorced him in 1998. He occasionally refers to her as his "ex-wife" during a three-hour interview. More often, he calls her his "wife."

He dreams of a reunion with her to help pass the time. Might they get back together?

"Sometimes I want that more than I want anything in the world," he says.

Will it happen?

He pauses for what seems like a long time. Then again, to him, every second that passes in there seems like a long time.

"That certainly won't be up to me," he says. "That will be up to her."

Many inside will miss McLain when he is granted the freedom he craves. He will be missed most from mid-May to mid-September. That's when the camp softball league plays, four nights a week. McLain is the commissioner of the league.

"I just make sure they don't run roughshod over my umpires and make sure they don't make any illegal trades. You have to watch that or the 10 best players all end up on the same team. Somebody's always up to something, trying to bribe the umpires or something else."

McLain, suspended three times by Major League Baseball Commissioner Bowie Kuhn during the 1970 season, had to suspend two players for a pair of games apiece during the 2001 McKean Camp Softball League.

Recognize These Guys?

When you've been around baseball for a while, you see all sorts of players. They come in different shapes, sizes, and temperaments. Most of them fit into one of these categories:

1. **Billy the Bandage:** An adhesive-tape worm. Keeps himself on pills and needles. . . . First in the whirlpool, first on the rubbing table, last on the field (a rub-tub-sub). . . . He has tried every medicine. Next week, embalming fluid. . . . Even the look he gives you is a hurt look. Not only are his ailments chronic, they're chronicles. . . . Always in the punk of condition.

2. **Lover Louie:** Never married, but he has had a lot of near Mrs. . . . Troubled by curves. . . . More effective at night—late at night. Will chase anything but a fly ball.

3. **Belligerent Basil:** One half of a fight looking for the other half. He'd climb a mountain to take a swing at an echo. . . . Loves a fight so much, he has been married six times.

4. **Porous Paul:** He couldn't stop a grapefruit from rolling uphill. Plays every hop perfectly—except the last one. . . . No matter where his manager puts him in the lineup, he can't hide him from the opposition. Leads league in runs-booted-in. . . . A holier-than-thou defensive debit.

5. **Orville and Out:** The pitcher's best friend. As a hitter, he has ruined more rallies than tear gas. . . . Qualifies for trapeze act because his only attributes are a swing and a miss.

6. **Slow Freight Freddie:** It takes a triple to score him from third. . . . He not only runs like he has a piano on his back, he also stops and plays "God Bless America" on the way. . . . Nickname is E Pluribus Unum because he can't get off a dime.

7. **Percentage Patrick:** His mother must have been frightened by a computer because he is forever figuring. . . . Can't remember whether his team won or lost, but he can tell you his batting average to the final percentage point. . . . Officious with the official scorer.

8. **Conceited Charles:** In love with himself—and he has no competition. . . . A case of mistaken nonentity. . . . Suffers from I strain. . . . On his 24th birthday he sent a telegram of congratulations to his mother. . . . Hasn't an enemy in the world, but all his friends hate him.

9. **Stuffer Sam:** If calories counted in the official averages, he would be leading the league. . . . Way out in front. Always exceeding the feed limit. . . . Far from his old sylph. . . . Sure to get his just desserts.

10. **Raver Ralph:** Named year after year as the game's Most Voluble Player. . . . A man who pops off even more than he pops up. Often is thrown out spieling. . . . Mama's little yelper. . . . Approaches every subject with an open mouth. His future is in the radio or TV booth.

11. **Money Man Marvin:** Only sign he doesn't miss is the dollar sign. . . . Spends more time with his agent than with his teammates. . . . Doesn't care if the game is on the line—only if his signature is. . . . Would rather see a pitch from his broker than from a hard-throwing opponent.

—E.H., April 1992

"One guy tried to defame one of my umpires with a litany of profanity," he explains. "Another guy threw his bat in anger. If you just throw the bat, that's not so bad. If you throw it in anger, no."

Commissioner McLain took action, and the players apologized.

As did former nemesis Bowie Kuhn when Charlie Finley tried to dismantle the A's overnight, McLain says he has voided trades.

"Being the commissioner," he says, "there's always someone pissing and moaning to me about something."

That cloud that moves in and out of McLain's world blows in and settles on him, changing his mood in a blink.

"In a setting such as this everything bothers you," he says. "You don't have any responsibilities. You don't have to pay rent. You don't have to pay the light bill. You don't have to work. You don't have to pay car insurance. You don't have to take care of kids. Everything is reduced to such a microscopic level that everybody makes a big deal out of every little thing and for no reason, really."

The cloud drifts away again, though not far away, never very far away. He thinks about one of the teams and can't help but smile.

"The league is a sitcom waiting to be written," he says. "If you could videotape this one team we had, you could sell it and retire. The whole team was black guys who couldn't play a lick and they were hilarious to watch. La Familia, an all-Latin team, won the championship. They're great kids and they can really play. All the best ballplayers I've seen in prison have been Spanish kids."

"Why not play?" he is asked.

"Please," he says. "I'm too old. My knees are so bad when I walk a mile and a half on the track I practically need a wheelchair to get back to my room."

Harwell isn't in northern Pennsylvania to announce these games, though McLain suspects he could make them seem interesting.

"I always compared him to a franchise player," McLain says. "He's always had the ability to take the worst ballgame and make it sound like it was still worth listening to."

Harwell and McLain often went to a music store in Kansas City when the Tigers played on the road against the Royals. They took turns playing the organ there.

Who was the more skilled organ player?

"Oh, please," McLain says. "I think Ernie will tell you there was no contest."

Harwell agrees. McLain has far more talent at the organ.

"I only play well enough for my family to hear me," Harwell is fond of saying.

McLain still has an audience.

"I'm terrific at the High Mass on Sunday here," he says.

He remembers fondly the days when his audiences were larger, even if he is a little embarrassed thinking back to how he dressed then while performing.

"Nehru jacket," he says, his head slowly moving from side to side. "Medallion, tight pants with bell-bottoms, white belt, white shoes."

In a word: *mod.*

Now he wears prison blues and sometimes sings them, too. After the Tigers won the 1968 World Series, he was in great demand.

"I did the *Joey Bishop Show* a lot," McLain remembers. "Regis Philbin was his sidekick. Real nice guy. If you did the *Joey Bishop Show*, Johnny Carson wouldn't have you on, so I never did Carson. I was on the *Ed Sullivan Show*, and he paid serious money for those days, and I was on with the Smothers Brothers."

McLain was the warm-up act for comedian Shecky Greene at the Riviera.

"It went well, except for the first night when I was shitting all over myself because I was so nervous," McLain says. "We had just won the World Series and all the big acts were there to see me."

That sort of pressure was the exception, he says. He talks about the interactions he had with the crowds, and the stress leaves his face and is replaced by a smile.

"We had an act where if we didn't know a tune someone from the audience mentioned, they would get an autographed ball. A woman might say, 'Lullaby to Susie.' We'd fake it and sing."

He turns the clock back 33 years and sings: "A lullaby to Susie, she's so lazy."

Reliving that moment in time, he is enjoying himself.

"The woman would say, 'No, that's not it. Give me the ball.' We'd tell her, 'You have to sing the song first to get the ball.' She would sing the song and make a complete ass of herself. But the people would do anything to get that ball. Four guys were with me, all from Detroit, none of them ballplayers. I'd play golf all day and do the shows at night. The money was great. I was making I think $15,000 a week doing that."

The money in baseball, McLain reminds, wasn't yet great. He recalls having made $30,000 in 1968, the year he went 31–6, the first year of back-to-back Cy Young Awards.

"The GM offered me a big raise to $60,000," McLain remembers.

Here's how that negotiation between McLain and Jim Campbell went, according to McLain's recollection.

Campbell: "We're going to give you a raise to $60,000."

McLain: "I want $100,000."

Campbell: "You want what?"

McLain: "I want $100,000."

Campbell: "Even Kaline isn't making $100,000."

McLain: "I don't care about Kaline."

Campbell: "Are you kidding? OK, I'll tell you what then, I'll give you five minutes to accept $60,000. And at the end of five minutes, I'm taking away $10,000 for every minute you don't sign it."

McLain: "We just won a World Series and drew 2.5 million fans and you would really do that?"

Campbell: "Yes I would."

McLain: "Give me the pen."

The money he made endorsing Pepsi made up the difference between what he wanted and what the Tigers were willing to give him.

"That night we won the pennant in Detroit was just a terrific night," McLain says. "It didn't matter if you were black, green, yellow, or white. Everybody celebrated the same thing. After the riots in '67, that ballclub kept that town together. It was a powder keg. We were talking at every school, every YMCA, every high school. That team had an awful lot to do with keeping that town together. I don't think any of us were smart enough at the time to realize we were maintaining the sanity of the city, but that's exactly what we were doing."

His mind rolls back a year from magical 1968, and the cloud rolls back into the room. The Tigers finished a game behind the Red Sox in 1967, their season ending when second baseman Dick McAuliffe grounded into a double play for the first time all season.

"What a time to do it," McLain says. "I got blamed for us not getting in."

An ankle injury kept him off the mound in the final days of the season.

"Those allegations that organized crime tried to take my ankle out, talk about stories that just got out of control," he says.

How did the injury occur?

"At midnight, I was falling asleep to *The Untouchables*, and I heard something fall in the garage and I got up to see what it was and hurt my foot when I got up," he recalls. "All of a sudden the Mafia stepped on my toes? Why would they not want me pitching? You had almost a sure thing when I was pitching. The FBI cleared me, said there was nothing to those rumors, but they put that in the last paragraph of the stories. Why wasn't that in the first paragraph? A lot of people don't read to the last paragraph."

OK then, Denny is told, tell a true story from your days pitching for Mayo Smith's Tigers.

"Second and third, nobody out, seventh inning in a game up in Boston," he starts. "Dalton Jones, a good hitter at the time, Yaz, and

175

Ken Harrelson were due up. Mayo tried to take the ball out of my hand with a 2–0 lead. It seemed like 10 minutes he was out there, screaming at me to give him the ball. All he had to do was turn around and ask the umpire for another ball, but he didn't think of that."

The mound exchange went like this, according to McLain.

Smith: "Denny, I'm gonna take you out of the game."

McLain: "Like hell you are. They haven't hit a ball hard off me all day. Now get back to the dugout."

And Smith went back to the dugout.

"I struck out the next three guys on nine pitches," McLain says. "I come back to the dugout and he's sitting there with his head down, not even looking at me. I said you better look at me. Don't you ever come out there again."

Did he ever come out again?

"Yes, he did," McLain says with a smile. "Only this time I *wanted* him to take me out of the game. I was pitching against the Orioles. Bases loaded, nobody out, and I've only thrown three pitches in the inning. First three guys hit line-drive singles. One to left, one to center, one to right. Boog Powell's the next hitter. He was a .260 lifetime hitter who hit about .910 against me. That S.O.B. owned me. I wanted out this time. Mayo came out, and Freehan came to the mound. Mayo turned to Freehan and said, 'How's his stuff?' Only time Freehan ever got off a line in his life. He had the personality of an infected pimple. Freehan said, 'How would I know? I haven't caught anything yet.' Mayo told me, 'I don't have anybody loose. You're going to have to pitch to him.' Freehan asks me, 'How do you want to pitch him?' I said, 'What, after six years you finally want to know?' I tried to throw him a fastball inside, and it came in right over the plate, nut high. He hit it right at me. Triple play and we win the game. I came back in the dugout, went right to Mayo and said, 'I told you to stay off that mound.'"

What about the Joe Foy story? True story? Did you really groove a pitch to him to keep him from getting sent to the minors?

"True story," he says. "If I can get him out any time, the last thing I want is for him to get sent to the minors. I'd do that with about one guy per club. I knew I could get them out any time I needed to."

And the Mickey Mantle story? Did you really groove one for him so he could pass Jimmie Foxx with career home run No. 535?

"Oh, sure," McLain says. "He was my guy. On one leg he outplayed the American League. When there was a crowd at that park, there was only one major leaguer on the field. He stood out from everybody else that much. And he was just one good old boy. I don't think he had a serious moment in his life."

Another true story: a few days after his high school graduation, McLain made his professional debut in Harlan, Kentucky. He pitched a no-hitter, struck out 16, borrowed a friend's car, drove it 600 miles home to visit his girlfriend in Chicago, and went AWOL from the team.

"She tried to elope with me and her father sent the cops after us," McLain remembers. "She and I ran away between starts, and her dad threatened to kill both of us."

Too dominant for the rookie league in Kentucky, McLain gained a promotion to the next level and pitched for an affiliate in Clinton, Iowa. He was told not to leave Clinton, so naturally he left Clinton and headed for Chicago any time he felt like it.

"I was making $550 a month, plus $2 a day meal money, and I could never figure out how they caught me every time I went to Chicago. There was a toll bridge I'd have to go across on the three-hour trip back. After my first trip, the next day the manager came by and said, 'By the way, that's $100.'

"What do you mean?

'Didn't we tell you not to leave Clinton? You went to Chicago.'

"What makes you think I did?

'We know you did and it's $100. And next time it will be $200.'

"A week later I did it again and the manager came over and said, 'That's $200.'

"What for?

'You went to Chicago again last night. And next time it will be $500.'

"Now I'm thinking it's got to be a conspiracy and someone is surreptitiously watching me at the toll bridge. There was another toll bridge 15 miles away. I used that one. The next day I get back and he says, 'Come on, let's go, we've got to talk.'"

Here's how McLain remembers that talk going:

The manager: "You didn't pay us the $300 and now you owe us $500 for last night, so that's $800 you owe us now. Why did you keep going to Chicago?"

McLain: "Look, it's $500, so you know I'm not going to go again. Why don't you just tell me how you've been catching me?"

The manager: "The general manager's brother works nights at the toll bridge."

McLain: "OK, that explains the first two. How did you catch the third time? I went across a different bridge."

The manager: "The guy who normally works that bridge was sick that night and the GM's brother was filling in for him."

He shakes his head, as if to say, "Just my luck."

Aside from his duties as commissioner, McLain's daily job at the camp is to "hand out cleaning supplies," from 7:30 A.M. to 2:30 P.M.

He says he has written two books—one a novel, one a book of baseball anecdotes—and has 800 pages of notes on life inside the prison system. He spent part of the eighties in prison after being convicted of racketeering and cocaine smuggling. He spent two and a half years of a 23-year sentence before gaining his release on a procedural matter.

Even on the inside, life changed on September 11, 2001.

"When that happened, you could hear a pin drop in here," he says. "The good thing was some people in here figured out who the president was. I don't think some of them knew until that happened."

He watches CNN, when he can pry the remote away from other inmates who desire to watch less cerebral shows.

"Put three broads on a beach and they'll watch it," he says. "It doesn't matter if the world is ending on the other station, they'll still watch the three broads on a beach."

When McLain is asked what is the first thing he plans on doing upon his release, he leans forward, drops his chin, and raises his eyebrows in such a way that his expression says, "You can't possibly be so naïve as to not know the answer to that question. Nice try, but I'm not falling for your Columbo act, pal."

When he speaks, these are the words that come out: "You mean the second thing? I think I've got the first thing pretty well covered. The second thing I'm going to do is go to Morton's, get one of those great big rib eyes, a baked potato, salad with Roquefort, and broccoli with hollandaise sauce. And then I'm probably going to go to bed again."

He likes his chances of landing a morning radio show in Detroit like the one he had between convictions. He's funny, opinionated, informed, controversial, offbeat. In short, he has the perfect makeup for a radio talk show host.

Above all, he is haunted. The scene he never saw he sees repeatedly. Every day. It won't go away. His daughter Kristin died at the age of 26 in 1992 in a traffic accident. Denny McLain's waking nightmare will never change.

"Time does not heal it," McLain says. "It does not get better. It never gets better." Talking about it doesn't make it better and it doesn't make it worse. Nothing could make it worse. "She ran into a truck at 2:15 in the morning," he says. "The truck had its lights off because the reflection from the lights kept the driver from seeing the little driveway he was trying to back his 18-wheeler into at 2:15 in the morning. She came over the rise and never saw it. She was going 55, going the speed limit. A cop came to the house at 3:30 in the morning and knocked on the door. Her husband was in the air force and she was living with us at the time.

A cop came to the door and as soon as I opened the door, he said, "Oh my God, not you, Denny. I didn't make the connection."

"What, what is it?"

"It's Kristin, she's in bad shape. You have to get to the hospital right away." She was dead before we got there. I'm the one who talked her into moving from Tampa. The horrible guilt I feel over that every day, you couldn't possibly understand."

The guilt is not deserved, McLain is told by the millionth person for the millionth time. His response rings truer than anything else he says during the three-hour visit. It is delivered out of the side of his mouth in such a way as to make it clear the time has come to change the subject.

"Easy for you to say," he says.

McLain caused most of his own problems. He doesn't own up to all of his transgressions, including the pension fund theft, which he dismisses as a paperwork snafu, a simple matter of not having "dotted the *i*'s and crossed the *t*'s." Yet, he punishes himself for the cruelest of all hands dealt him. He blames himself for an accidental tragedy for which he deserves not an iota of blame. He has sentenced himself to a lifetime of guilt for the harshest of all losses a father could endure. He's wired differently than most, which makes trying to understand him a test of one's patience.

Since first meeting his friend Harwell, McLain has been through so many changes. He swiftly fell from the hottest story in baseball to ex-ballplayer status before reaching the age of 30.

"I've been addicted to everything I've ever done in my life," McLain says. "My wife said that about me, and she was absolutely right. It's a good thing I never tried cocaine. I never even tried it once."

His addictions included Pepsi, bowling, gambling, golfing, and gambling on golfing.

"I wasn't interested in spending four hours on the golf course to win $50," he says. "If I was going to be out there four hours, I wanted to win or lose at least $2,000. . . . I gambled on football and basketball and got my ears waxed. I never bet on baseball. I don't know enough about baseball to bet on it."

The most he ever won gambling?

"I won $115,000 in an hour and 15 minutes playing baccarat in Atlantic City."

Did he walk away?

"Of course," he says, shocked at the question. "I was born at night, not last night."

The most he lost?

"I never lost a lot at one time. I never accepted a line of credit at a casino and never took more than $10,000 to a casino with me. I would never sit in a corner all night or bet every piece on the board. I was never like that. I bet maybe three games a day. I wasn't the degenerate who bet every game. I never cost us anything with my gambling."

The most he ever lost on one game?

"Oakland hadn't lost to, I think it was Denver, since Rin Tin Tin was a puppy," he says. "I bet $15,000, which I didn't have by the way, on Oakland, and Oakland lost by 35 or 40 points."

McLain had so much going for him and lost it all. Through all the changes in McLain's life, his pal Harwell has remained doing the same thing he's done since long before he first extended his right hand and introduced himself to a can't-miss teenager named Denny McLain.

"What a lucky guy," McLain says. "Patience. Pure patience. If I could have one virtue that he has, that's what I would want. Patience never has been a quality of the McLain clan. He's always had it."

McLain smiles when he remembers how he used to needle Harwell.

"I always told him maybe you've been doing the same thing for so long because you can't do anything else," he says. "He's blessed to be in that position all his life. And he always worked with good people. Everyone who worked with Ernie had that graciousness and style, and it probably came to them from being around Ernie. That was the way he always carried himself, and Ernie expected no less of them. He's always been a perfect gentleman, a man blessed with the great virtue of patience. And tolerance. Ernie will tolerate anyone. I think of myself as being pretty tolerant, but I'll tolerate them and move on. Ernie tolerates them and keeps on visiting them."

McLain attended the press conference at Tiger Stadium the day Harwell announced he had been fired, effective at the end of the 1991 season. He was vocal in his support of Harwell. More than 10 years later, he isn't sorry the firing took place.

"After it happened, Ernie got better again," McLain says. "He got more life. Not that he was ever bad, but he got better. You know, if you wear the same clothes every day, you start to look the same after a while. I thought it wasn't the worst thing that happened to him."

McLain is impressed when informed Harwell is back on a 162-games-per-year schedule.

"How old is he, 70-what?" he asks and is told Ernie is 83. "Oh my God, I didn't know he was 83. He's 83? He's old as dirt."

Old as dirt, young at heart, and happy as a lark, that's Ernie Harwell at 83.

Denny McLain at 57 sees a return to morning radio in Detroit in his future. As the clock ticks down on the allotted three hours for the visitor, McLain's visitor gives the obligatory speech aimed at reaching the inmate the way nobody has reached him. McLain is told it would be best to keep life as simple as possible upon his release. Land a morning talk show and leave it at that.

"I don't know if that will be enough," he says.

He doesn't mean it won't be enough to support himself financially.

"I just mean enough," he says. "I've never been real good at simple. For some reason, I've always need complexity in my life."

The cloud drifts back into the room. Time is up. Denny McLain is three hours closer to freedom.

Chapter 14

Walking the Walk

Joe Falls of the *Detroit News*, a fearless writer and fearful flier, grew queasier with each bump and shake on the turbulent Tigers team flight. Belts were fastened on every lap, hands gripped armrests tightly, and worried expressions were easy to spot. Falls had trouble believing his eyes when he saw Tigers pitcher Dan Petry get up out of his seat and sprint down the aisle of the plane, the turbulence bouncing him off seats all the way. Petry didn't stop until he reached his destination, the open seat next to Ernie Harwell.

Petry stayed seated next to Harwell until the turbulence passed and all those tight grips eased. Once Petry returned to his seat, Falls, seated across the aisle, assumed his familiar role of asking an athlete a question. Unlike so many questions asked by sportswriters, this time the man asking the question had no clue as to the answer the question would trigger.

"Dan, what was that all about?" Falls asked. "Why did you run up the aisle like that in the middle of all that turbulence and sit down next to Ernie Harwell?"

"Well," Petry said, beginning his explanation, "I thought to myself: this could be serious, and if Ernie Harwell is going to somewhere now, I want to go with him."

Petry knew that if the plane went down, Harwell eventually would be going up for eternity, and he wanted to go with him.

Through the years, Harwell has impressed those who travel with the Tigers with a deep spirituality that shows itself more in his actions than his words, more in his walk than his talk.

Jim Hawkins covered the Tigers beat from the 1970 season through 1980, which made him an expert on the rigors of travel a baseball team endures during a six-week spring training and a six-month, 162-game regular season schedule. Even for young, well-conditioned, extraordinary athletes, the travel is a grind when everything is on schedule and snafu-free.

"Sometimes you get in at two, three in the morning," Hawkins says. "Other times, you get in and the rooms aren't ready. The bus driver will get lost on his way from the airport and the players will be screaming, 'Hey, Busie, you better . . .' Here's Ernie Harwell, the guy who had the most right to complain because he was by far the oldest one on the trip, and not once, not once, did I ever hear him complain. Never said a word. I think that says a lot about his character. Another thing I've always liked about Ernie is with him it's never been, "Look at me, I'm going to chapel." If you want to talk to him about religion, he'll talk to you. But he's truly humble. He's happy with his faith, and that's what matters. He's not trying to shove it down anybody else's throat."

Harwell begins every meal, public and private, by saying grace. He's not bashful about introducing God into a conversation if he thinks it's appropriate. It never was more appropriate than on August 16, 1990.

Warner Fusselle visited Harwell's home on that day with a camera crew to shoot a cover story for ESPN's *Major League Baseball Magazine.* Harwell warned his friend Fusselle that if the phone rang, he would need to excuse himself and answer it. He explained that a nurse had called to inform him that a teenager who was threatening to commit suicide first wanted to talk to Ernie Harwell. As the camera crew was setting up, the phone rang and Harwell answered it within earshot of Fusselle and the crew.

"Hello, thank you for calling," Harwell told the teenager. "Make sure to listen tonight because Paul Carey and I are going to dedicate the pregame show to you. I understand you're going through a tough time right now. We all do from time to time. You might be feeling like nobody cares about you, but that's not true. It's never true. The Lord always cares about you. He always loves you. You're in God's hands and no harm can come to you when you're in God's hands. And we care about you, too."

Harwell was the only one who could hear the teenager, but everyone in the room was able to figure out what he said next, based on Harwell's animated response.

"No, I have to disagree with you on that," Harwell said. "I believe Trammell is more valuable than Fielder because he does so many more things to help a ballclub win a game than Fielder does."

Harwell lives by the tenet, "Always tell the truth, that way you don't have to remember what you said," even if that means disagreeing with a teenage boy threatening to commit suicide. Harwell never heard from or about that boy again, which can be filed in the no-news-is-good-news category.

Harwell was raised in a religious household, but it wasn't until midlife that his spirituality began to direct his life more completely.

"As a youngster I had been a Christian," Harwell says. "My family believed in God. We felt like if we stayed out of everybody's way and did good deeds we'd get to heaven. I never really surrendered myself to Christ."

That change in his life came in 1961, the only spring training he spent alone, without anyone from his family.

Baseball History? You Can Look It Up

People send me all kinds of things. I get snap-shots of babies and dogs, most of them named Ernie and wearing Tigers caps. I get wedding and graduation invitations and photos of "The House by the Side of the Road." Also, there are baseballs to sign and questions to answer.

It's good to know folks are interested in baseball and take time to write.

I appreciate their participation.

I was rummaging through my desk recently and found some Bible-style questions on baseball that George Bloom of Defiance, Ohio, had sent me a few years ago. With updates and changes, I pass some along.

- What advice did pitching coach Dave Duncan give St. Louis Cardinals starter Andy Benes? Answer: "And you shall pitch it within and without." —Genesis 6:14
- How do we know Joshua was with the Cubs and not the White Sox? Answer: "And he pitched on the northside." —Joshua 8:11
- What did Reds manager Ray Knight ask Hal Morris when Hal messed up the hit-and-run? Answer: "But can you not discern the signs?" —Matthew 16:3
- What did Rangers starter Bobby Witt tell closer John Wetteland? Answer: "Thy right hand upholdest me." —Psalms 63:8
- How did Billy Martin and Earl Weaver react to bad umpiring? Answer: "They cried out and cast off their clothes and threw dust into the air." —Acts 22:23

- How did Babe Ruth tell Red Sox manager Ed Barrow that he wanted to be an everyday player instead of a pitcher? Answer: "Let me now go to the field." —Ruth 2:2
- What did Orioles manager Davey Johnson tell catcher Chris Hoiles about Tigers speedy center fielder Brian Hunter? Answer: "Let him that stole, steal no more." —Ephesians 4:28
- What was Tigers slugger Tony Clark thinking when he tried to score standing up and was tagged out? Answer: "Therefore I shall not slide." —Psalms 26:1
- What did Braves manager Bobby Cox say to pitcher John Smoltz about the Cardinals lineup? Answer: "Thou shalt fan them." —Isaiah 41:16
- Why did Hall of Fame pitcher Gaylord Perry have trouble with the ball one afternoon? Answer: "Because it lacked moisture." —Luke 8:6
- What did Twins manager Tom Kelly tell Paul Molitor when he sent him in to pinch-hit with the bases loaded? Answer: "Bring these men home." —Genesis 43:16

—E.H., May 1997

"I was in Lakeland and something told me to go over to listen to Billy Graham in Bartow," Harwell remembers. "God was speaking to me, a small voice I guess you could say, telling me I should go over there. Billy Graham was having an Easter service. When he gave the invitation to surrender your life to Christ, I went down and did that. That was the watermark of my life. It made my outlook completely different. Now my outlook is I have a relationship with Jesus and He is the dominant factor in my life."

In walking the Christian walk, Harwell has conducted himself in such a way as to gain praise from Tigers fans who want to meet him, aspiring broadcasters who send him their tapes for review, and countless other strangers.

"I just try to live my life the way He wants me to," Harwell says. "I try to be kind to people, no matter who they are. One thing I have done is I have tried to help young announcers. I've listened to tapes, talked to them about what they could do to improve or to find opportunities. It's something I feel I have to pass along. I've seen so many people in the public eye turn people off, and I decided I wasn't going to be like that. Often, when someone meets me, it will be the only time. You could really hurt someone's feelings. I just try to live by the old golden rule: do unto others as you would have them do unto you."

During the season, Harwell attends Baseball Chapel at whatever ballpark the Tigers are in on Sunday, which figures because he was involved in the founding of Baseball Chapel.

Bobby Richardson, second baseman on the great Yankees teams during the Mickey Mantle years, finally nagged Mantle, a notorious runner of the night, and Whitey Ford into attending church on Sunday. Mantle and Ford were mobbed by autograph seekers, which turned them off to the idea of returning to church any time soon.

Richardson shared that story with Detroit sportswriter Watson Spoelstra, who related it to Harwell. Spoelstra and Harwell discussed the idea of having a private service where players could worship without becoming distractions. At first, they met at hotels. For years, the worshippers have convened at ballparks.

"Waddy came to me and asked me to help him get it started," Harwell says. "I told Waddy early on I think we'd be a lot better if we took it away from the hotel and brought it to the clubhouse so that guys would be in their own environments. I guess that would be my one contribution to Baseball Chapel."

Today, Baseball Chapel has grown to the point that an average of 300 major leaguers per week and nearly 3,000 minor-league players attend.

"We now provide chapel service for every major and minor league team and quite a number of the independent leagues as well," says Vince Nauss, president of Baseball Chapel, based in Ocean City, New Jersey. "Basically, where professional baseball is played, we have somebody assigned to speak in each city."

For years, Harwell would speak at Chapel. Once while speaking, Harwell spotted California Angels manager John McNamara, a man's man not easily moved to emotion, tearing up. Harwell's message: "No. 1, first things come first. Seek first the kingdom of God. Second, I have problems, but He's here to help me. No. 3, when God is by your side, nobody can do anything to you. We know what the final score is. We're just playing out the game."

Harwell no longer speaks at Baseball Chapel. Now he listens.

"Ernie's been a very faithful participant and supporter of Baseball Chapel for decades and a great man of God, from my experience," Nauss says. "He's marvelous to listen to. I was shopping somewhere and saw the Bible on tape with the voice of James Earl Jones, and the first thing I thought was how much I'd love to hear Ernie read the Bible on tape."

Harwell settles for reading the Bible for himself, trying to follow the tenets of Jesus. Figuratively, and on a couple of occasions literally, he walks the path Jesus walked.

During one of Ernie and Lulu's visits to the Holy Land, a particularly informative tour guide was giving the group an insightful history lesson at the Church of St. Peter in Gallicantu, when one of the men in the group asked the guide a question. The guide was startled by the familiarity of the voice.

"He stood there and looked at Ernie in amazement," Lulu remembers. "He said, 'You're not Ernie Harwell are you? I'm from Detroit and

I've listened to you all my life.' We talked to him for quite a while, and he told us all about growing up in Hamtramck."

The Harwells invited the tour guide, Robert Bialowicz, to their hotel that evening to join them for dinner. He quickly accepted the invitation, and the Harwells assumed he had a means of transportation from his home, at the church where he worked, to the hotel. He did. He had feet. Bialowicz had no other means of getting there than to traverse the Kidron Valley.

Upon their return to Michigan, the Harwells looked up Bialowicz's mother and informed her that her son, who had gone to Jerusalem for a music festival, had found a good job as a tour guide and was doing well. She was grateful to the Harwells for sharing that news, and her response was a lament echoed by mothers worldwide: "You know how boys are. They never write letters."

By the time Bialowicz looked up the Harwells, he had returned home and had become a police officer in Westland.

On another visit to the Holy Land, on a visit to Jacob's Well, Lulu and several others on the tour stayed on the bus, fearing it was too dangerous to venture into Arab territory. Ernie had no such fears and used that bouncy walk of his, the one that just as easily could belong to a junior high school boy on his way to a game of touch football, to get in position to add a few more morsels of history to his elephantine memory.

A minister by the name of Jim Rose, whom Ernie had come to know when living in Florida, baptized him in the Jordan River on January 8, 1985, at the breathtakingly beautiful cove where historians believe John the Baptist baptized Jesus as a dove that symbolized the Holy Spirit appeared.

"It was cold," Harwell remembers. "I tell you it was freezing. About six of us went in, one by one, full immersion. Poor old Jim had to stay in there for everybody."

Harwell's friends agree he is humble about his faith and doesn't force it on anyone. Harwell is the first to acknowledge he is more aggressive in letting others share in another driving passion in his life. He does not wait to be asked about the song lyrics he writes while seeking someone to put a melody to them.

Chapter 15

Sing Every Song

Struggling composers and starving lyricists are quick to agree that in the music industry it's not necessarily *what* you know that leads to fame and fortune as much as *whom* you know.

A writer of sports all his life, Ernie Harwell decided to take his writing talent in another direction after moving to Detroit. He took to writing lyrics for songs and encouraged Lulu to do the same. Lulu gave it a brief stab and quickly determined it wasn't her thing. Ernie became hooked for life.

If only he could find a composer to put the right music to his words. Thumbing through a music magazine one afternoon, Harwell's eyes were drawn to an advertisement placed by a composer seeking to join talents with a lyricist, and something told Harwell that this was his man.

In the advertisement, the man boasted of having written music for Robert Goulet and Barbra Streisand. Harwell had his doubts as to whether a man who walked among the giants of the industry would bother to take the time to even write back to a relative novice. Figuring he had nothing to lose, Harwell sent a letter to Larue Dickson, the man who had composed melodies for Goulet and Streisand.

Dickson got back to a grateful and excited Harwell, who had a hunch he had scored his first major breakthrough as a songwriter. They arranged a meeting.

"So you've written for Robert Goulet and Barbra Streisand," said Harwell, excited to hear about what that experience was like. "Tell me about it."

"Yes, I composed melodies that were perfect for them," said Dickson, an older gentleman. "And I mailed them to them. I never did hear back from them, but I did write the songs for them."

That admission had the effect on Harwell of a sewing needle jabbed into a balloon. Deflated though not defeated, Harwell decided to give Dickson a try, nevertheless.

Harwell gave Dickson the lyrics to a song he had entitled "Upside Down," a song about a world askew, a world in which a singer wants to be a comedian, an actor wants to sing, and so on.

The melody that the unpublished Dickson put to it was to Harwell's liking. Now they had to find someone willing to perform it, no easy assignment.

That's where Harwell's friendship with George Toles came in handy.

Toles had a decided advantage in lining up heavyweight guests for his music and interview radio show in the sixties on WJBK in Detroit. Celebrities frequently passed by his office on the way to doing the mid-day television show in the studio down the hall.

"I snagged them and asked them to come on my show," remembers Toles, now working for an advertising agency in Seattle. "Most of them were good about giving me their time."

Steve Allen and Herb Alpert stopped by. So did Tony Bennett, Edgar Bergen, Mel Blanc, Pat Boone, Vikki Carr, Wilt Chamberlain, Mike Douglas, Peggy Fleming, Connie Francis, Andy Griffith, Ernie Harwell, John Havlicek, Gordie Howe, Homer and Jethro, Al Kaline, The Kingston Trio, Peggy Lee, Jerry Lewis, Archie Moore, Tiny Tim, Lawrence Welk, and Adam West.

Of all the famous voices to pull up a chair next to Toles to chat, none ever sounded any sweeter to Toles than did the voice of the Tigers.

"His diction is absolutely flawless," Toles says. "And it's sort of rounded by that sweet Georgia clay accent. There is not a consonant Ernie doesn't love and embrace. That *d* always comes through. Most announcers will drop the *d*. They'll say, 'He slides into secon'.' Not Ernie, with Ernie, it's 'He slides into second.'"

Toles admired Harwell for more than his voice. He also admired his breadth of interests that extended well beyond the baseball diamond.

When Homer and Jethro were in studio with Toles, one of them said, "Man, we sure would like to see a baseball game while we're in town."

Anybody involved in baseball knows there is no more thankless and bothersome task than arranging for tickets to be left for someone. Last-minute cancellations, mix-ups as to where to pick up the tickets, and complaints about seat locations make it a no-win situation for the baseball insider carrying out a ticket request.

Toles was well aware of all those factors and under normal circumstances would not have volunteered a friend to arrange for tickets. He viewed this situation as worth the trouble for Harwell.

"I knew Ernie was a neophyte songwriter who had eclectic taste in music," Toles remembers. "I knew part of what he liked was country music. I thought he would enjoy meeting them."

Toles told the musicians: "Ernie Harwell's a good friend of mine. I'll see if I can get you some tickets through Ernie."

Toles called Harwell, who not only arranged for the singers to get through the turnstiles, but for them to visit him in the screened-in booth that hovered closer to home plate than any other in baseball.

"Are you sure?" one of the musicians said. "We don't want to get in his way."

"You won't be in his way at all," Toles told them. "He's looking forward to meeting you."

Hammer's First Hit Was with the A's

His name was Stanley Burrell. He used to bring us the lineups in the radio booth at Oakland County Coliseum. They called him Hammer because he looked like Henry "Hammerin' Hank" Aaron. He wore a green and gold baseball cap with VP on it.

Indeed, Athletics owner Charlie Finley even introduced Stanley as his vice president at a press conference. Finley had discovered Burrell in the Coliseum parking lot, pitching pennies and dancing around with his teenage pals. Stanley's brothers worked in the A's clubhouse, so he was always hanging around.

When Stanley joined forces with Finley, the Oakland franchise was in bad condition. The team had slipped in the standings, and Finley's visits became less frequent. He continued to run the Athletics and his insurance company from Chicago.

Only a few relatives remained in Oakland to man the front office. There were no full-time scouts. And the team's radio rights were passed off to a small University of California station in Berkeley.

At $7.50 a game, Stanley Burrell became a part of this scene. When Finley needed to follow the A's games from Chicago, Stanley phoned him the play-by-play. The Hammer even talked himself into the radio booth a couple of times and did his own play-by-play. That career came to an abrupt halt when the station's general manager turned on his car radio.

"Get that kid off the air!" he ordered.

Hammer had other ideas of self-promotion. He went to Frank Cienzcyk, the A's equipment manager, and told him, "Mr. Finley wants me in an A's uniform with a hammer on the back."

"When Charlie calls me and tells me that, you'll have the uniform," Cienscyk told him.

The players looked on Stanley as a spy. "It was scary," said Steve McCatty, a Troy native pitching for the A's at that time. "We'd look up at the press box, see Hammer on the phone, and realize that our careers might depend on what a teenage kid was telling Finley back in Chicago."

Fast-forward to 1990.

It's Game 3 of the AL playoffs. On the mound to throw out the ceremonial first pitch is Stanley Burrell, the Hammer. Except now he's known as M. C. Hammer, music superstar.

He's M. C. Hammer, Grammy winner, seller of 7 million albums, rap artist and multimillionaire.

But he couldn't have made it to the cover of *Rolling Stone* without the A's. First Finley discovered him, then two Oakland players provided him with seed money for his record company.

Stanley Burrell, the A's former vice president, was on top of the world.

—*E.H. , June 1991*

That was an understatement.

"He was elated he was going to get to meet some recording artists," Toles remembers.

Harwell was not so elated as to lose his wits, however. Harwell came to the game prepared.

"Songwriters are worse than insurance salesmen," Harwell says, looking back on the meeting. "Any time they get a shot at somebody, they'll take it."

After making Homer and Jethro feel the way he makes all visitors to the booth feel, which is to say right at home, he got around to letting them know he enjoyed more than just listening to music.

He whipped a piece of paper out of his pocket.

"I have a song here that I worked on with a friend," Ernie told the boys. "I don't suppose you would want to see it, would you?"

"Sure," one of them told him. "We'll record it on our next RCA album."

Harwell told himself, "It can't be this easy, can it?"

It can. He never heard back from them, until, sure enough, Homer and Jethro recorded it on their next album. Ernie broke the news to Dickson. Finally, after all those years of dreaming and after all the years of enduring the snickers of friends who told him to stop fantasizing, one of his songs was recorded, and not by just anyone.

At long last, Larue Dickson could tell his friends that he had the last word and the last word was "I told you so." He could tell them, but even after Homer and Jethro recorded the song, few friends not named Ernie Harwell would believe Dickson had anything to do with it. Unfortunately for the old melody man, the record company that gave Harwell proper credit forgot to put Dickson's name on the record.

"He was so disappointed," Harwell says. "This was his last chance at a little fame, and they forgot to use his name. I felt for him."

Dickson's name does appear alongside Harwell's in all other official listings of the song. Theirs was a one-song collaboration. Not everyone with whom Harwell collaborated had to run an ad in a music magazine and stretch the truth immensely to attract lyricists.

Sammy Fain wrote the Hollywood scores for the Walt Disney hits *Alice in Wonderland* and *Peter Pan*. He collaborated with Irving Kahal on his most famous hit, "Wedding Bells Are Breaking Up That Old Gang of Mine," first performed by Gene Austin and a quarter-century later made known to another generation when performed by The Four Aces.

Born Samuel Feinberg on June 17, 1902, in New York, Fain also worked with Ernie Harwell. Fain captivated Harwell with tales of his start in the music business, when he sold sheet music to dime stores, which was then purchased by comedians to use in their acts. Harwell also enjoyed tales of his years as a singer and pianist in vaudeville shows and in Hollywood, where he was brought by Warner Brothers to work when talking motion pictures came about.

Harwell keeps a tape of a melancholy love song entitled "Our One Sweet Summer" in his car. Fain once recorded a demo of it.

"Typical composer," Harwell says, as the voice of Sammy Fain is missing as many notes as it's hitting. "Can't sing a lick."

The desire to find a home for "Our One Sweet Summer," and so many other songs, burns as strongly within Harwell as it would if it were his only occupation, his only source of income.

Ask him his favorite among the songs he has written and he'll not only answer, he'll break into song:

> Kick those childish covers off;
> Answer love's alarm.
> You'll find out who you are
> In somebody else's arms.
> You're gonna wake up wiser, baby,
> When you wake up to love.

Chuck Boris, a singer and guitar player, put music to and sang several of Harwell's lyrics. One such song, "I Don't Know Any Better," was performed by B. J. Thomas and was selected for inclusion on his compact disc entitled *The Very Best of B. J. Thomas*.

The Harwell song most familiar to baseball fans old enough to remember Hank Aaron's successful pursuit of Babe Ruth's home-run record is entitled "Move Over Babe, Here Comes Henry," written with former Tigers pitcher Bill Slayback. NBC gave it big exposure during its "Game of the Week" as Aaron closed in on 714, a number burned by Ruth in the brain of every baseball fan.

Slayback, something of a Renaissance man, had a talent for oil paintings, ink drawings, and furniture building, and he even built his own recording studio. He wasn't the only one who recorded the song. It was hot enough that Popcorn Wiley also recorded it.

Aaron was involved in the marketing of the record as well. His image in uniform and his autograph were on the cover of the record sleeve.

The man who as a boy got the Babe to sign his shoe, got the man who broke the Babe's record to sign his record jacket [more than 40 years later].

One of Harwell's songs, published in 1978, is entitled "Nobody's Perfect."

> Shakespeare used the wrong word once,
> And Welk ran out of the bubbles.
> Lincoln worried about his warts,
> Life is full of troubles.
> So if I act the perfect fool,
> Don't treat it like a crime.
> 'Cause nobody's perfect all the time.

Nobody's perfect all the time, not even a Hall of Fame broadcaster. When Harwell makes a mistake in the booth, he corrects it and moves on.

"I don't see what good it does to dwell on it by apologizing over and over," Harwell says. "All that does is get in the way of describing the game."

Harwell's most embarrassing mistake occurred during a broadcast of a West Coast game at such a late hour for Detroit listeners that Harwell did not receive a single irate letter or phone call. Either that or listeners simply couldn't believe their ears and dismissed what they thought they heard as fatigue having played a trick on them.

With the score tied 1–1 in the eighth inning of a game against the Angels at Anaheim Stadium, Dave Collins of the Angels stole home.

Umpire Rich Garcia called him safe, which drew Tigers manager Ralph Houk out of the dugout for an argument.

As he described the scene unfolding at home plate, Harwell said, "Bill Freehan is there too. Now Freehan is beating his meat at home plate."

Harwell meant to say Freehan, the Tigers' standout catcher, was beating his mitt. The mistake is immortalized on a bootleg tape that includes tirades from managers Tommy Lasorda and Earl Weaver.

Harwell never heard a word from the front office about his unintentional, graphic use of slang on the air. The same could not be said for other unfortunate words he spoke intentionally in 1973, again in a game against the Angels, this time at Tiger Stadium.

Harwell, partner Ray Lane, and engineer Howard Stitzel were in the booth waiting out a rain delay when Tigers public relations director Hal Middlesworth called to inform them that the game appeared headed for postponement and would be rescheduled as part of a doubleheader the next day. Middlesworth said not to make any announcement on the air until he officially announced the postponement over the press box intercom.

Shortly after that phone call, Middlesworth apparently made an announcement in the press box informing, "If the game is canceled it will be made up tomorrow as part of a doubleheader." Harwell, Lane, and Stitzel did not hear the word *if* over the scratchy intercom. Harwell went on the air and called off the game, thus making more history. He became the only broadcaster in history to postpone a game. Not only that, he postponed a game that was played after all. As is his custom, Harwell swiftly left the ballpark. So did many of the fans at the park listening to the radio.

Ernie and Lulu were on the Lodge Freeway, on their way to see Ronnie Dove's concert, when Lane spoke directly to his partner over the radio: "Wait a minute, folks. We've just received word the game has not been postponed. Ernie, the game's on. Come back, come back, wherever you are."

He came back and arrived in the booth in the second inning.

Lane remembers: "GM Jim Campbell called us into a meeting the next morning, and we took a terrible beating about that. It was one of the very few times I've ever seen Harwell flustered. His hands and knees were going up and down. When Ernie postponed the game, the people who were sitting in their cars outside the stadium waiting for word drove off. A lot of the affiliates from around the state only stayed on the air late at night to carry the games. When they heard Ernie's announcement, they shut the transmitters off and went home and lost the revenues for that game. It's funny to talk about now, but nobody was laughing then."

The Tigers also issued refunds to the fans duped by Harwell's announcement. Harwell, Lane, and Stitzel were called to Campbell's office and were given a tongue-lashing from the man they all admired greatly.

They weren't in danger of losing their jobs over that, but there was another incident that grew so hot that Harwell began to hear rumors that he was in danger of getting fired.

Harwell's selection of José Feliciano to sing the national anthem for Game 5 of the 1968 World Series on October 7 set off a firestorm of controversy. His bluesy rendition of "The Star-Spangled Banner" triggered nonstop phone calls to the network and the Tigers. It was blasted as unpatriotic.

Harwell's other choices, Margaret Whiting and Marvin Gaye, were well received.

Harwell met Feliciano at the airport and enjoyed hearing from him on their ride to Tiger Stadium that he had listened to Harwell announce Dodgers and Giants games when he was a boy growing up in Harlem.

After introducing Feliciano to the Tigers he wanted to meet, Harwell accompanied the singer to center field where the two men and Feliciano's guide dog, Judy, stood as the man who took The Doors' tune "Light My Fire" to a new level of popularity, sang the anthem.

Harwell complimented him when he finished. The crowd voiced another viewpoint, sending boos down from the stands.

The Tiger Stadium switchboard lit up with angry callers. Newspapers across the country gave the controversy front-page play, and Harwell was bombarded with phone calls, some from irate fans, others from reporters seeking an explanation. Harwell was unapologetic at the time and remains so decades later. He does not count the choice of Feliciano as one of his career mistakes.

"I felt he did it in a good way," Harwell says. "It was sort of stylized, but he did it that way because that was his style and he was just paying tribute to the country. If you heard it now, it would be very mild compared to some others you hear today. It's just that he didn't do it like Lucy Munroe, Kate Smith, or Robert Merrill did it, and people weren't used to it. And it was a fractious time. The hippie movement was on, and he sang it with a guitar, which some people considered to be a hippie instrument. His hair was long, and because of his blindness he wore dark glasses, which were sort of a symbol of a cool cat. A lot of people put all that together and thought he was being disrespectful, which he wasn't in any way. It was amazing the reaction was so reactionary."

Harwell feels stronger than ever that Feliciano's anthem was both well done and appropriate.

"There are so many terrible ones now with all these wanna-bes trying to get attention for themselves," Harwell says. "His wasn't that way at all. They murder the song now. Before September 11, I felt they played the anthem too often. In peaceful times, I would like to see them only sing it on Opening Day, Fourth of July, and Veterans Day. With it being played every day, people don't pay attention and give it the proper respect."

Harwell witnessed a bigger mistake than he ever committed when the Tigers were in Chicago to play a doubleheader against the White Sox on July 12, 1979.

Bill Veeck owned the White Sox at the time. Twenty-eight years earlier, as owner of the St. Louis Browns, Veeck orchestrated the most famous promotion in baseball history. He signed midget Eddie Gaedel to a contract and sent him into a game as a pinch-hitter against the Tigers with explicit instructions *not* to swing the bat. He told Gaedel that rooftop snipers would shoot him if he took a swing. Gaedel took a walk and was banned from baseball the next day, and Veeck was chastised for not showing proper reverence to the grand old game. The runt stunt is looked back upon with fondness by many today. Harwell, nine years away from calling Tigers games, was a Giants announcer then and did not witness it.

Harwell was on hand for the infamous Disco Demolition Night at Comiskey Park. Steve Dahl, a disc jockey at Chicago radio station WLUP-FM, had taken to blowing up disco records and was drawing big crowds at venues such as shopping malls.

Veeck's son, Mike Veeck, who was convinced the popularity of disco killed the careers of many musicians, including his own, thought it would be a good idea for Dahl to bring his act to Comiskey Park.

Dahl promoted the event on his radio show, urging baseball fans to bring disco records in exchange for tickets discounted to 98 cents.

"It was complete chaos," Harwell remembers. "People began to throw albums on the field. They were flying out there like Frisbees, hitting people. They built fires in the stands. It was completely out of control. The people who came that night weren't even baseball fans. They just wanted to have a good time and party. It was like the people were from another planet. They put Bill Veeck on the mike to try to calm people down. He had no effect. And then Harry Caray got on the mike. They didn't even listen to Harry. The only way they stopped them was with the riot police. They lined up on the field with helmets and billy clubs and marched onto the field and that's when everybody skiddooed. It got a little scary there for a while."

The field was so torn apart that the White Sox were forced to forfeit the second game of the doubleheader.

"That promotion wasn't such a great idea," Harwell understates. "But I thought the Eddie Gaedel promotion was a great one. I didn't think that made fun of the game at all. I thought it was great for the game."

Harwell never has made a habit of destroying songs. He would rather write them and listen to them.

To ride shotgun to Harwell on a trip to the ballpark is to listen to songs written by him and sung by others on tape. If the passenger is lucky, Harwell might even sing along with one of them while bobbing his head this way and that.

> Sing, sing, sing
> Every song.
> Dance, dance, dance
> All the day long.
> Life is a party
> That doesn't last long.
> So dance every dance
> And sing every song.

"We thought that would be a good tavern song," he says. "A perfect song for reunions."

> Pull up a memory,
> Stay for a while.

Harwell had collaborated with renowned composer Johnny Mercer, a man who counted among his works "Moon River."

After Mercer's death, his estate, seeking someone to put new lyrics to an old song of his entitled "My Harvest Time Letter of Love," contacted Harwell.

"It was about a guy sitting on a porch, which nobody does anymore, writing a letter, which people don't do anymore, and it was about harvest time, which doesn't apply now," Harwell says. "I thought I would write a song for a reunion. I don't know what came of it."

Through 2001, Harwell has had 65 songs recorded. It's the ones that haven't been recorded that eat at him, such as the one Motown purchased and planned to have Marvin Gaye sing.

"Nothing ever came of it," Harwell says with more than a hint of regret.

His finances secure and his baseball fame immortalized in Cooperstown, Harwell nonetheless is as hungry to get discovered as any struggling artist.

Those even mildly familiar with the name Ernie Harwell consider Harwell's voice and the way he uses it to describe baseball games as his natural gift. Those who know his life story are aware he had to take lessons just to learn how to talk without embarrassing himself.

His natural gift, his first gift, was writing. He has used it to write everything from sports columns to lyrics to books. In addition to covering 30 spring training games and all 162 regular-season contests during the 2001 season, Harwell continued his duties as a weekly columnist for the *Detroit Free Press*.

While spending winters living in Dunedin during the 1970s, Harwell never claimed to be the best writer on the block. Erskine Caldwell, author of best-selling novels *Tobacco Road* and *God's Little Acre*, and his wife lived next door to the Harwells. The couples socialized often. When Erskine died, his widow, Virginia, gave the typewriter he had used to write his books to Ernie.

Harwell's fourth book, *Stories from My Life in Baseball*, is a collection of his columns that have appeared in the *Detroit Free Press*. As a baseball columnist, Harwell is neither mean-spirited nor apologetic for the athletes. He blends wry humor with an encyclopedic recall of details from generations past. In one column, he is able to expose Willie Horton as a hypochondriac, yet he does so with a touch that leaves Horton even more likable to the reader: "Always treating each ache or pain with an overdose of exaggeration, he was the Tigers' Moaner Lisa. To Willie, a simple headache loomed as a brain tumor. The sniffles indicated at least pneumonia, and a boil on his leg meant immediate amputation."

In another column that leaves the reader laughing, Harwell predicts from experience what his next book signing will be like. In another dripping with common sense and humor, he details pet peeves, including those silly hotel key cards that often don't work in contrast to the old-fashioned keys that always worked. In that column he poses the question: "Do maids and housekeepers take college courses in how to yammer loudly in hotel corridors at 7:30 A.M.?" He also wonders: "Why do most hotels ignore climatic conditions and set their thermostats according to the calendar?"

In his column, just as on the air, his is not a voice that yearns for "the good old days." He sometimes draws on experiences from the good old days to put today's events in perspective, but he never slips into the habit of bemoaning today's world in comparison to yesterday's.

The first three books Harwell authored ranked among the best-selling baseball books of the years they were published. *Tuned to Baseball*, published in 1985, is autobiographical in nature. He also authored *Diamond Gems* and *The Babe Signed My Shoe*.

Those artistic achievements all found homes. It's his songs, every last one of them, that he yearns to lend immortality with music written and performed by others. No one should be surprised to stumble upon Harwell in the middle innings of a dog-days-of-August game with one eye on the game being played before him and the other eye scanning the classified ads of an obscure music magazine, an eye in search of a modern-day Larue Dickson.

Even if Harwell finds him, he's not likely to make a song Harwell's most famous piece of writing. That would be neither a book nor a column, rather an ode to baseball that captures Americans' bond with the sport about as well as any piece of literature ever has.

Chapter 16

The Game for All America

Under normal circumstances, Cooperstown is the one haven from boos for baseball fans. But there was nothing normal about baseball in the summer of 1981. A players' strike erased the middle third of the season, and two winners were crowned in each division. Ill will toward the game ran rampant, even after the opponents in the labor dispute reached agreement.

The Hall of Fame induction ceremonies took place one week before the resumption of the season. Jack Buck worked as master of ceremonies that afternoon in Cooperstown. In his introductory speech to kick off the ceremonies, Buck twice mentioned the impending resumption of the season and twice was booed loudly. The people were angry and felt betrayed by the game they loved.

If ever baseball was in need of someone to step to the plate and hit a home run for the sport, this was the time. Ernie Harwell, who that day became the first active announcer given the Ford Frick Award, came through in the clutch for baseball with a speech that rekindled passion for the game in so many who felt spurned.

After a warm introduction from Hall of Fame slugger and Mets broadcaster Ralph Kiner, Harwell quickly charmed the crowd.

Here's the text of his speech, supplied by the Hall of Fame:

Thank you, Ralph Kiner, and thank you folks for that warm Cooperstown welcome. This is an award that I will certainly cherish forever. I praise the Lord here today. I know that all my talent and all my ability comes from Him, and without Him, I'm nothing, and I thank Him for His great blessing. I'd like for you to meet my very best friend, and she is my best friend despite the fact that this month we celebrate our 40th wedding anniversary. Lulu Harwell. Lulu, will you stand up please. My son Bill, right next to her, his wife Diane, their youngsters, my son Gray, his wife Sandy, and their three youngsters, and my daughters, Julie and Carolyn.

I'm very proud of this award, but I'm even more proud of my family. You know the life and times of Ernie Harwell could be capsuled in, I think, two famous quotations, one from a left-handed, New York Yankee pitcher and the other one from a right-handed English poet. The Yankee pitcher, Lefty Gomez, once said, "I'd rather be lucky than good." And the poet, Alfred Lord Tennyson, once wrote in his epic poem "Ulysses," "I am part of all that I have met." Well, I know that I'm a lot luckier than I'm good. I've been lucky to broadcast some great events and to broadcast the exploits of some great players.

When I went to Brooklyn in 1948, Jackie Robinson was at the height of his brilliant career. With the Giants,

I broadcast the debut of Hall of Famer Willie Mays. When I went to Baltimore, the great Brooks Robinson came along to replace my good friend George Kell at third base. And in my 22 years at Detroit, it's been a distinct privilege to watch the day-by-day consistency of Hall of Famer Al Kaline. Yes, I'm lucky that I've been there and I've been at some events, too. I want to tell you about one that Ralph mentioned, Bobby Thomson's home run October 3rd. I felt a little sorry for my Giant broadcasting partner that day, Russ Hodges. Ole Russ was going to be stuck on the radio. There were five radio broadcasts, and I was going to be on coast-to-coast TV, and I thought that I had the plum assignment. Well, as you remember, it turned out quite differently. Russ Hodges' record became the most famous sports broadcast of all time. Television had no instant replay in those days, and only Mrs. Harwell knows that I did the telecast of Bobby Thomson's home run. When I got home that night after the telecast she said to me, "You know Ernie, when they turned the camera on you after that home run I saw you with that stunned look on your face, and the only other time I had ever seen it was when we were married and when the kids were born."

That other saying, I'm part of all that I have met, I think that would have to begin with my wonderful parents back in Atlanta. When I was a youngster, five years old, I was tongue-tied. They didn't have much money, but they spent what they had sending me to speech teachers to overcome the handicap. I know that a lot of you people who have heard me on the radio probably still think I'm tongue-tied, but through the grace of God, officially I'm not tongue-tied any more. Also, I'm a part

Going to Bat for Shoeless Joe

Ted Williams went to bat for Shoeless Joe Jackson.

The famed Boston Red Sox slugger supported a drive to elect the disgraced outfielder to the Hall of Fame.

Although many efforts have been made to clear Jackson of his involvement in the infamous Black Sox scandal of 1919, none has succeeded.

Jackson was a career .356 hitter for the Athletics, the Indians, and the White Sox in 1908–1920.

"I've put a great deal of study into the issue," said Williams, elected to the Hall in 1966. "And I truly believe that Jackson belongs in the Baseball Hall of Fame. He was an outstanding and dominant player of his era. While alive, he served his 60-year sentence of being banned from the game. I think his suspension should be lifted. After that maybe we can get him into the Hall of Fame."

In 1997 Williams met with board members of the Society for American Baseball Research to present his views. The research group agreed to provide Ted more background on Jackson and to discuss his proposal at its convention in Louisville, Kentucky, that summer.

Williams also wanted to enlist former players and media to support his drive for Jackson.

I served six years with Williams on the Hall of Fame veterans committee. From my personal experience I know he is very thorough and dedicated. Also, he is an open and forthright advocate once he believes in a cause. Certainly, Jackson could have no better supporter because Williams has tremendous prestige and respect among baseball people.

"I became interested in Jackson's case after seeing the film *Eight Men Out*," Williams said. "I began to read all the books and articles about his banishment from baseball. Sure, he took the money, but he tried to return it and Harry Grabiner, the White Sox official, told him to keep it."

From his early playing days, Williams heard constant praise of Jackson's hitting prowess.

"Ty Cobb told me that Jackson was baseball's greatest natural hitter," Williams said. "Also, Babe Ruth said he copied his swing from Jackson."

As a rookie, Williams learned more about Jackson from his teammate and manager, Joe Cronin, and from Red Sox executive Eddie Collins.

"Eddie was on that Black Sox team," Williams said. "He never discussed the game-throwing charges, but he did often tell me what a great hitter he thought Joe Jackson was."

Williams is convinced that Jackson, who died in 1951, should be exonerated. "Remember," Williams said, "he was never proven guilty in a court of law."

I'm sure Ted met some opposition in his support of Jackson. But he convinced me that his cause is right.

—*E.H., May 1997*

of the people that I've worked with in baseball that have been so great to me: Mr. Earl Mann of Atlanta, who gave me my first baseball broadcasting job. Mr. Branch Rickey at Brooklyn. Mr. Horace Stoneham of the Giants. Mr. Jerry Hoffberger in Baltimore, and my present bosses, two of the greatest ever, Mr. John Fetzer and Mr. Jim Campbell. I'm also a part of the partners that I've worked with, and there have been so many great ones, beginning with Red Barber and Connie Desmond at Brooklyn and continuing on to my present partner, WJR's Paul Carey.

But most of all, I'm a part of you people out there who have listened to me, because especially you people in Michigan, you Tiger fans, you've given me so much warmth, so much affection, and so much love. I know that this is an award that's supposed to be for my contribution to baseball, but let me say this: I've given a lot less to baseball than it's given to me, and the greatest gift that I received from baseball is the way that the people in the game have responded to me with their warmth and their friendship. Yes, it's better to be lucky than good, and I'm glad that I'm part of all that I have met. We're all here with a common bond today. I think we're all here because we love baseball.

Back in 1955—Ralph referred to this—I sat down and wrote a little definition of baseball to express my feelings about this greatest game of all. And I know that a lot of things have changed since then, especially in this strike-filled year. But my feelings about the game are still the same as they were back then, and I think that maybe yours are too. And I'd like to close out my remarks for the next couple of minutes, with your indulgence, to see if your definition of baseball agrees with mine.

Harwell then recited a slightly shortened version of "The Game for All America."

Baseball is the president tossing out the first ball of the season and a scrubby schoolboy playing catch with his dad on a Mississippi farm; a tall, thin old man waving a scorecard in the corner of his dugout. That's baseball.

And so is a big fat guy with a bulbous nose running home one of his 714 home runs.

There's a man in Mobile who remembers that Honus Wagner hit a triple in Pittsburgh 46 years ago. That's baseball. And so is a scout reporting that a 16-year-old pitcher in Cheyenne is the coming Walter Johnson.

Baseball is a spirited race of man against man, reflex against reflex, a game of inches. Every skill is measured, every heroic action or failing is seen and cheered or booed and then becomes a statistic.

In baseball, democracy shines its clearest. The only race that matters is the race to the bag; the creed is a rulebook and color merely something to distinguish one team's uniform from another.

Baseball is a rookie, his experience no bigger than the lump in his throat as he begins the fulfillment of his dream and it's a veteran too, a tired old man of 35 hoping that those aching muscles can pull him through another sweltering August and September.

Nicknames are baseball, names like Zeke and Pie and Kiki and Home Run and Cracker and Dizzy and Dazzy. Baseball is the clear, cool eyes of Rogers Hornsby, the flashing spikes of Ty Cobb, and an overage pixie named Rabbit Maranville.

Baseball, just a game, as simple as a ball and bat and yet it's as complex as the American spirit it symbolizes. A sport, a business, sometimes almost even religious. The fairytale of Willie Mays making the brilliant World Series catch and then dashing off to play stickball in the streets with his teenage pals. That's baseball.

So is the husky voice of a doomed Lou Gehrig saying, "I consider myself the luckiest man on the face of the earth." Baseball is cigar smoke, hot roasted peanuts, *The Sporting News,* Ladies' Day, down in front, "Take Me Out to the Ballgame" and "The Star-Spangled Banner."

Baseball is a tongue-tied kid from Georgia growing up to be an announcer and praising the Lord for showing him the way to Cooperstown. This is the game for America. Still a game for America. This baseball.

Thank you.

Harwell's definition of baseball was the hit of that summer day in Cooperstown, a day in which Hall of Fame inductees Bob Gibson and Johnny Mize also captivated the audience. Country boys forever are big hits with their speeches at baseball's most hallowed grounds and Mize, from rural Demorest, Georgia, was as country as they come. Here is an excerpt from his speech:

In our little town in Demorest, probably if it had this many people in it, it would tilt. I was 15 years old, a sophomore in high school, and Harry Forrester, coach at Piedmont College, came up to me one day, I'd played a couple of baseball games, and he says, "Come out for the college team." I said, "You gotta be kiddin'." So he talked me into it. I think it was something like a Tuesday morning I went out, he said, "Well, come out and at least put on a uniform." So I went out. Friday I was put in as a pinch-hitter, so I started out as a pinch-hitter and ended up as a pinch-hitter. So I got a base hit, and the next day I started, and I finished the season. The next year the county took over the high school and the [college] boys wanted to know if I was going to play with them, and I said, "I can't. I'm in high school." They said they'd talk to the coach. So they said something to Mr. Forrester, and he said, "Well, we'll fix it up. You can take one subject in college, and you can play on the team." So I went out for the team, and they didn't mention the subject and I didn't mention it either. Then we came around to next year and I just automatically started playing when they started the first practice, and I set probably the only record that will never be broken. I don't know of any guy today that will play three years of college ball while still in high school.

The more sophisticated Bob Gibson also traced the roots of his Hall of Fame career to his childhood:

My baseball career started, I guess, basically when I was about 10 years old. When I was born, I was relatively sick, and my older brother, Josh, came to the hospital where I was and told me if I got well—I had a bout with pneumonia—he told me if I got well he was going to get me a baseball bat and glove and he was going to teach me how to play baseball. Well, that ended up pretty much true to form. He got me a baseball glove. He's the one responsible for me learning all the fundamentals of the game, and by God did he teach me fundamentals. I never thought we were ever going to get a chance to really play in a ballgame. And it wasn't just baseball. He had a knack of getting me involved in baseball, basketball, track, or whatever else, and he taught me the fundamentals of all the games to a point that I was always a little bit ahead of kids my own age, so I would never play with those kids. I would always play with older kids. Because I knew the fundamentals so well and they were still learning them and I didn't have time to wait.

One warm day in Cooperstown couldn't heal all the wounds born from one of baseball's most ugly work stoppages, but it was a start. Whatever ill will toward baseball lingered in Detroit was washed away in one sweet summer, the summer of 1984.

Chapter 17

1984

The 1970s were packed with characters at Tiger Stadium. Billy Martin managed. Ron LeFlore, who played ball in prison before playing it for the Tigers, ran wild on the bases. Mark "the Bird" Fidrych talked to the baseball, dropped to his knees to manicure the mound dirt, and generally put on such an entertaining show that he drew huge crowds everywhere he went.

Harwell was on hand when the Tigers discovered LeFlore early in the 1973 season. Harwell, Martin, Frank Howard, and Tigers community relations director Lew Matlin visited a state prison in Jackson to talk to the inmates.

"Billy, I heard there's a lot of racial tension on the Tigers? Is that true?" one of the prisoners asked.

"Nah," Martin answered. "Willie Horton and Frank Howard are roommates on the road. How would you like to try to break into that room?"

Horton remembers a night when several Tigers rooms, all in a row, were broken into on the road. The one room that wasn't broken into was the one with the door wide open. The bed was too short for

Howard, so he slept on the floor. He also slept with the door open in order to get fresh air that night.

"I think they took one look at Frank lying there and didn't want any part of him," Horton remembers with a laugh.

After the Tigers' contingent was done speaking to the gathered inmates, they were given a tour of the prison. By the time Martin met LeFlore in the prison hospital, several prisoners had informed the manager about the phenom within those walls. LeFlore asked Martin for a chance, and Martin said he could have a tryout. The manager kept his word. Shortly before gaining his release, LeFlore was allowed to go to Tiger Stadium for a tryout witnessed by Harwell. After his release, he underwent another tryout at Butzel Field and was signed on July 2, 1973. He led the American League in runs and stolen bases in 1975 and spent five seasons with the Tigers, and during that time was a dinner guest at the Harwell home.

In 1976, the Bird ruled the Tigers' roost. Harwell enjoyed his company and chronicled his malaprops, including "I'll have the last hearsay" and "a hit's as good as a walk."

The 1970s had no shortage of entertaining moments, but in order to endure as special Tigers, a championship is required. No one can ever say the 1984 Tigers, managed by Sparky Anderson, weren't special.

The Tigers finished second to the Orioles in 1983 and were in need of a big-brother figure to take it to the next level. Before the 1984 season, they landed that big brother in Darrell Evans. His lefty power swing was suited to the right-field porch at Tiger Stadium, and his veteran presence was welcomed in the clubhouse.

"We called him Pops," remembers All-Star shortstop Alan Trammell, now a coach for the Padres. "Pops put us over the top. We were young, but we had a little experience. And we were hungry."

They also acquired a left-handed reliever by the name of Willie Hernandez without much fanfare. He proved to be the difference for the Tigers.

During that era of Tigers baseball, Paul Carey, Harwell's broadcast partner who had such a deep and resonant voice that columnist Mike Downey termed it "the Voice of God," never will forget the final day of spring training in 1984. A sportswriter from St. Petersburg, Florida, had done a story in which he quoted several people's predictions of where the Tigers would finish. Carey picked them for third.

Carey and wife Nancy enjoy retirement in Michigan during warm months and drive south for the winter, living on a Gulf Coast island not far from Pensacola, Florida. Both stay busy reading for the blind and dyslexic.

"Kirk Gibson got on my case something awful," Carey remembers of his prediction. "He and Lance Parrish both jumped all over me: 'Third? Where have you been?' They sure proved me wrong. They had the makings of a championship team, and they knew it. I'm not sure the media knew it, but the players knew it."

The Tigers came out of the blocks like Carl Lewis. No team before or since matched the 35–5 start of the Tigers. They won their first 17 road games. Big crowds, aware something very special was brewing, packed Tiger Stadium early on.

Anderson, famous for overhyping young prospects, found himself trying to douse flames for a change.

"Don't get too high. Don't get too high," he repeatedly warned everyone. "A lot of things can happen. It's a long season."

Not long enough for the Blue Jays to overcome the Tigers' 35–5 start.

Sparky and Ernie became close friends during that summer and walked and talked together every morning on the road.

Trammell and Lou Whitaker, the long-standing double-play combination, formed the heart of the championship team. After winning a Double A Southern League championship for the Montgomery Rebels, Trammell and Whitaker were brought to Detroit together in September

Sparky Always Had a Special Touch

Everybody has a Sparky Anderson story. I have two, and each reflects his human touch—one with his players and one with his public.

When Sparky's Reds played the Orioles in the 1970 World Series, he had a second-string catcher named Pat Corrales. In his third year of backing up Johnny Bench, Corrales was finishing the sixth year of his undistinguished nine-year career.

The Orioles were leading the series, three games to one. The final game at Baltimore's Memorial Stadium found the Birds ahead, 9–3, in the ninth. It was all over—just a matter of three more outs. Mike Cuellar retired the first two Reds easily. One to go and the Orioles were champions.

Corrales was watching from the dugout. It was his first World Series and his last. Anderson looked down the bench toward Corrales.

"Pat," he told him, "get up there and hit for Hal McRae. You deserve to be in a World Series, and this might be your only chance."

Pat grounded out to third baseman Brooks Robinson and the series was over. But he had batted in a World Series—thanks to a thoughtful manager.

My other Anderson story happened in 1984, the year the Tigers started 35–5. Sparky's team had won 17 consecutive road games. His picture graced the covers of magazines, and his name was in headlines across the country. He and I were having breakfast at our Anaheim hotel when a fan approached our table.

"Hi, Sparky," he said. "I'm a great fan of yours. I live in San Diego now, but I was living in Cincinnati when you managed that

Big Red Machine. You have always been my hero. Without a
doubt you are the greatest manager ever."
   Sparky beamed. Silently, he listened and just nodded his
head. Then, the man spoke again.
   "And by the way, Sparky, what are you doing these days?"
   Sparky gave him a polite smile and returned to his eggs and
bacon.
   But that fan's question gave Anderson a conversation topic
for the rest of the trip. Sparky always understood the mind of the
baseball fan and the player.

—E.H., July 2000

1977. They watched from the dugout as the Tigers played the final
game of a homestand, and then they boarded the team charter bound
for Boston, where they would make their major league debuts the next
day in the second game of a doubleheader.

By the time the Tigers evolved into a championship-caliber club,
Trammell and Whitaker had shown why they would be remembered
as one of the great double-play combinations in baseball history.

Jack Morris, the American League's best starting pitcher in the 1980s,
was the ace of the staff. Hernandez was such an automatic save that he
won both the Cy Young and MVP Awards in 1984, 16 years after Denny
McLain won both awards for the Tigers. Other similarities between the
1968 Tigers (103–59) and the 1984 Tigers (104–58): neither team had a
100 RBI man. Both teams led the league in runs and home runs.

Kirk Gibson, once a star receiver at Michigan State, took on leadership status by breaking up double plays with an exclamation point and
by consistently delivering in the clutch. Gibson had an abundance of
speed and strength, and what he lacked in grace he compensated for
with passion.

"He brought the intensity," Trammell says. "I've never been around any player like Kirk Gibson, and I say that because of his intensity. If you weren't feeling all that well and you saw him ranting and raving, putting a game face on, it rubbed off on you. To see him day in and day out mentally strapping it on like that helped us all. That man was as intense a player as anybody I've played with. He would will himself to accomplish things. To me, our two best clutch hitters were Gibby and Lou Whitaker. They just had a knack for the timely hit."

Gibson's knack never was more noticeable than in the World Series. After the Tigers swept the Royals in the best-of-five American League Championship Series, Gibson eliminated the Padres in the fifth game of the World Series by hammering a pair of home runs at Tiger Stadium.

"When he hit that second home run, that was the first time I felt like we got it," Trammell says. "If we didn't win that game, we would have had to go back to San Diego. We really wanted to win it at home. We had clinched the division at home and we clinched the pennant at home, so we got to clinch all three at home."

That meant the Tigers didn't have to return to San Diego. Even if the Series had been extended to a sixth game, Carey wasn't going to make the trip West. He had a far more important duty to attend to than announcing a World Series game or two. His wife Patti's memory began failing her.

"Something was obviously wrong with Patti," Carey recalls. "We were all packed and ready to go to Chicago to play the Cubs, figuring they were going to win the pennant. Then the Padres came from behind and won the Series, so we wound up going to San Diego. The wives were invited to go along, and I invited Patti, but then I quickly realized there was no way she could go along. Her memory was really bad. I went to San Diego with no idea what was going on with Patti. I made long-distance calls to make arrangements for her to go to Beaumont Hospital in Royal Oak to have her looked at. I was

Ernie and Reggie Jackson before the All-Star game at Tiger Stadium on July 13, 1971. Photo courtesy TV Sports Mailbag, © 1989.

In his first visit to Comerica Park, Ichiro Suzuki requested a meeting with Ernie. On the right is Ichiro's interpreter, Brad Lefton. Ernie Harwell personal collection.

Ernie interviews Roger Clemens at Boston's training camp. Photo courtesy of Francis G. Tate.

Two Hall of Famers: Ernie and George Brett. Ernie Harwell personal collection.

A hug for Ernie from Ken Griffey Jr. Photo courtesy of Bill Eisner, © 1999.

Ernie with Seattle manager Lou Piniella. Photo courtesy of Bill Eisner, © 1999.

Ernie with another Iron Man, Cal Ripken Jr. Photo courtesy of Bill Eisner, © 2000.

They both overcame childhood speech handicaps: Ernie and James Earl Jones. Ernie Harwell personal collection.

Joe Torre tells Ernie he saw him on NBC-TV when Bobby Thomson hit his famous "Shot Heard 'Round the World" home run on October 3, 1951. Photo courtesy Bill Eisner, © 2000.

Tiger great Al Kaline chats with Ernie. Photo courtesy of M. Cunningham, © 1998.

Ralph Kiner welcomes Ernie into The National Baseball Hall of Fame. Photo courtesy of Richard Collins.

Ernie and grandson Josh Harwell visit John Smoltz. Ernie Harwell personal collection.

Ernie and Lulu backstage with José Feliciano. Ernie Harwell personal collection.

announcing a World Series, but Patti was foremost on my mind the whole time. She had a craniotomy scheduled for the same day as Game 6, so I told the station there was no way I could go to San Diego for Game 6."

Before the week was out, Carey learned his wife had an inoperable brain tumor. He was told she had an estimated nine to twelve months to live. She died six months later.

"I couldn't have had anybody better to work with than Ernie Harwell at a time like that," Carey says. "He was there to befriend you, to talk to you, to listen to you. He had lost his brother, with whom he was very, very close, and he knew Patti very well. She knitted him a big, heavy wool sweater to wear to the ballpark. Ernie was very fond of her."

And Carey remains very fond of Harwell.

"He was the easiest guy you could ever work with," Carey says. "Extremely tolerant and kind. Just welcomes everybody. I had done pregame shows in '58 with Van Patrick and Mel Ott and then in '59 with Van and George Kell after Mel got killed in an automobile accident. Back then, the station only carried night games, and there weren't that many night games. A big, mobile studio pulled up in front of the stadium and I'd do the pregame shows. Then when Ernie came, he did the pregame shows and I was kind of glad. Then in '64 our station took over the origination of the broadcasts and I became the producer of the Tiger network. Then in '73 I began working with him in the booth. You're elbow to elbow with someone for 19 years and you get to know them pretty well."

Carey still marvels at Harwell's mental abilities that gave him an edge as a broadcaster.

"He has a great ability to remember verbatim what somebody tells him on the field and then bring it up on the air," Carey says. "I'd get the gist and forget half of that by the time I got to the booth. He remembered every word. He has a great capability for that, plus one other trait I've never seen anybody else duplicate. Certain players are hard to reach. I had a good relationship with players, but because I was also engineering for 16 of the 19 years, I couldn't spend a lot of time on the field. Ernie was always able to get down there. There was always some player who wasn't talking to the press, had a chip on his shoulder and decided not to talk to any member of the media. What got me, pretty soon this guy would be telling Ernie things he wouldn't be telling his wife, personal things. The player would just unload. Players known to be standoffish warm up so quickly to Ernie. It's an amazing trait, just something that's within his chemistry. Every city we'd go to, every ballpark we'd go to, he would introduce himself to every rookie he sees, and they would know him by first name after that."

One such player with a reputation for being standoffish with the press was future Hall of Fame first baseman Eddie Murray.

Yet, on March 7, 1991, when the Tigers were in Vero Beach to play an exhibition game at intimate Holman Stadium, Harwell was in mid-broadcast, on the roof of the press box, when he noticed a familiar face had climbed the rickety stairs to deliver a message.

"A man in the stands wanted me to deliver this to you, Ernie," Murray said with a smile.

The note was from a man who wanted to say hello to his parents back home in Monroe.

Now more than ever, major league ballplayers are suspicious of the motives of those approaching them for conversation. They forever are weary of being used. They often wonder: Why is this person being so nice to me? What's he angling to get from me? An autograph? An interview? Investment money? In Harwell's case, they never wonder any of that. Trammell explains why.

"The first thing that comes to mind when I think of Ernie Harwell is how he treats everybody the same," Trammell says. "Rookie, veteran, somebody not involved in baseball in any way. It doesn't matter. He treats everybody the same. I can honestly say there is nobody better that I've met in all facets of life. He's a great announcer and a great human being. I miss him. I really do miss him."

Carey doesn't miss the travel involved in covering a major league team. He marvels at how Harwell has resumed a full schedule.

"Here we are more than 10 years later, and he's still doing it," Carey says.

The former broadcast partners communicate via e-mail.

"He's so concise," Carey says of Harwell. "I can't condense my words the way Ernie can. I'll have several questions for him and the questions will fill a couple of screens. He'll answer every question and he'll do it in three lines. He would have been a good rewrite man, a good editor. He transferred it to broadcasting too. It comes through in his ability to interview. He can phrase a question in 12 seconds that would take most of us 30 seconds to ask."

Carey and Harwell miss working together. Theirs was a close personal relationship and a seamless working one. Carey was fortunate in that he worked only with Harwell and never had to follow him.

Chapter 18

A Suffocating Shadow

As sidekick to the colorful and comedic former catcher Bob Uecker on Milwaukee Brewers broadcasts, Pat Hughes never was going to be the most high-profile man in the booth. As Ernie Harwell's replacement in Detroit, Hughes could have become the No. 1 man. So when Harwell suggested to Hughes that he apply for his job in the summer of 1991, Hughes thought about it . . . for about half a second.

"I knew it was going to be a no-win situation," Hughes says. "Similar to replacing Vin Scully or Jack Buck, you just can't do it. No matter how good you are, you're still not Ernie Harwell. My kids were very young and I could have moved, and certainly I could have used the money, but I knew it would be a no-win, short-lived endeavor. If Vin Scully decides to retire, he would almost have to be in charge of handpicking his successor, and there would have to be a picture of Vin with his arm around you on the cover of the *LA Times* for it to work."

The fact that Harwell didn't retire and was, in effect, fired only made the task of his successor all the more daunting. A decade later, Hughes expresses no regrets. He is the Cubs' play-by-play man on radio and performs a similar role on television broadcasts of the Marquette University basketball games, where he has a front-row seat for Michigander Tom Crean's remarkable rebuilding of a dormant giant back into a national power.

Working with Uecker on Brewers games and the late great Al McGuire on Marquette games, Hughes knows the pull that legends have on the adoring public.

Once while in Louisville, after Brian Wardle's dramatic buzzer-beater gave Marquette a victory, McGuire and Hughes were prepared to take a cab to the airport when McGuire had a better idea.

"'Let's hitchhike,' McGuire suggested. 'Somebody will recognize me and they'll want to take me to the airport.' We're hitchhiking and these young kids, about 22 years old, stopped. One of them said, 'Hey, you're Al McGuire.' Al said, 'That's right; me and my partner Pat here need a ride to the airport.' They told us to get in, and Al had them laughing all the way, telling stories about John Wooden and Denny Crum and arguing with officials."

After they thanked the thrilled kids for the ride, Hughes turned to McGuire and said: "Now you're going to turn in a receipt for that cab ride on your expenses, aren't you?"

Replied McGuire: "Nah, Pat. I got enough big scams going. I don't bother with the small stuff."

Moments such as those made riding shotgun to a legend quite all right with Hughes.

Rick Rizzs, the No. 2 announcer to Mariners fixture Dave Niehaus, enjoyed that role as well. Yet, the desire to be the main man always burned within him.

"My goal was to be a No. 1 guy," Rizzs says. "I remember when I first went to the big leagues and had a chance to meet Ernie Harwell, I said to myself this is what I want to be, the No. 1 guy who gets involved in the community and is the guy in the community forever and then gets to pass the torch. I wanted to be like Ernie and my partner Dave Niehaus, where you turn on the radio, hear their voices, and say, 'OK, it's springtime.' Then when the opportunity came to actually be the next Ernie Harwell, I figured what the heck, if I get support from the station and get support from the Tigers, it could possibly happen. I applied for the job."

The bad news: Rizzs not only applied for the job, he landed it. Big Foot couldn't have filled the shoes of Ernie Harwell.

"It was like I was broadcasting the seventh game of the World Series every day for three years," Rizzs says. "The scrutiny was unbelievable. If I made a mistake on the air, it was in the paper the next day."

"Once, I got blasted for saying Lou Whitaker was the greatest second baseman in Tigers history, and that's not even close to what I said," Rizzs says. "Charlie Gehringer is the greatest second baseman in Tigers history. Everybody knows that. All I said was that Lou Whitaker had joined Joe Morgan as the only second baseman to achieve some statistical combination. The writer admitted he was wrong, but he never wrote a retraction."

Right from the start, Rizzs was not blind to the shadow of Ernie Harwell.

When Harwell suggested to Rizzs that he apply for his job in a conversation behind the batting cage, Rizzs initially expressed a sentiment similar to that of Hughes.

"No, I feel sorry for the poor son of a gun who replaces you, Ernie," Rizzs told him.

"Why don't you apply? You can handle it," Harwell reassured him.

The more Rizzs thought about it, the more the idea appealed to him. He put together a resume and a tape and sent it to the Tigers. Doc Fenkell phoned him to let him know he liked the tape. The Tigers brought Rizzs in for an interview while the rest of the world was growing bags under their eyes watching the classic seven-game World Series between the Braves and Twins.

Rizzs met with Fenkell, Bo Schembechler, Jeff Odenwald, Jim Long, and WJR program director Phil Boyce. The Tigers talked about

By the Numbers, 1984 Tigers Edge 1968 Team

WARNING: This column contains statistics. They may be harmful to the casual reader.

You might know that I don't care for statistics. I think we have too many meaningless ones in baseball. However, today I'm making an exception in order to answer a question a fan asked on WDFN. The question: If the 1968 Tigers played the 1984 Tigers, which team would win?

The only way to find an answer was to dig into the records and cite statistics. My conclusion: it would be a close matchup, but the 1984 team would win.

When you look over the figures, there is an amazing similarity between the teams.

The 1968 team won 103 and lost 59. The 1984 champs were 104–58. In 1968, Baltimore, in second place, finished 12 games back. In 1984 the runner-up Toronto Blue Jays were 15 back. Each Tigers team led the league in runs. It was 671 in 1968 and 829 in 1984. Each led in homers. The 1968 team hit 185; the 1984 group had 187. Neither team boasted a player with 100 RBIs. Jim Northrup, with 90, topped the 1968 team; in 1984, Kirk Gibson was the best with 91. Each team had a Cy Young Award winner and an MVP. Denny McLain won both honors, and in 1984 Willie Hernandez did it in relief.

A comparison, by position:

First base: I'll take Norm Cash over Dave Bergman. Bergman outhit Norm, .273 to .263, but Cash had 25 home runs and batted in 63 runs. Bergman had 7 homers and 44 RBIs.

Second base: Lou Whitaker over Dick McAuliffe. Each knocked in 56 runs. Whitaker batted .289 to Mac's .249.

McAuliffe out-homered Lou, 16 to 13, but Whitaker was a better fielder.

Shortstop: Alan Trammell over Ray Oyler. Oyler batted only .135 with one home run and 12 RBIs. Trammell hit .314 with 14 homers and 69 RBIs. Trammell is the only regular who hit .300 for either Tigers team.

Third base: The statistics favor 1984's Howard Johnson over Don Wert. However, I'll pick Wert because he was a much steadier fielder. Wert hit .200 with 12 home runs and 37 RBIs. Johnson batted .248, hit 12 home runs, and knocked in 50.

Left field: Willie Horton over Larry Herndon. Horton led the team in homers with 36. He batted .285, and his RBI total was 85. Herndon hit .280 with 7 home runs and 43 RBIs.

Center field: Chet Lemon was much stronger than Mickey Stanley in each batting department. He outhit Mickey .287 to .259. He hit 20 homers to Stanley's 11. And his RBI total was 76 to Mickey's 60. Both were fine defensive players, but Stanley was much steadier. Lemon was a poor baserunner; Stanley had great baseball instincts.

Right field: Kirk Gibson over Northrup. Gibson batted .282, had 27 home runs, and 91 RBIs. Northrup hit .264 with 21 home runs and 90 RBIs. Northrup was the better defensive player.

Catcher: Here's where I go against the stats: Bill Freehan over Lance Parrish. Lance had better power. He hit 33 homers to Freehan's 25. He knocked in 98 runs to Bill's 84. Freehan had the better average, .263 to .237. I take Freehan because he was such a superior defensive catcher.

Pitching: A slight edge to the 1968 team. McLain overshadows everybody with 31–6 and a 1.96 ERA. He pitched 336 innings. The 1968 staff racked up 19 shutouts compared to 8 for the 1984 staff. Its ERA was 2.71; the ERA of the 1984 team was 3.49.

The 1984 pitching star was Hernandez. He was in 80 games, had a 1.92 ERA, won 9 and lost 3, and had 32 saves. Jack Morris was the super starter. He won 19 and lost 11 with a 3.60 ERA. Other 1984 stalwarts were Dan Petry (18–8), Milt Wilcox (17–8), and Aurelio Lopez (10–1).

Besides McLain, the 1968 regular starters were Mickey Lolich (17–9), Earl Wilson (13–12), and Joe Sparma (10–10). John Hiller (9–6) and Pat Dobson (5–8) did most of the relieving.

Reserves: The 1968 team had Al Kaline, who played in 102 games and hit .287. It also had the premier pinch-hitter, Gates Brown, who batted .370. However the 1984 Tigers had more bench strength. They boasted Tom Brookens, Ruppert Jones, Johnny Grubb, Marty Castillo, and Rusty Kuntz.

Manager: Sparky Anderson over 1968 skipper Mayo Smith. Anderson was much more into the game, more alert, and a much better strategist.

—E.H., August 1994

a one-year offer with two years at the club's option. Rizzs told them that wouldn't cut it and handed them his counterproposal, a three-year deal with perks, including a car, which the Mariners had provided him in Seattle.

"You're right, Rick," Schembechler told him. "A one-year deal wouldn't be right."

Rizzs returned to Seattle feeling as if the meetings had gone well. On November 17, 1991, his 37th birthday, Rizzs was making waffles for his son, Nick, at 7:00 in the morning, preparing to drive him to school when the phone rang.

"We want you to be our guy, Rick," boomed the unmistakable voice of Bo Schembechler on the other end of the phone.

Rizzs accepted the offer and got everything he had requested except a car—an ironic twist, he thought, because he was headed to the Motor City.

"When I hung up the phone my first thought was, 'Oh my gosh, what did I do? I love it here in Seattle. They've treated me so great.' It all happened so quickly," Rizzs remembers. "My life changed."

Not necessarily for the better.

Bob Rathbun, whom Rizzs came to "love like he was my brother," was hired as the No. 2 man, replacing the retiring Paul Carey.

The radio broadcast of the first exhibition game for the Tigers has more significance than for any other club because of Harwell's signature recital of a Biblical passage that signals the beginning of spring more than any calendar ever could.

> For lo, the winter is past,
> The rain is over and gone;
> The flowers appear on the earth;
> The time of the singing of the birds is come,
> And the voice of the turtle is heard
> In our land.

This would be the first spring in many years that the people of Michigan would not hear those reassuring words. This was news. This was big news.

When Rizzs and Rathbun settled into the booth, the eyes of scrutiny settled in on them, never to leave. A Detroit television camera's eyes were trained on the two new voices of Tigers baseball, and the camera's ears, a giant microphone, were in place as well. Columnists were in the booth to record the first words in their notebooks. Thirty seconds before the curtain was to be lifted on their careers, ESPN's Dick Vitale, a buddy of Rathbun's, burst into the booth with a loud hello.

The two new men said all the right things about replacing a legend. They made it clear they weren't going to try to copy Harwell's style, knowing that to do so would be to invite failure. Their styles were as different as could be from that of Harwell, which only intensified the criticism. Rizzs is talkative and given to excitement. Harwell believes dead air is a misnomer, believes that the sounds of the ballpark enliven a broadcast, and remains calm during big moments. Harwell avoids using statistics whenever possible. Rathbun relied on them heavily.

The day after getting through their first spring training broadcast without incident, Rizzs and Rathbun picked up the Detroit newspapers available in Lakeland. To their horror, they saw the *Detroit News* had decided to run a poll inviting listeners to share their thoughts on the new tandem's debut.

"I'm thinking, oh my God, then a few days later the results came out, and it came out to be about 50/50," Rizzs remembers. "I thought it was going to be about 90/10 against us. I told Bobby that's a victory for us. One teacher from a broadcasting school was one of the negative comments printed. He said I talked so much he felt like he wanted to grab a hammer and smash something. I called him and said I wanted to talk to his class, tell them how I got in the business. I wanted to tell them how I do a ballgame and how everybody's different."

During the regular season, Rizzs spoke to the class.

"During that speech I said, 'Sometimes when people hear me they feel like they want to grab a hammer and smash something, and that's OK. It takes a while before you get used to a new style.' I visited with the instructor afterward and he apologized," Rizzs recalls. "I told him not to worry about it. At that point, I decided I was going to try to make one fan at a time."

Ernie's spring shadow mushroomed when the tandem made its first appearance in the Tiger Stadium booth on Opening Day. A local radio station had printed 10,000 Ernie Harwell faces, attached them to a stick, and handed them out to fans entering the stadium.

As Rizzs and Rathbun walked from the parking lot to the stadium entrance on a brisk and bright April afternoon, one smiling Ernie Harwell face after another greeted them. A few hundred protesters stayed outside and refused to go in as a means of letting the Tigers know how they felt about the decision to fire the beloved broadcaster.

Throughout the game, an airplane with a "Where's Ernie?" streamer flew overhead. At one point, Rizzs stuck his head out of the booth, looked skyward, and aired his frustration: "He's in Cincinnati!" he said, as if speaking to the streamer. Harwell was working the Reds opener for CBS radio.

For nine innings, spectators chanted, "We want Ernie! We want Ernie! We want Ernie!"

Rizzs turned to Rathbun and said: "It can't get any worse than this. If we survive this, we'll be all right."

When Rizzs and Rathbun looked out to center field, they saw a gigantic banner that said, "We want Ernie!"

"It had to be 4 feet tall and 20 feet long," Rizzs remembers. "It was out there the whooooooooooooooooooooooole year. Bob and I stared at that all season long."

As tough as it was, it beat reading reviews in the newspaper or on the radio. Rathbun's reliance on stats inspired a joke making the rounds in Detroit. It went like this: "A statistics convention came to Detroit and they had Bob Rathbun as the keynote speaker. Ten minutes into his speech, a guy in the crowd stands up, says, 'Enough with the stats already!' and walks out."

The "good-bye baseball!" home-run call of Rizzs didn't make anybody forget Harwell's more understated "long gone!" call.

The waters were rough for Rizzs and Rathbun, and they didn't get any calmer when news broke that Mike Ilitch was buying the team from Tom Monaghan. Rumors spread that Ilitch, eager to show he cared about the sentiments of the team's following, wanted to bring back the most popular broadcaster in Tigers history.

Harwell was doing the CBS "Game of the Week" on radio every Saturday and had a schedule of 14 broadcasts of California Angels games. When the Tigers visited Anaheim as rumors of Harwell's possible return to the booth filled the newspapers and airwaves of Detroit, Harwell stopped by the booth to see Rizzs and Rathbun.

Seeking to break the ice, Harwell said something to the effect of, "I don't want you boys to be nervous about what you've been reading back home in the newspapers."

Rizzs, who had looked up to Harwell for years and had considered him a friend, spoke for himself and Rathbun: "To be honest with you, Ernie, we are concerned about what we've been reading. What are your plans? Do you plan on coming back?"

Replied Harwell: "I have to keep my options open. If I'm asked back, I'd have to consider it."

Remembers Rizzs: "I just looked at Bob and said, 'whoa!'"

After the ownership change was completed, Harwell was asked back and accepted the invitation. The plan was for him to come back in the radio booth for one final season, 1993. Rizzs was guaranteed six innings in his contract, and Harwell would do the middle three innings. Rizzs didn't like that setup because he didn't feel it was fair for Rathbun to be relegated to pregame and postgame duty. He gave up two of his innings to Rathbun.

Because Rizzs became protective of his "brother" Rathbun, his friendship with Harwell became strained during the 1993 season the three men spent sharing the booth. Harwell received a Siberian shoulder from Rathbun, who would, according to several Tigers employees, not even say hello to Harwell when they passed each other in the booth. When the press informed the public of the cold-shoulder treatment, Rathbun's already low popularity in Detroit took another hit.

From 1994 through 1998, Harwell worked out of the TV booth, and rather than finding the lighter schedule to his liking, he found it made the job more difficult.

"I felt like I lacked continuity, not being at every game," Harwell says. "I didn't feel like I really knew what was going on in the game."

He returned to the radio booth and a full schedule of 162 games for the 1999 season.

Meanwhile, Rizzs and Rathbun, who originally had signed three-year contracts with an option for a fourth year, had the fourth year guaranteed at the urging of Long. They never worked that fourth year, however. Frank Beckmann and Lary Sorenson replaced them before the 1995 season.

Rizzs returned to his job in Seattle, as the popular No. 2 man to Dave Niehaus, and Rathbun found work announcing in Atlanta.

Harwell had urged the public to give the two new men a chance when they first arrived on the Detroit scene. When things got particularly heated for them, both men had hoped Harwell would try to tell his friends in the press box to lighten up. Harwell, a writer all his life, knew better than to presume to tell other writers, friends or not, what opinions to write.

After Rizzs and Rathbun left Detroit, Harwell reached out to both men to melt the frost in their relationships. When the Mariners visited Tiger Stadium in 1998, Harwell visited Rizzs in the booth and brought tears to his eyes.

Jack Brickhouse, legendary voice of baseball in Chicago, had just passed away. Aware of how Rizzs had looked up to Brickhouse, Harwell stopped by to express condolences over his passing. Engineer Kevin Cremin and Niehaus were in the booth with Rizzs.

"Ernie worked his way between me and Dave and was standing off to my right shoulder," Rizzs remembers. "He leaned down a little bit and said, 'Rick, I'm sorry for the things I did or didn't do that made your job tougher than it should have been.' I said, 'Ernie, I appreciate that. I love you. Thank you very much.' We hugged and then he turned and walked out of the booth. We took a lot of crap there from writers for three years, but it got better the longer we were there.

When Ernie came in and said that, I felt closure. All the stuff we took for three years and we were trying our darndest to do the best job we possibly could. It just wasn't good enough for certain people. For Ernie to come in and say that was really special. I think the world of him, and I always will."

Harwell wrote a note with similar sentiments to Rathbun, who responded with a letter that included the words, "Apology accepted." Rathbun did not offer any apologies in the letter for the cold shoulder he showed Harwell during their year together in the Tiger Stadium booth.

Chapter 19

Mentoring Voices

When Toronto Blue Jays announcer Jerry Howarth told his two young sons, Ben and Joe, that they were going to "Ernie's house" many spring trainings ago, the boys couldn't wait to get there. When they arrived, rang the doorbell, and saw Ernie Harwell standing at the door, one of the boys burst into tears, unable to mask his disappointment.

"You said we were going to Ernie's house," the boy wailed at his father. "That's not Ernie!" The boy thought his father meant Ernie from *Sesame Street*, Bert's sidekick.

Ernie Harwell had the opposite effect on another son of a broadcaster. Duke Castiglione, son of Red Sox play-by-play man Joe Castiglione, was about to do his first sports talk show for New York 1, a cable network in New York City. Duke was so nervous that he feared he was about to vomit.

"Ernie called me and told me he went through the same thing when he started in Georgia," Duke remembers. "He told me everyone goes through that and told me everything was going to be fine. That was all

I needed to hear from him to feel better. I still call him for advice from time to time."

Duke's father also sought the comfort of Harwell's words when he was getting lambasted for being "boring" after his first year on the job in Boston, in 1983. Harwell told him what he tells all men new to a city: "People get comfortable with an announcer in time, and just being there a while can be the most important thing."

Generations of broadcasters have sought advice from Harwell, who vowed he would never turn his nose up at those trying to learn the trade when, as a young announcer, he witnessed others doing just that.

"He told me to keep doing what I was doing and not worry about the critics," Joe remembers. "I've always been impressed by his descriptive, low-key manner. He's never interfered with the game. And he doesn't dwell on the past like a lot of seniors do, and he certainly could with all he's experienced."

Through the 2001 season, Pat Hughes had done play-by-play for the Twins for one year, the Brewers for twelve, and the Cubs for six. He continues to seek the advice of Harwell.

"When the Cubs were 0–14 in 1997, I called Ernie to ask how I should be covering the losing streak," Hughes recalls. "He said: 'Don't make excuses for the team. You're covering a bad team, just lay it out there. Baseball fans are smart enough to see through you if you're making excuses anyway. If the pitcher gives up eight runs in three innings, that will speak for itself. You don't have to say he stunk. Everybody knows he stunk.' I'll never forget the four things Ernie felt were essential to be a good broadcaster. He told me you have to have the enthusiasm of a fan, the reactions of an athlete, the impartiality of an umpire, and the background knowledge of a writer."

Hughes and Harwell once discussed the finer points of the business at the English Room of the Pfister Hotel in Milwaukee.

"We discussed the difference between a ballplayer and a broadcaster," Hughes says. "For a ballplayer, every single minute he's out there, a guy on the other team is trying to make him look bad. As a broadcaster, if you really are on top of your game, there is nothing to stop you."

Ron Menchine was the last radio voice of the Washington Senators. He was in the booth for their final game September 30, 1971.

"I thought when I got the job in 1969 I had a lifetime job," Menchine says. "I never would have imagined they would be gone after my third year."

Menchine, then a sophomore at the University of Maryland, got his first big break when Harwell returned his phone call instead of blowing him off in 1954.

"He invited me out to the Stadium and made arrangements for me to tape record myself announcing baseball games in Baltimore," Menchine recalls. "Bob Wolff arranged for me to do the same thing at Senators games."

Menchine appreciates how Harwell has maintained his humility: "He never turned into one of those egomaniacal jerks who really think they're something special, and let's face it, there are a lot of those in television and radio."

Without the help of Harwell and Wolff, Menchine wouldn't have been able to tell stories that still make him laugh from his career in broadcasting.

Menchine called the Fiesta Bowl for NBC radio the year Marcus Allen won the Heisman Trophy for USC. The Trojans were beaten handily in the Fiesta Bowl by a Penn State team that featured Todd Blackledge at quarterback and Curt Warner at running back. Darryl Rogers, the former Arizona State coach, handled the color commentary.

After the announcers finished interviewing the players from Penn State, Rogers, still on the air, marveled at the intelligence of the Nittany Lions.

"That's the first time I've ever heard players from a college team interviewed where I didn't hear the words *you know* one time," Rogers said, busting up Menchine then and now.

Enberg Prospered Despite My Advice

Isn't it amazing how friendships sometimes develop?

In the early 1960s I got a phone call in my room at Los Angeles' Ambassador Hotel.

"My name is Dick Enberg," the caller said. "I'm from Michigan and I'm a teacher at Northridge College. Could I drop by and say hello?"

My answer was yes. Dick came by and we went out for an early dinner. Then I invited him to sit in our radio booth and watch the Tigers/Angels game. I discovered that he was from Armada, Michigan, and had attended Central Michigan University, where he had worked on the radio.

"I can do a better job than a lot of the announcers I hear today," he told me. "I'm teaching now and helping coach our Northridge baseball team, but I still believe I can be a competent announcer."

His words proved prophetic. Within a few years he had graduated from TV boxing and wrestling to become the network TV voice of the Los Angeles Rams.

Meanwhile Dick and I developed a friendship through the years. Later at a Los Angeles sportscasters' luncheon, Dick called me aside.

"I've got a chance to be the Angels announcer," he told me. "But I'm not sure I want to try it. With football I haven't been away from home very much, but the baseball schedule demands a lot of traveling. I have a good marriage and I don't know what effect travel might have on it."

"I wouldn't worry about travel," I told him. "A good marriage can certainly withstand those difficulties."

"Do you think I should take the Angels job?" he asked.
"I do," I told him. "Doing baseball day-to-day will be a great showcase for you. And it can lead to all kinds of success."

Dick took the Angels job and was an immediate success. His marriage was less successful; it ended in divorce before his first baseball season was over. So much for my marital advice!

But now Enberg is remarried and has gone on to become a premier network voice. He has broadcast outstanding sports events all over the world for NBC-TV and is regarded as one of the best in his profession.

I don't get to see him as much as I used to. But I remember those good dinner conversations in Los Angeles and Dick sitting in the booth during our Tigers broadcast.

He is a great announcer and deserves all the honors that have come his way. And next time, Dick, I'll do better with my advice on marriage.

—*E.H., June 1996*

Tom Davis, a veteran of the Baltimore media scene, approached Harwell in 1969 and asked him to critique tapes for him.

"It was like going to college learning from him," Davis says. "He felt like baseball was a romance between the pitcher and batters. He always felt the announcers didn't use the batters' and pitchers' names enough. A lot of guys just say, 'Here's the 2–2 pitch.' He says: 'Palmer's in the stretch. The 2–2 delivery to Robinson, he hits a fly ball to left.' He's always stayed to a basic game plan. He's always been very informative by staying very basic. He never has fallen into the trap of using the clichés. Another little thing he told me was to say, 'Groundball to second, Alomar picks it up and throws it to first,' not 'Groundball to Alomar.' Always say the position first. He has all these little techniques. He's a college of baseball knowledge."

Chuck Swirsky knew he wanted to be a sportscaster from the time he was five years old. When his father died when he was only 11, Swirsky had an uncle who lent his nephew a hand in trying to fulfill his career dream. He arranged for Chuck, who lived in Seattle, to spend his summers in Baltimore at the house of family friend Vince Bagli, a Baltimore sportscaster.

Bagli took Swirsky on trips to Memorial Stadium, where he would sit in the booth with Ernie Harwell and observe the pro at work. Harwell has written Swirsky monthly ever since, and the friends talk on the telephone weekly.

Swirsky fulfilled his dream and has worked for WGN in Chicago, WJR in Detroit, and, most recently, as the play-by-play man for Toronto Raptors games.

"He told me to report what you see in front of you, told me that in the sixth grade," Swirsky remembers. "The other things he told me were, be accurate, never assume, and be polite. I'll go into a game and I'll never assume. I'll go to the assistant coach and ask, is anybody hurt? I'll never be caught in a position on the air, if a player doesn't play, of not knowing why. When I was 11, Ernie told me to always go up and introduce yourself, don't wait for somebody to come to you. The other thing he told me is it never hurts to be nice."

It never hurt to be nice to colleagues from other stations, either. Rob Parker and Mike Stone, billed as "the Odd Couple" for the show they cohosted on the new all-sports radio station WDFN, were touched when Harwell told them he wanted to take them out for lunch. When they arrived at Thanasis in Windsor, the restaurant's marquee said: "Welcome to the Odd Couple."

To appreciate how long Harwell has been mentoring broadcasters, consider that Hall of Fame announcer Herb Carneal, the legendary voice of the Twins and a former partner of Harwell's in Baltimore, said, "Ernie really took me under his wing and showed me the ropes. I had never traveled until I traveled with Ernie. I stopped traveling in 1997, and Ernie's just catching his second wind."

Sometimes, Harwell helps young broadcasters by doing nothing more than setting a good example. Harwell doesn't take himself so seriously as to believe that anything that occurs during a baseball broadcast is worthy of panicking.

Kirk Gibson grew up listening to Harwell call Tigers games and got to know him well when he starred for the Tigers. The first time they were paired in the booth to call a game on TV, a technical screwup resulted in the camera staying on them when it was supposed to cut away. The intense Gibson stood there staring into space, fuming on the inside. The mellow Harwell delivered the exact punch line on the air that Gibson needed to hear to put the moment in perspective.

"Well, don't worry about it, Gibby," Harwell said, "three hundred million Chinese don't know what just happened."

Chapter 20

2001

Well into the 2001 exhibition season, uneasiness spread throughout the Mariners' organization. Many trained baseball eyes watched Ichiro Suzuki hit so softly they wondered how on earth he won seven batting titles in any league. The seven Gold Gloves he won in Japan, everyone could understand that. But the bat they had heard so much about, where was the bat? The Mariners needed a new star to soothe the loss of the great Alex Rodriguez to the Texas Rangers, a baseball team in football country. They needed Ichiro to be the guy. The more they saw him slap the ball with so little authority, the more they worried they could never replace A-Rod, whose record 10-year, $252 million contract sent shock waves throughout the professional sports industry. They doubted themselves for believing Ichiro could be at least a small part of replacing baseball's best player. He didn't look like "one of the five best baseball players in the world," as Mets manager Bobby Valentine had called him a few years earlier. Valentine has more enemies than most in baseball, but even they acknowledge he has a wealth of knowledge and is a sound baseball man. Valentine has no greater strength than evaluating talent and accurately projecting performance. Could Valentine really be that far off base? Could Major League Baseball really be that much better than the version of professional baseball played in Japan?

Ichiro's mediocre play gave rise to such questions. Veteran Mariners manager Lou Piniella, never accused of having too much patience, grew antsy and asked hitting coach Gerald Perry to tell Ichiro he needed to start driving the ball. Perry did as he was told, and Ichiro responded in a universal language. He winked at Perry. The hitting coach could live long enough to grow confused enough to forget his phone number, his address, his dog's name. He never will live long enough to forget that wink. The next day against the A's in Peoria, Ichiro smoked a home run and two doubles. It was at that moment that the mythical powers attributed to this marvelous baseball player completed their cross-continental trip. In no time, the questions surrounding Ichiro changed.

People began asking: Can baseball really be as easy as this man makes it look? Did he really make that throw from the right-field corner to third base on the fly and with that much velocity and such a small humpback? Has the time come to scout more ardently in Japan, once thought to be a fertile ground for only pitching talent? Have body stereotypes fooled scouts into thinking some great Japanese players don't have the builds to make the transition to the major leagues, packed with Paul Bunyanesque sluggers?

Reggie Jackson—has God ever blended a greater mix of intelligence and athletic ability in one man's DNA than in this complex man's?—looks at the muscles of so many of today's hitters and feels sorry for them well in advance of their woes. Jackson built his muscles a natural way, with good genes and rigorous conditioning exercises.

"They're going to get into their fifties and weird things are going to start happening to their bodies—tumors, other mysterious ailments," Reggie says, while listening to baseballs crash into seats during an especially sunny, particularly loud batting practice. "They won't have any idea why. I'll know why."

Home runs beget attention, television ratings, dollars, macho points, even wins. Home-run lust so overpowers some baseball players that vague, long-range health risks become incidental. Baseball bans many performance-enhancing drugs, but the ban is as meaningful as outlawing ice fishing in the Sahara because baseball doesn't test for the banned substances. It's an honor system. Home-run lust, shared by owners who enjoy the financial benefits of hooking the public, comes first. Faraway health fears place second. Honor comes third.

Not with Ichiro. His talent is genuine, not enhanced by anything but the adrenaline that must flow in large quantities, based on his penchant for delivering his best performances when the stage is the grandest, the lights the brightest, the competition the most skilled.

Ichiro's slight frame and slender build make him stand out among the behemoths. Especially when wearing sunglasses, which he always does in street clothes, Ichiro emits more the aura of a rock star than a ballplayer. He might not look the part, but he plays the part as completely as anyone in the game. He doesn't hit many home runs, though it takes only witnessing him in batting practice, where his power is on display, to realize that if he wanted to go that route, he could hit many more in games. He hits them deep into the seats in batting practice, much the way Wade Boggs did. He slaps them to all fields in games, much the way Boggs did. As a hitter, Ichiro reminds many of a young Rod Carew.

In the 2001 All-Star Game played in front of an adoring public at Seattle's Safeco Field, Ichiro beat out an infield hit and did so in such a manner as to enhance his mythical aura. His last stride looked elongated, as if he had the power to stretch his limbs the way cartoon characters do on a whim. A Seattle baseball public that once cheered with such verve for Ken Griffey Jr., A-Rod, and Randy Johnson has taken passion to another level in its reverence for Ichiro, a star so esteemed that all references need only include one name.

Tape Trick Is a Story That Sticks

Reporter to New York Giants rookie, circa 1920: "Are you married?"

Rookie: "You'll have to ask Mr. McGraw."

This terse exchange illustrates the control and power a big-league manager once wielded over his players. Today, it is different. Managers and coaches are not complete masters over their charges anymore. A new technique is required.

Here, for example, is a story a modern big-league coach told me about how he corrected one of his players (not wanting to reveal the player's identity, I've given him a false name):

"We had a shortstop named George Zender who was playing awful. He couldn't concentrate. My manager told me to work with him.

"A big-leaguer doesn't want to be taught. Your presentation has to make the player think it's his idea. You can't say, 'This is the way to do it,' or 'I have a suggestion for you.' The player won't listen. If I tell him he's not concentrating, he'll just blow me off. He'll say: 'I've been playing this game 18 years and I know what I'm doing. Leave me alone.'

"So here's what I do.

"I know exactly when George comes to the ballpark every day. I make it a point for three straight days to walk by him with two videotapes in my hand. I say, 'Hi, George,' and keep walking. On the fourth day, George can't contain his curiosity. 'What are you doing?' he asks me.

"'I've got these tapes of you in action,' I tell him. 'One when you won your Gold Glove. The other for your last few games. I can't find anything wrong with the way you're fielding the ball.'

"'I told you, there's nothing wrong,' George says.

"'It's not really worth showing to you,' I tell him.

> " 'Oh, come on, tell me,' he says.
> " 'Well, when you won your Gold Glove,' I explain, 'you always looked at the ball a little bit longer after you fielded it. Now you're lifting your head too soon before you throw. But it's so close you really can't tell the difference.'
> " 'Oh, yeah?' he says. 'I bet I can tell the difference.'
> "Now I can show him the videos. He takes a look and tells himself he has discovered his flaw. He makes the correction and begins to play better.
> "I have accomplished my purpose in three ways:
> "1. I didn't burden him with a lot of teaching about mechanics.
> "2. I gave him an excuse he could adopt as his own.
> "3. I told him to concentrate without mentioning the word.
> "Let me make a confession. I never looked at those videos. I sat in the video room for three days with the lights off. If George had ever checked the room, he would have discovered my web of intrigue."
>
> —E.H., July 2000

Not unlike Yankees shortstop Derek Jeter, Ichiro is one of those instinctive athletes who forever is in the right place at the right time making the right bang-bang decision. Such ballplayers influence the outcomes of games more profoundly than statistics could ever capture. This is not to say that Ichiro didn't have big numbers; he most certainly did. He finished his first season with a batting title—he won seven of those in Japan—and a stolen-base crown.

Ichiro sparked the Mariners to a record-setting start and finish. The M's won a major league record 116 games. His throws from the outfield, so accurate and delivered with such stunning velocity, overshadowed his work at the plate. And the public didn't know a great deal more about the man behind the game at season's end than was known about him on Opening Day. He revealed little of himself in interviews through an interpreter with members of the American media, and for a time, he even stopped talking to the horde of Japanese media that followed his every move.

Yet when Ichiro made his first visit to Comerica Park, one member of the Detroit media didn't need to introduce himself. Ichiro sent word well ahead of time through an intermediary that he wanted to meet legendary Tigers broadcaster Ernie Harwell on the day the Mariners first visited Detroit on July 31, 2001. The meeting occurred three days after closer Todd Jones singled out Harwell as the man he would miss most if he was traded to the Twins.

The intermediary who arranged the Ichiro meeting was a gentleman named Brad Lefton. A freelance writer and documentary filmmaker, Lefton splits his time living between Japan and the United States. Lefton brokered a deal with Ichiro that gave him closer access than anyone to the mythical aura that surrounded baseball's best story of the year. Ichiro granted Lefton and his film crew access in exchange for having unedited copies of all the tapes. Ichiro has a rich appreciation for major league baseball's great tradition, and he wanted his entire first year on film as a keepsake.

Lefton explains how it came about that this superstar so famous that in a poll of the most recognizable figure in Japan, the emperor finished second, one spot behind Ichiro, wanted to make sure he met a broadcaster from Detroit.

He says he first met Harwell in early September of 1999. He was on assignment for a magazine that is the closest facsimile Japan has to *Sports Illustrated*. It is entitled *Sports Graphic Number*.

"The article was about the final month of Tiger Stadium and about Ernie Harwell," Lefton remembers. "I spent the whole day with him."

Lefton watched in amazement as a procession of players from the visiting team came up to Harwell to shake his hand, to ask him how he'd been doing, to wish him well.

"All right, Brad, what do you say we get going up to the press box?" Harwell suggested.

"Oh, great," Lefton answered. "One of the best parts about coming to Tiger Stadium is riding the elevator with Sara Simpson." Simpson is the elderly elevator woman at Tiger Stadium and then Comerica Park.

Baseball fans across the globe would die to have the access to ballplayers that is afforded members of the media.

"Do you get to talk to the players?" fans repeatedly ask baseball writers.

"No," baseball writers routinely answer, "We don't get to talk to the players, we *have* to talk to them. It's our job."

Given the choice, most visiting baseball writers would prefer to ride the elevator up and down over and over in the hours leading up to games at Comerica Park. That way they would get to spend more time with the sweet and beloved Sara Simpson.

"Oh yeah, Sara's a doll, but we're not going to see her today," Harwell told Lefton.

Remembers Lefton: "I thought, 'Oh no, what happened to her.'"

"I don't ride the elevator," Harwell told Lefton. "We're going to walk up."

"I look down at his feet and he's wearing sneakers," remembers Lefton, who is built more like modern home-run hitters than like Harwell or Ichiro. "We climbed up through the seating area, across the catwalk, and into the old radio booth at Tiger Stadium. He lost me twice on the way there. I couldn't keep up with him he was walking so fast. He kept on getting stopped by people in the crowd, and I still couldn't keep up with him. His energy was unbelievable. It seemed like everyone who was there stopped him to shake hands or ask for an autograph or pose for a picture. He gave time to everyone who stopped him. He acted like it was the first time anyone ever stopped him each time, acted so grateful to be asked for an autograph."

The radio booth at Tiger Stadium was like no other. It was small and in some ways primitive. And it was the best radio booth ever. It hovered over the field by itself and was closer to home plate than any other before or since. On days when crowds were small, and there were many such days and nights, players standing on second base could hear the man in the booth identifying the hometown of the lucky fan who caught the foul ball.

The booth was not unlike the man who sat in it all those years in that it wasn't enhanced by flowery trimmings, and it brought the listener closer to the games than any other; it brought the listener the best seat in the house via the most dulcet pipes in the house.

During his day with Harwell, Lefton witnessed streams of people congregating at the catwalk that led to the booth, staking out a position in hopes of chatting with him during the middle innings.

Lefton chronicled the day and the rich histories of Harwell and Tiger Stadium. During spring training preceding Ichiro's rookie season, Lefton gave him a stack of newspaper and magazine clippings.

"They were mostly stories about the ballparks we were going to go to and some of the people he might have a chance to meet along the way," Lefton says. "He read it, took it all in, and we sat down and talked about the things we'd like to do. One of the first things Ichiro told me was that when we go to Detroit, I want to meet that announcer."

The meeting took place on the grass next to the batting cage, the third-easiest place to find Harwell at a ballpark, ranking behind the radio booth and the ice cream stand.

"Ice cream is his weakness," Lulu says. "He found a new flavor that he really likes: Chunky Monkey."

Harwell and Ichiro didn't talk about ice cream. Here's how the conversation went, with the help of Lefton acting as translator:

Harwell: "How do you like our new ballpark?"

Ichiro: "Too big."

Harwell: "No, it's tailor-made for you. (Pointing) Jim Thome hit one between the flagpole and the Al Kaline statue. And it's shorter down the right-field line here than it is at Fenway, so that ought to be good for you."

Ichiro nodded with an expression that suggested his opinion of the park was changing for the better.

Harwell: "It's been very nice meeting you. I wish you great success and we have great expectations for you."

Ichiro: "If I could contribute to major league baseball in my career only a fraction of what you have contributed, it would be very meaningful."

Lefton says he thinks, "Ernie was very touched by Ichiro saying that."

Lefton is aware Harwell is not a schmaltzy man, so he was moved himself by seeing how much that meant to the veteran broadcaster.

Lefton laughs when he thinks of Harwell's response to a question during his original interview of him.

"I asked Ernie what memento he wanted to take with him from Tiger Stadium," Lefton recalls. "I said it with a completely straight face and complete sincerity. I expected him to say the chair he sat in all those years, or maybe the microphone."

He said neither.

"The thing I want most is the urinal in the visiting clubhouse," Harwell told a shocked Lefton.

"Of all the things you could take from Tiger Stadium, why would you want that?" Lefton asked.

"Because every Hall of Famer from Babe Ruth to Mark McGwire used it," Harwell answered.

Lefton saw Harwell a couple of months later and asked him if he ever got the urinal.

"No," a disappointed Harwell reported. "Lulu wouldn't let me bring it home. I tried to tell her how nutritious it would be for her garden. I told her what a good thing it would be for her roses, but she didn't think it was a very good idea." Somehow, their marriage survived that disagreement and the Harwells celebrated their 60th wedding anniversary in the summer of 2001.

Harwell could have gone on and on listing the names of baseball greats who also relieved themselves in the urinal of the closet-sized visiting clubhouse at Tiger Stadium. Only one of those all-time greats can boast three seasons of at least 60 home runs.

Sammy Sosa's 2001 season was packed with thrills. He reached the rare home run milestone for the third time in four seasons and played a better right field and ran the bases more aggressively than he had in years. His Cubs contended until fading at the end. Already an icon with Chicagoans and Latin Americans throughout the country, Sosa won the hearts of all Americans when he once carried the American flag during his signature sprint through the Wrigley Field outfield at the beginning of games.

Sosa will remember one more special day when he looks back on his latest special season. He will remember the day a familiar old face captivated a room full of millionaires by reciting a poem.

Cubs manager Don Baylor and Harwell first met when Baylor was a rookie with the Baltimore Orioles. Much to the delight of Rochesterians treated to one of the greatest minor league teams in history, the 1971 Red Wings, Baylor and Bobby Grich waited longer than most stars to get to the big leagues because the Orioles were so loaded. Baylor quickly learned that part of making it to the big leagues is meeting the friendly announcer from Detroit.

Harwell and Baylor developed a friendship over the years, and it spiked to a new level when they were represented by the same attorney, Gary Spicer, who brings them together for dinners whenever possible.

One such dinner occurred when the Cubs visited Detroit to play the Tigers in midseason. After the first game of the series, Spicer took out

Baylor and his wife Becky, Ernie and Lulu Harwell, and Cubs coaches Sandy Alomar and Gene Glynn.

During the dinner, Baylor asked Harwell to recite "A Game for All America" for Alomar and Glynn. Harwell obliged.

"Those guys were blown away," Baylor remembers with a smile from behind his desk at Wrigley Field. "The next day, on short notice, I asked Ernie if he could come over to the clubhouse after chapel. Frank Tanana was having chapel on the other side. I started out telling them about Kaline and Horton, those names on the wall. Look to the right and you see a Harwell. This is Ernie Harwell. He's alive. I told them that because every time you see someone on the wall, you think they're gone. Here's one who's alive and well. They were in awe. Joe Girardi and Sammy Sosa and all those guys who played in the American League, they all know Ernie. He's always had time to talk to people, no matter what."

Baylor remembers Harwell's message to the Cubs: "You're playing in a great era of baseball. You're one of the 800 players privileged to play this game. You're the best in this game. Nobody's better."

Not standard fare for a man in his eighties.

"Ever since I've known him that's the way he's talked," Baylor says. "Always positive things. Never negative things. Never players are making too much money. I've never heard that from him. Never. When he came in our clubhouse when I was a young player in Baltimore, he came over and introduced himself and he was a fixture in the clubhouse. Everybody knew him, and you didn't have anything to hide from him. And he was always talking about baseball. The changes have driven a lot of baseball guys out of the game. Earl Weaver and Gene Mauch always talk about modern-day players coming in and the changeover. You hear people say: 'When I first came up to the big leagues guys were reading *Sporting News*. Now it's the *Wall Street Journal*.' It's true. A lot of today's players don't know who's pitching tomorrow or who played before them. Any time I'm around Ernie I'm always picking his brain about how it was back in the old days. I was always interested in that, especially when Ernie talks about Jackie Robinson."

Baylor points to his left, to a framed picture on the wall of Jackie Robinson's first at-bat, a gift from legendary Cubs clubhouse manager Yosh Kawano.

"Ernie grew up in the South," Baylor says. "Pee Wee Reese grew up in the South. But you could never tell they were from the South unless you heard them talk. You couldn't tell by they way they treated you, as a minority player. They didn't really care. They didn't see color. And Ernie doesn't see the color of your uniform either. With Ernie, if you're on the other ballclub, it's no big deal."

The corkboard behind his desk is empty but for two items: a Cubs pocket schedule and a copy of Harwell's "The Game for All America." Baylor takes it down and begins reading from it:

"Baseball is a spirited race of man against man, reflex against reflex. A game of inches. Every heroic, every failing is seen and cheered—or booed. And then becomes a statistic. In baseball, democracy shines its clearest. Here the only race that matters is the race to the bag. The creed is the rulebook. Color is something to distinguish one team's uniform from another."

"That's poetry," Baylor says.

When Baylor had Harwell talk to his players, he asked him to recite his definition of baseball, which marked the first time Harwell had done so in a major league clubhouse. Prior to that, he had only recited it in the clubhouse of the minor league West Michigan Whitecaps, invited to do so by manager Jim Colborn, the same man who years later discovered Ichiro for the Mariners.

"They were mesmerized, Sammy Sosa, some of the newer guys, everybody was just taken by him," Baylor recalls of Harwell's recital.

Afterward, Sosa and several other players had Harwell autograph baseballs for them.

"Players really respect him," Baylor says. "He's not taking rips at players. He's like Red Barber. It's the game. It's about the game. It's about all the little nuances of the game, the hit-and-runs, the missed signs. That's the way Ernie and my other guy in Los Angeles, Vin Scully, call a game. They can describe a game almost like you're sitting there. 'And the man from Saginaw catches that foul ball.' You got to be kidding me? How great is that? Ernie Harwell and Vin Scully can make changing a flat tire sound exciting."

Harwell believes the play-by-play man's role is to report the news of the game and news about players to the extent it affects their play. He does not view reporting gossip of trade rumors and other such developments as within his realm.

"When Billy Martin was managing the Tigers he would tell me about how they were looking to get rid of this player or trade for that player," Harwell says. "I told him not to tell me those things, because if it leaked out I didn't want him thinking I was the one who leaked it."

In part because of that approach, Harwell is able to talk loosely with players.

"Players not playing, a lot of them are inside listening to the announcers," Baylor says. "They form opinions if they like the announcer or don't like the announcer, based in part on if he's taking shots at teammates. Ernie tells you about the game. He'll say he's 0 for 4, but it's not a rip. It's never: 'How in the world can he swing at that pitch?' It's: 'He went after a bad one.' Players notice that because as a player you know there are times when you can go after a pitch that's bad, but it's not like you recognized it was a bad pitch when you swung at it."

Harwell's exalted status in baseball stretches well beyond the borders of Michigan, far beyond the Midwest, as one late-night phone call he received late in the 2001 season proved.

On the night Barry Bonds broke Mark McGwire's single-season home-run record, Ernie and Lulu didn't stay up to watch him do it.

It was past midnight when the phone rang, and Harwell pulled an old line out of his memory banks: "That's all right. I had to get up to answer the phone anyway."

It was someone from one of the many branches of the Fox empire, calling for Harwell's perspective on the inflated home-run totals and whether that tainted the record. It did not, Harwell answered.

"Take records as they come," Harwell said. "Babe could have bounced balls for home runs. He had a short fence at Polo Grounds and at Yankee Stadium. There are a lot of factors. To me, a record is a record. You have to accept what the circumstances are at the time. They used to say about Joe Louis, 'How can you say he's great? He boxes bums.' Well, those were the only guys he could box at the time. I do feel home runs are getting too frequent and have lost some of their appeal. There was a time when pitching was so dominant and that changed. I think we'll get another cycle and the home runs will drop to where maybe 30 or 35 home runs would be a good target for a home-run hitter. Fifty home runs should be extraordinary, and it's not that way anymore, and we just have to accept that for now."

Harwell has been around long enough to know not to use the word *unprecedented*. When talented young left-hander Rick Ankiel of the Cardinals experienced outrageous control problems in 2001, Harwell was reminded of having seen it before. Kevin "Hot Sauce" Saucier was untouchable coming out of the Tigers bullpen in 1981. He couldn't find home plate in 1982, and couldn't find it ever again.

When the mother of Northwestern football player Rashidi Wheeler filed a wrongful death lawsuit after her asthmatic son died during pre-season conditioning drills, Harwell dipped into his clip files to offer a little historical perspective.

He pulled out a story he had written for the *Saturday Evening Post* about an incident that happened 21 years before he was born. The headline to the story: "HOW A WOMAN SAVED SOUTHERN FOOTBALL."

Von Gammon, an 18-year-old player for the University of Georgia, died of a brain concussion October 30, 1897, one day after suffering the injury in a game against the University of Virginia played in Atlanta. Harwell noted city councils from Atlanta to Chicago moved to abolish the sport. Georgia disbanded its team. The Georgia state legislature passed a bill that banned football. As the bill awaited the governor's signature, the deceased player's mother appealed to the state legislature, the governor, and the university trustees to save the sport. She wrote a letter detailing her son's love of football. "Grant me the right to request that my boy's death not be used to defeat the most cherished object of his life," Roslind Burns Gammon wrote. She signed the letter "Von Gammon's mother." Still on display at the University of Georgia is a bronze plaque commemorating both Von Gammon and his mother. The plaque was a gift from the University of Virginia.

If Harwell calls a game in which a team wins and doesn't get a hit, he'll know not to call that unprecedented. He announced just such a game already, on April 30, 1967, when Steve Barber and Stu Miller, pitching for the Orioles, combined to no-hit the Tigers and lost 2–1. Barber walked 10 and hit two batters before being removed in the ninth with two outs. Harwell has covered seven other no-hitters: Rex Barney (September 9, 1948), Hoyt Wilhelm (September 2, 1958), Joel Horlen (September 10, 1967), Steve Busby (April 27, 1973), Nolan Ryan (July 15, 1973), Jack Morris (April 7, 1984), and Randy Johnson (June 2, 1990). If Harwell calls a no-hitter in the first decade of the 21st century, it will extend his streak to seven consecutive decades of calling a no-hitter. If he calls a perfect game, it will be his first.

The wisdom Harwell can share based on life experiences stretches beyond the baseball diamond. After the September 11, 2001, attacks on the World Trade Center towers and the Pentagon left the nation and so many of its citizens in a state of emotional inertia, Harwell was able to reassure them that the haze would be lifted.

"That feeling of helplessness, of floating in limbo," Harwell noted. "Things you ordinarily would do lie there and pile up. It's the same feeling I had when Pearl Harbor was bombed. I had been sent down to Jacksonville in early December to cover the baseball convention. I went down with an engineer and interviewed Connie Mack, Joe McCarthy, and Lou Boudreau. I was excited about getting back and putting it on the air. On Sunday, Pearl Harbor happened, and by the time we put the stuff on the air on Monday, it was meaningless to me. After the initial shock, you realize life's got to go on and you begin to return to your normal routine."

Harwell's normal routine remains working 162 regular-season Tigers games a year.

Chapter 21

Forever Young

Lulu Harwell awakens slowly from a slumber and hears the soothing racket that signals all is right in her world: clack, clack, clack, clack, clack. The sound of a whirring jump rope hitting the floor tells Miss Lulu her husband has awakened and is partaking in his morning ritual: Ernie jumps rope 300 consecutive times and then heads for the trampoline, jumps on his left foot and then his right, forever belying that birth certificate that reads January 25, 1918.

Soon he will be on his way out the door to read to schoolchildren, one of his favorite off-season pastimes. He is signed on to broadcast 162 regular-season games and a full slate of exhibition games at the age (is just a number) of 84. Ernie and Lulu, who have seven grandchildren, were looking forward to spring training for more than baseball reasons. They were anticipating the birth of their second great-grandchild.

Harwell's special gift of dwelling in the present and not yearning for what he sarcastically refers to as "the good old days" so enriches those moments when someone rekindles a fond memory. One such moment came when he received a letter dated September 17, 2001, from a Reisterstown, Maryland, man by the name of Richard Liebno.

Dear Mr. Harwell,

I have written (and rewritten) this letter so many times I hope I can finally get it right.

I write to thank you (at last) for a great kindness you performed 40-plus years ago when you were announcing for the Orioles.

I was eight or nine years old and had suffered an attack of rheumatic fever, which confined me to a wheelchair for the summer. My grandfather's company had season tickets (mezzanine box!) to Memorial Stadium, and he arranged to get me to a Yankee (hated them then, hate them now) game for my birthday. I didn't quite understand why we left for the stadium so early, but I accepted that elevator rides were necessary.

When we arrived, I got the VIP treatment to our seats and then got to meet you. Wow. Pretty cool. My friends (we had six seats) were really impressed. And then you took my wheelchair (and me) on a tour of the bowels of the stadium. The next thing I knew we were in the Orioles (third-base) dugout, and I was meeting all my heroes and getting autographs. Brooks, Marv, Willie, Gus; I was in heaven.

I still have a stuffed dog I named Gus (big and just as slow). You then wheeled me out (I was on cloud nine) and took me over to cloud ten, the Yankee dugout. Whereas the Orioles were my heroes, the Yankees were icons. Meeting Whitey Ford, Mickey Mantle, Bobby Richardson, and all these other larger-than-life athletes will always be an incredible highlight of my life. My only regret is, over time, I lost my autograph book. And you, in your compassion, made it all possible.

In subsequent years, when I traveled, I always tried to find Tigers games on the radio to hear your voice. And each time, I smiled and silently thanked you for that most magical day in Baltimore. It's a memory that I treasure greatly, and I owe it all to you.

I realize that to you it was a small thing, but I just wanted you to know how BIG it was to an eight-year-old. Thank you for creating one of the most memorable days of my life.

Respectfully,

Richard Liebno

The nicest surprise of 2001 for Harwell came on the day Harwell made a speaking appearance at the Hall of Fame in Cooperstown in November.

An elderly African-American gentleman in a wheelchair looked up at Harwell and said, "Hello, Ernie. I'm your old friend."

"Oh, what's your name?"

"Jocko Maxwell."

Harwell could hardly believe his ears. Maxwell, 93, had authored the first piece of fan mail ever sent to Harwell. That letter started a pen-pal correspondence that would stretch for decades. Maxwell had a radio show in New York way back when, but the two men never met until making each other's years on that special day in Cooperstown.

Eleven winters after his press conference to announce the bizarre decision to let him go, Harwell's popularity as a corporate spokesman is at an all-time high. From a financial standpoint, the greatest thing that ever happened to him was getting fired at the age of 73.

Gary Spicer, Harwell's attorney and longtime friend, spearheaded for Harwell the difficult transition from making appearances gratis to charging for them once his firing hiked an already high demand for his presence, voice, and name.

Some of My Favorite Things

This is purely personal.

If I had a life to live again, I would: Learn to be a handyman. . . . Eat more ice cream and less bran. . . . Read more of the Bible and less modern fiction. . . . Get to know the hotel managers. . . . Do more sightseeing when I travel. . . . Walk in the woods more often. . . . Try to be kind instead of correct.

I might be crazy, but I like a lot of foods others can't stand. My list includes okra, figs, prunes, grits, broccoli, spinach, and grapefruit. My favorite food is corn bread. Corn on the cob is a close second. My least favorite food is liver.

I like: dogs and cats, quiet dinners, sunrises, radios, popcorn, movies, good conversation, soft-spoken ladies, kids with baseball gloves, Thanasis Restaurant in Windsor, walking into a baseball stadium and seeing the green grass and the bright sunshine, letters from old schoolmates or friends from my years in the marines, baseball in the daytime, a smile and a kind word.

I don't like: stamp machines, pushy autograph seekers, plastic packages wrapped too tightly, artificial turf, bad grammar, people who can't get past "the good old days," newspaper coin boxes, rain delays, fried food, people who don't identify themselves on the phone . . . and those who give you only their first name, self-serve gas pumps, intricate telephone-answering systems with no human voices, presectioned grapefruit, media overkill, lumpy oatmeal, long-winded speakers, people who end statements with "OK?", ethnic jokes, committee meetings, highway construction and detours, envelopes that won't stick.

Here are some of my favorites. Big-league city: Milwaukee. Hotel: Pfister in Milwaukee. On-the-road restaurant: Hausner's in Baltimore. Ballpark: three-way tie among Coors Field, Camden Yards, and Jacobs Field. Tree: dogwood. Flower: rose. Writer: John Updike. Pop singer: Nat King Cole. Movie: *My Cousin Vinny*. Song: "Vincent."

—*E.H., July 1998*

"What better spokesperson can you have from an integrity standpoint, and you get his voice as part of the package," Spicer says, explaining why Harwell is in such high demand. "Ernie and I arrived in Appleton, Wisconsin, for an appearance of his and the windchill was 40 below zero. We assumed it would be canceled. It not only was not canceled, they had TV monitors wired to other parts of the building to accommodate the overflow crowd. His income outside of baseball has increased 20-fold from what it was before the termination."

Harwell's presence at Comerica Park is even more noticeable than it was at Tiger Stadium. A recording of his voice welcomes patrons to the main entrance of the park, and the huge black-and-white photograph there is not of Ty Cobb or Al Kaline, but rather of a much younger Ernie Harwell talking into an enormous microphone.

Unpleasant memories of the termination remain a sore spot with men and women who grew up listening to the Tigers on the radio, from inner-city Detroit to the Upper Peninsula, and every picnic in between.

"Ernie Harwell is a sound of summer in Detroit," says *USA Today* baseball writer Chuck Johnson, who was born in 1954. "It's been that way for as long as I can remember."

Johnson was reared six blocks north of Grand Boulevard on Marston, between Beaubien and Brush.

271

"Twenty-five-cent bus ride and a nickel transfer," Johnson remembers fondly of the trip to Tiger Stadium.

The other sounds of summer in the Detroit of Johnson's youth: "Motown. The Supremes, the Temptations. The Four Tops. Marvin Gaye. The Contours. You don't remember the Contours?"

Bent over slightly at the waist, his left fingers snapping, Johnson breaks into song with a high-pitched voice that whistles him back in time: "Do you love me?"

"Those guys, Tom Monaghan and Bo Schembechler, they just proved they didn't know what Tiger baseball is all about," Johnson says, with more than a hint of disdain. "Ernie Harwell is Tiger baseball. When I first heard the news they were trying to fire him I was like, 'What? They've got to be crazy. Fire Ernie Harwell.' Even people who didn't go to the games still listened to Ernie Harwell, a sound of summer in Detroit."

The exact evolution of the worst public relations disaster in Detroit sports history remains a mystery.

"It doesn't matter," Harwell says. "All that matters is everyone is forgiven."

Sometimes sad eyes talk louder than words. One gets the sense that if one day Harwell bounced off the trampoline to pick up the phone and heard a familiar voice from the past calling from Arizona, or a famous voice from the University of Michigan campus, he sure would appreciate the closure the voices would bring.

At the same time, he won't let the mystery consume him. Life's too good for that. The sun shines too brightly in the Florida springs, and the games that stretch across the summer pack too many thrills for an eternal optimist and lover of baseball to obsess on anything negative.

To run into Harwell is to run into a happy man, as Mike Siano of MLB Radio discovered a few springs ago.

"I'm surprised to see you down here," Siano told Harwell. "Why are you here so early?"

"Oh, I don't know," Harwell said with a smile. "Maybe they think I need the practice."

And then the old man blessed with the young spirit rocked onto his tiptoes.

"Ball one . . ."

He settled back onto his heels and then rocked back onto his tiptoes once more.

"Ball two . . ."

Afterword

grew up in Little Rock, Arkansas, and for as long as I can remember I've been interested in baseball history. I remember that when Babe Ruth died in 1948, I cut the story out of the newspaper. I had to write a booklet about what I wanted to be when I grew up for an eighth-grade assignment. I wrote about how I wanted to become a baseball player. But it wasn't until I got to know Ernie Harwell—we met in 1955 when I broke into the big leagues with the Orioles as a teenager—that I realized how little I knew about baseball's past. My sense of history was a drop in the ocean compared to Ernie's.

Ernie invited me to his and Lulu's house when the twins were just babies, and he showed me his collection of *Baseball Guides* and *Sporting News* magazines. I couldn't believe my eyes. He must have had every *Sporting News* ever published. I felt like I was in the presence of a real baseball historian.

When I broke into the big leagues a few people really looked after me. George Kell, who was also from Arkansas, was one of them, and Ernie Harwell was another. I'll never forget that.

The public's reaction when the Tigers decided they were going to fire Ernie just shows you what kind of an impact he has on people. When you're playing, you never think about the impact you have. But when I was a broadcaster I felt it when I heard from people—like the little old lady in Cumberland, Maryland, who stayed up past midnight to catch the broadcast of the Orioles game from the west coast.

Ernie Harwell is arguably the best who ever announced, right there with anyone who ever did baseball games. And he's a warm, wonderful gentleman. He never has changed. And his voice has never changed. I guarantee that if you sat someone down who was unfamiliar with baseball players names and told them to listen to Ernie calling a game from 1955 and another one from today, that listener wouldn't be able to tell you which game was played 47 years ago. That's how ageless his voice is, how timeless his approach is. The only thing I can figure is that he found the fountain of youth and did more than drink; he must have gargled from it too. He's always been someone who has been able to come up with the right word for anything that might be happening—not only for baseball, but for anything.

Even before I met him, he already had experienced so much baseball history. He was traded for a player, started out under Red Barber, was in the booth when Bobby Thomson hit that home run.

Here he is, more than a half century later, still with that perfect pitch. He hasn't lost a thing off his fastball. How many of us can say that?

—Brooks Robinson
January 2002

Appendix

The Ernie Harwell Sports Collection

In 1965 and again in 1968, Detroit Tigers Hall of Fame broadcaster Ernie Harwell donated his personal collection of sports material and memorabilia to the Burton Historical Collection at the Detroit Public Library. Initially heavily focused on baseball, the Ernie Harwell Sports Collection has grown to become the second largest public collection of sports history in the country. The collection consists of over 40,000 photographs, 6,000 baseball cards, 2,000 books, assorted yearbooks, scorebooks, programs, guides, and millions of clippings in an extensive assortment of subject headings.

Individual and team photos of players, managers, and broadcasters make up the most often used part of the collection. Photographs of Ty Cobb were used in the 1994 movie *Cobb*, starring Tommy Lee Jones, and in countless books, newspapers, and different kinds of periodicals, including *Sports Illustrated* and *Michigan History Magazine*. Practically everyone who ever wore spikes is represented here.

The baseball card collection, with thousands of cards, traces the development of those precious pieces of cardboard from the cigarette cards of the 1880s to the ever-popular Topps cards of the 1960s. The collection contains a near-complete run of Spalding and Reach baseball guides, as well as the DeWitt, LaJoie, and Beadles books. Yearbooks, scorecards, and programs cover every team and period of baseball history. Beginning with the early New York teams of the 1880s through the present seasons' Red Book and Green Book, a researcher can identify rosters, statistics, and scores for all games.

The countless newspaper and magazine clippings that made up Ernie's own database of facts can be searched by subject headings such as umpires, gambling, errors, or scorekeeping, or by individual players' names. That also includes managers and umpires such as "Steamboat" Johnson.

The book section of the Harwell collection contains an excellent selection of biographies, team histories, and sports histories. For instance, every book written by or about Ty Cobb is here, including the rare book *Bustin' Em*, written by Cobb in 1914.

The collection does not ignore the other sports, either. Football, hockey, boxing, golf, auto racing, horse racing, soccer, and tennis are amply represented.

Index